Images of Modern America

WHITE SOX PARK'S AMAZING VENDORS

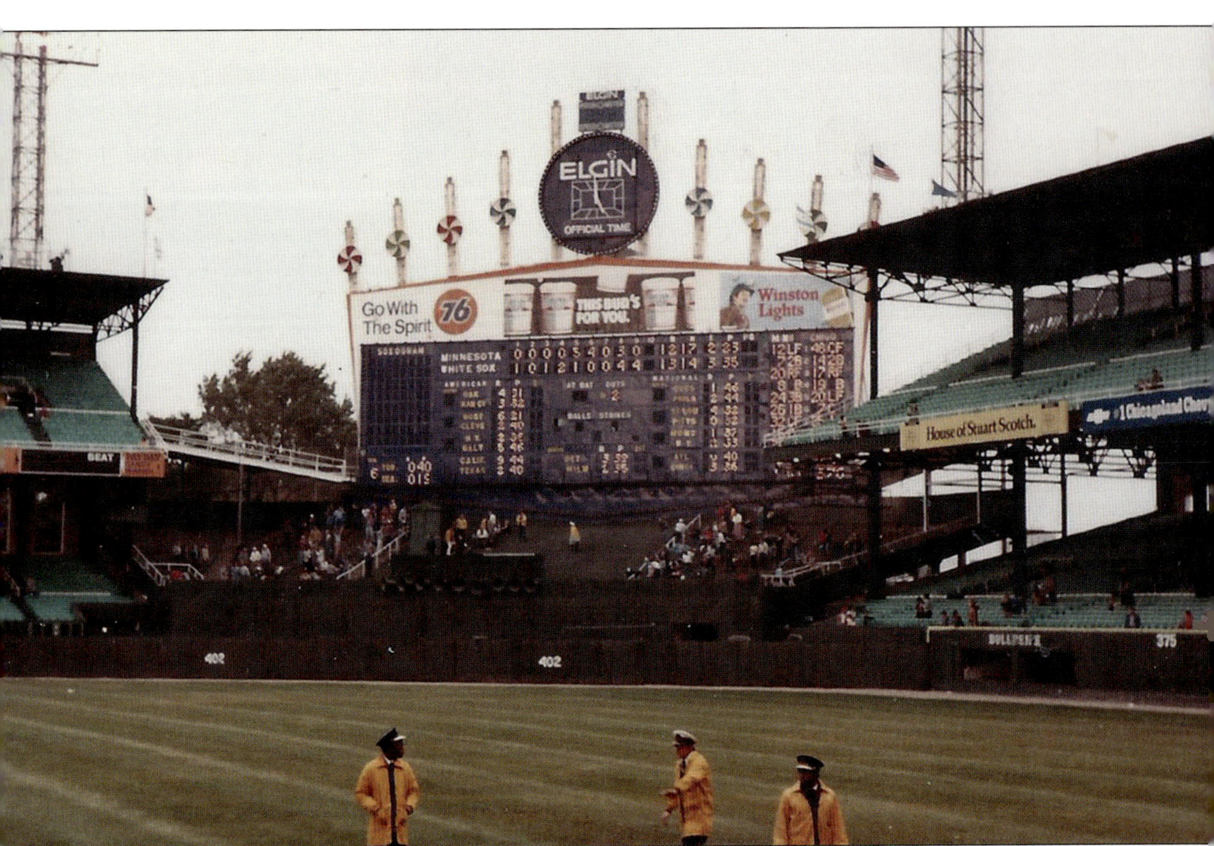

The iconic "exploding" scoreboard at Comiskey Park blasts its amazing news for the season's final game on October 4, 1981. A magnificent eight-run rally in the last two innings resulted in a memorable 13-12 victory for the Chicago White Sox. However, this season was stained by a horrendous two-month summer strike that not only ruined the team's chances, but also meant its vendors would have to survive the winter missing one-third of their earnings. But the South Side sun would come out again the next season—and forever!

Front Cover: US Army Vietnam veteran Sherwin Tycher salutes to the fans with a bag of peanuts as the White Sox wave goodbye on the last day of the 1980 season.

Upper Back Cover: In 1978, David Shanker works his way through medical school selling hot dogs from "the boiler" on a warm July day. He would become a dermatologist.

Lower Back Cover (from left to right): Marty Schatzman uses the "high thrust" method of selling beer in 1979; co-author Lloyd Rutzky sells freshly baked pizza from a heated metal box in 1972; and Gary Newman sells cans of pop he needs to pour in 1975.

Images of Modern America

WHITE SOX PARK'S AMAZING VENDORS

Lloyd Rutzky and Joel Levin

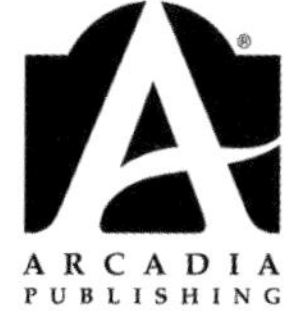

ISBN 978-1-4671-0324-4

Published by Arcadia Publishing
Charleston, South Carolina

Printed in the United States of America

Library of Congress Control Number: 2019930752

For all general information, please contact Arcadia Publishing:
Telephone 843-853-2070
Fax 843-853-0044
E-mail sales@arcadiapublishing.com
For customer service and orders:
Toll-Free 1-888-313-2665

Visit us on the Internet at www.arcadiapublishing.com

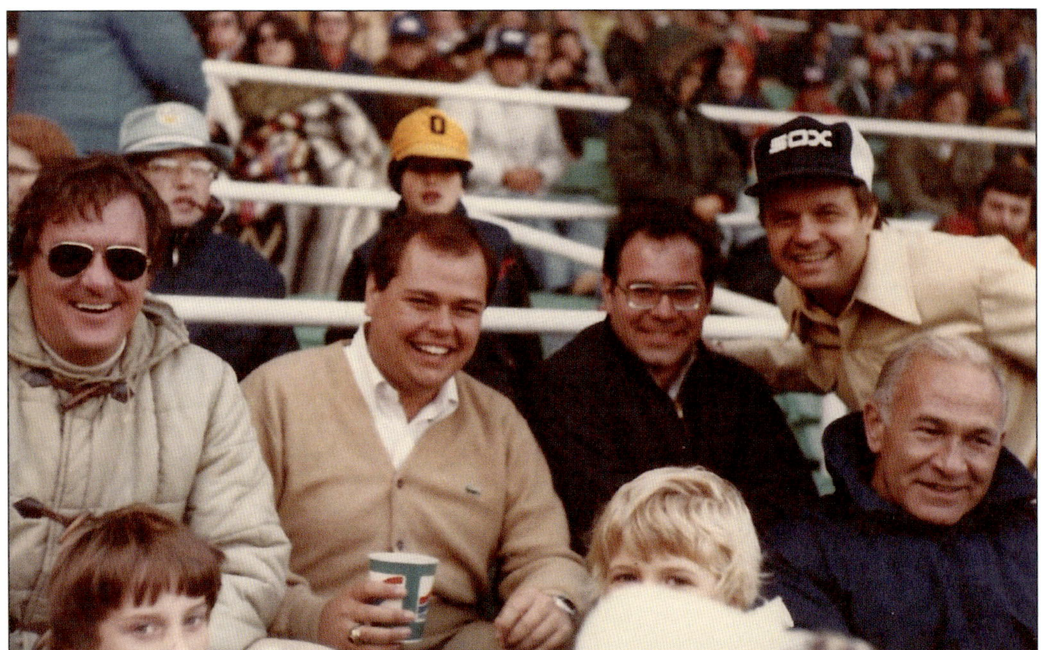

This book is dedicated to the White Sox fans who keep the amazing vendors of White Sox Park in business, like these four in Box 125 from Rensselaer, Indiana, who were frequent customers of co-author Lloyd Rutzky: (from left to right) Lanny Sigo, Herschel Cook, Jerry Gerrard, and Bruce Babcock. Sigo, a sportscaster, interviewed Rutzky for his radio program on WJCK on this day, October 2, 1977. Gerrard was a TV broadcaster who worked with WGN legend Arne Harris.

Contents

Acknowledgments and Introduction

It's almost too great to put into words. Almost. The experience of writing *Wrigley Field's Amazing Vendors* and seeing it come to life last year filled me with so much joy, I felt almost as eternally blessed as when I saw my two daughters being born—well, almost.

Witnessing my creation with co-author Joel Levin being rejoiced by my family and friends, my pictures and our words entertaining the world, was a one-of-a-kind miracle—and now it's happening again! Please, if I'm dreaming, don't wake me up from such utter ecstasy; especially because now, as a native South Sider, I can pay homage to my team, the White Sox.

Many might surmise my 54 years of climbing up and down aisles in the heat, the cold, and the rain for over 8,000 games could have been a struggle, an epic burden. But to me, it's been a magnificent obsession. I can only explain it the way Peter O'Toole did in *Lawrence Of Arabia* when he demonstrated his ability to extinguish a match with his fingers: "The trick is not minding that it hurts." There's no simpler way to describe what I think of my job other than "fun."

That was primarily why I began taking pictures nearly half a century ago of everybody I worked with and had fun with at the old ballpark. Even if they thought I was a screwball, taking pictures of strangers that nobody would ever care about. But oh my, they definitely do. They absolutely, definitely do, especially when people see a face from decades ago that is no longer around, a friend they thought was forgotten, as if they never existed. Until these books came to be, they existed only in their memories—but now, they are immortal.

Assembling what you now are holding in your hands could also have been likened to a laborious task. And it very well might have been if I hadn't been blessed with so much inspiration and assistance from others. Starting with my father, Jules Rutzky, who worked harder than anybody I've ever known but also instilled in me a love for baseball that steered me into finding an occupation I would enjoy participating in, even if it wasn't as a baseball player, but I still got paid to go to a ballpark. My mother, Pearl, earns a rich acknowledgment for her work ethic, which I embraced: "If you're going to do something, do it well." Accordingly, I must thank my beloved computer-expert wife, Helita, for everything she has done to not only make me desire to make her proud, but also for how much her technical assistance got me through some confusion about making Microsoft products achieve all that they're supposed to. I'm also in debt to my two daughters, Katie Rutzky Gerber and Liz Rutzky Forcier, for their invaluable knowledge of the intricacies of iPhones, the internet, and the art of cut and paste and copy that I needed to rely on to complete this project.

I have also been blessed with a great many friends who have supported my new career in book writing and done their best to promote its success, like Arnold Lipski, Mark Reiner, Abe Rapuch, Michael Ginsburg, Dave Levenson, Howard Wolinsky, Art Newman, Jack Beermann, Brandon Medow, Harlan Grabowsky, Cindy Fosco Gaborek, Dave Gaborek, Dave Hoekstra, David Kaplan, Gary Tuch, Steven Leahy, John Studnicka, Mike Rubin, Mike LaPapa Sr. and Jr., my union president Vince Pesha, and many others. Not to be forgotten are very helpful Arcadia staff members Stacia Bannerman, Jim Kempert, Erin Owens, and Leigh Scott. I've also been moved by two former vendors who have achieved mightily out of the park and have sent us fond words.

The first is John W. Rogers Jr., whom I have known since he was 10 years old—some 50 years ago—when he came to White Sox games with his dad. He later worked as a competing vendor and, still later, founded Ariel Investments, befriended fellow Chicagoan Barack Obama, and became one of the president's economic advisers (see pages 65 and 93):

In 1974, when I was 16 years old, I started my first summer job as a vendor at Comiskey

Park. My inspiration was Lloyd Rutzky, who used to sell pizzas at the ballpark to my father and me on Sunday afternoons.

> The experience of being a vendor was transformative for me. It was a job I looked forward to every single day because it combined my love of sports, my desire to stay physically active, and my motivation to become an entrepreneur.
>
> I started at the bottom selling Coke. I worked my way up to peanuts, then hotdogs, and finally the ultimate—beer! I ended my career as a proud Stroh's vendor at Comiskey and an Old Style vendor at Wrigley. I had reached the peak.
>
> I had the opportunity to meet and work with some extraordinary and wonderful people. I also learned valuable life lessons that remain with me to this day. To be strategic and maximize my selling time. I soon realized there was a direct correlation between my hard work and results. To be a successful vendor, one needed to be competitive and decisive. I have so much respect for the vendors with whom I worked, especially those like Lloyd, who have devoted over 50 years to their jobs. Every one of them inspired me to do my best work.
>
> I built some tremendous relationships over my seven summers, many of which I have maintained throughout my career—including my lifelong friend and Ariel colleague Charlie Bobrinskoy [see page 66].

The second is Mark Carman, a talented broadcaster now working for WGN radio. Among his credits are post-game White Sox shows:

> I started my vending career in 1992 when I was 18 "going on 12." My first memories are being afraid of walking up the steep upper-deck steps at the new White Sox Park, selling Dove ice cream bars for $3. I also hawked cotton candy, since it was light and only cost $1. In the early years, I was not motivated to make much money. Being at the ballpark seemed much better than being inside at some desk job or out in the fields detasseling corn, like some of my classmates at the University of Iowa were doing. There were plenty of days where I would enter the ballpark and consider working, but just kicked back and watched the game instead.
>
> My most embarrassing moment happened when I decided to take a nap in my bright yellow uniform before a midweek 1:05 p.m. start. I took a seat in the shade down the left field line, fell asleep, and ended up on Channel 7 Mark Giangreco's 10:00 p.m. sportscast as the "it-was-a-long-day-at-the-ballpark guy." Cameras in the ballpark are always rolling, even two hours before the game.
>
> There were many signature moments through the years, such as the 2005 World Series. I had checked out after last call and was underneath the bleachers when Paul Konerko hit his famous game two grand slam. It felt like the ballpark was going to collapse on top of me. During the 2008 blackout game, I was moonlighting as a vendor while starting out in media for WGN radio. During the game, I sold beer and then went on the field to interview Nick Swisher after the White Sox win over the Twins. I might have left out my pregame duties to my radio bosses. I hope they don't mind now, 11 years later.
>
> One of the best parts of being a vendor was the people I worked with each day from all walks of life—teachers, lawyers, musicians, garbage men, bus drivers, and some year-round vendors working all of Chicago's venues. It brings a smile to my face to see them captured in pictures here.

Chicago has supported two Major League Baseball teams for over 100 years. The Cubs have been playing the game on the North Side since 1876, and the White Sox have been safely at home on the South Side since 1901. It was only natural, then, that the release of *Wrigley Field's Amazing Vendors* in 2018 be followed up by *White Sox Park's Amazing Vendors* in 2019. Arcadia Publishing has, in fact, long recognized the intense and divided loyalties of the Windy City's diamond duo by producing 15 titles devoted to the history, stadiums, players, and managers of both teams.

Both books originated as a tribute to Irving Newer, a popular ice cream vendor who though legally blind and hobbled by old age continued to vend on his solitary journey in the stands of these legendary venues. Newer died in 1983, and Joel Levin, a former vendor and Chicago Public Schools teacher, had an idea when he saw Newer's photograph in *Forgotten Chicago*, an Arcadia publication from 2004, with Newer sadly unidentified. "This man was my friend," Levin thought, "and he absolutely, positively has a name and has not been forgotten!" Levin was then on a quest to right this wrong—and write it he must! He also knew that Lloyd Rutzky, a current vendor for both the White Sox and the Cubs with over five decades of experience, owned a private and previously unpublished treasure trove of personal photographs of his ballpark colleagues, including Irving Newer. The rest is history.

The authors first thought that one combined book with vendors from both ballparks would cover the field. However, after seeing the incredible volume of pictures in Rutzky's possession, it was determined that at least two separate volumes were needed to do justice to this never-before-explored topic. Also, with the rivalry so heated between the legions of both team's fans, it was thought best to give each park's workers their own book. The question then became, who bats first? With the Cubs having "seniority" in Chitown, they were designated the hitters. The White Sox have now tied the score with this new release.

Rutzky and Levin's collaborative efforts give readers the chance to vicariously experience the ballpark life. Whether vending beer, peanuts, or anything else on the ballpark's menus, readers will learn about every facet of what it is like to earn a living in this job so many fans have fantasized about. Readers are also treated to visits to places that are usually off limits or ignored by the general public, including commissary rooms, cashier's offices, checkout lines, and more.

White Sox Park's Amazing Vendors is organized into four chapters similar to its companion volume *Wrigley Field's Amazing Vendors*. But there are differences in content and focus. White Sox Family, the first and longest chapter of this book, emphasizes the team's commitment to the concept of an inclusive family. Included here are vendors, fans, security personnel, cashiers, forklift drivers, commissary workers, and even an electrician and a shoeshine man, all captured by Lloyd Rutzky's relentless camera. Of special note in this chapter is a two-page photograph of vendors waiting to work the 2005 World Series, the first Fall Classic to be played in the team's newest park, which they moved to in 1991. And contrasting with that is a picture of a vendor who claimed to have worked at the first World Series in the previous venue across the street in 1917.

Chapter two, Vendors Hit to All Fields, is a brand new idea that answers one of the questions fans always ask: "What do vendors do after they stop working at Chicago's ballparks?" These "other lives" are a vocational smorgasbord. Finance, law, medicine, politics, education, and the military are just some of the fields vendors have swung to successfully. A definite highlight here is a photograph of a young vendor counting his money in preparation for a business career that would eventually see him giving economic advice to a US president who was also a longtime resident of the Windy City.

The workers featured in this book also like to socialize in pretty much the same way the rest of the outside world does, which is what chapter three, Vendors Who Play Together, Stay Together, illustrates. And finally, chapter four, The Legends, not only features five remarkable individuals in vending history but also famed announcers and team personnel who have mingled with White Sox Park's amazing vendors.

Joel Levin would like to thank the following people who supported and encouraged stories of both Cubs and White Sox vendors and, in the process, made baseball fans everywhere the ultimate winners: Mitch Levin, Jerry Shencup, Dr. Paul Smulson, Michael Ginsburg, Jeff Ruetsche and Stacia Bannerman of Arcadia Publishing, the staff of the Chicago Teachers' Pension Fund "Redefining Retirement," Neil O'Shea of the Niles-Maine District Library, and Joan Waxman of the North Shore Senior Center.

A very special thank-you goes to my wife, Peggy Levin, and daughter Victoria, who have cheered on all my literary endeavors and are the best fans any author could hope for.

Unless otherwise noted, all images are from the collection of Lloyd Rutzky.

One

White Sox Family

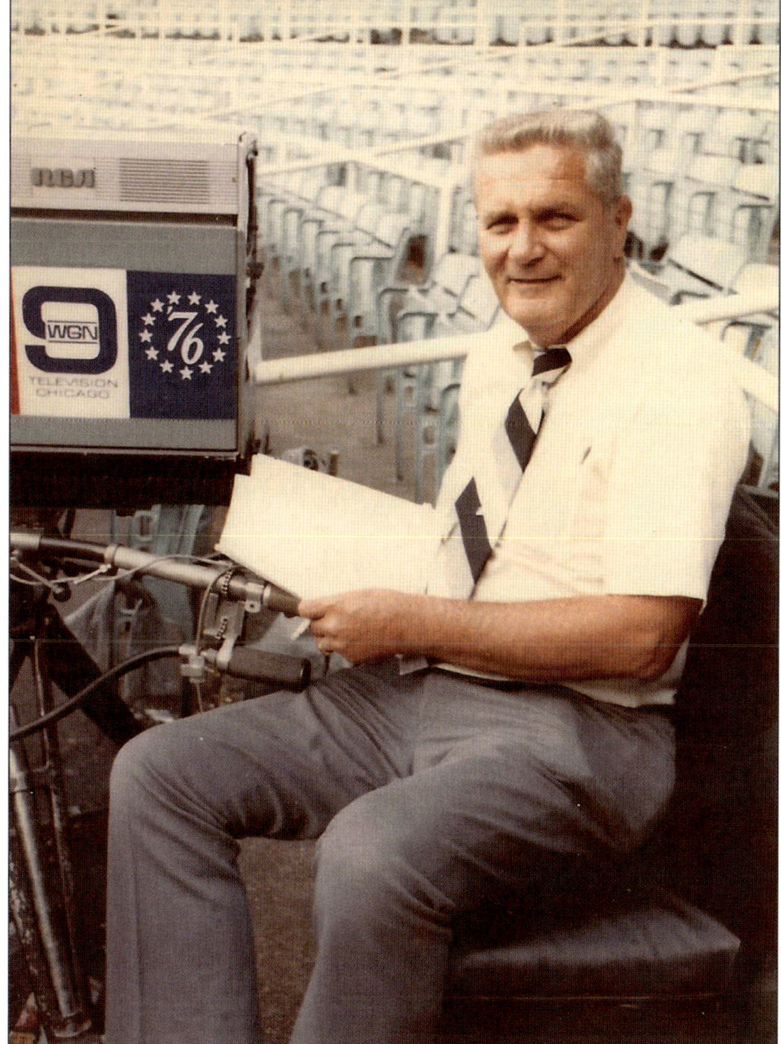

The year 2019 marks more than half a century of WGN-TV broadcasting Chicago White Sox games. Throughout three different periods—1948–1967, 1973–1981, and 1990 until the present day—White Sox baseball has been a welcome part of the Channel 9 family lineup. This cheerful-looking guy operating the red, white, and blue bicentennial-decorated camera in 1976 will now forever be enshrined in history with his "leadoff man" spot in this book. (Courtesy of Mike Gold.)

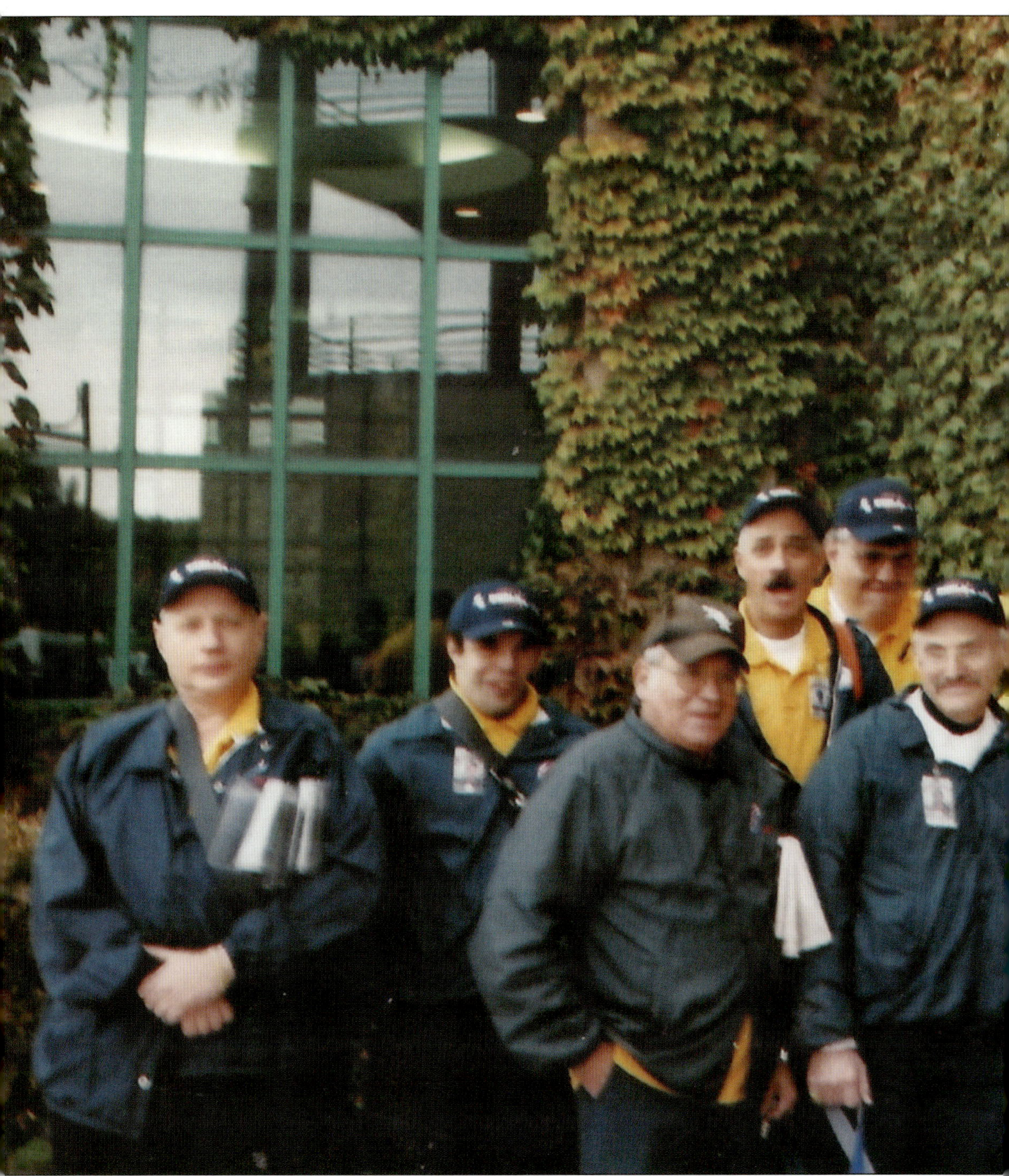

It was a proud day in White Sox Park family history that saw these vendors gathered outside on October 22, 2005. It had been 46 years since the "ChiSox" were in the World Series, and after sweeping the Red Sox in three games in the Division Series and knocking off the Angels four games to one in the American League Championship Series, the Fall Classic had returned to the South Side. The excited group here is, from left to right, Rus Nelson, Todd Smoler, Don Gerstein,

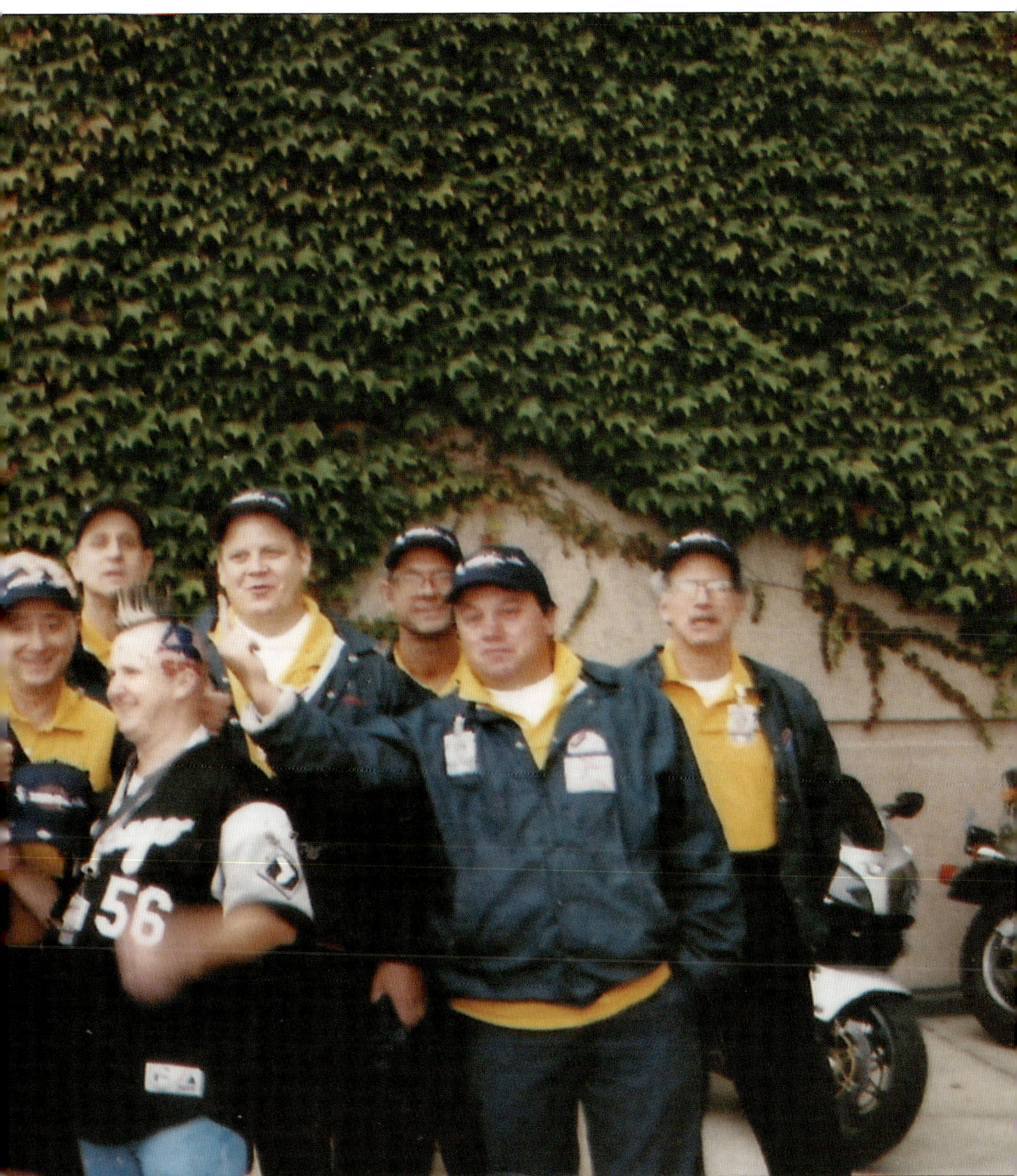

Ira Levin, Anthony Donato, Marv Mitofsky, co-author Lloyd Rutzky, Glenn Smoler, Joey Svec, David Mariotti, Jim Jelinski, Scott Wesolek, and Stephen Livingston. The Sox won that Saturday night, 5-3, and the next night here too, 7-6. They then completed a sweep in Houston of the Astros with 7-5 and 1-0 victories to become world champs on Wednesday, October 26. (Courtesy of Michael Ginsburg.)

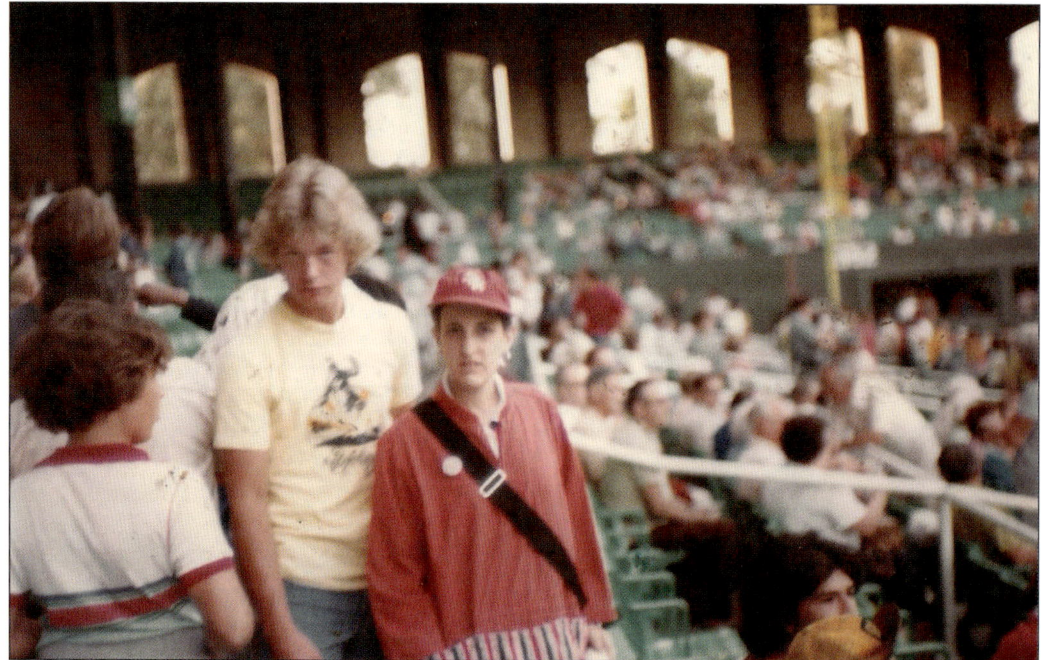

Seen above, Alise Rutzky, Lloyd Rutzky's "little sis," had a one-day vending career on July 9, 1979. She was credited with selling two loads of pop that day, but Lloyd had to help her with most of it. Lloyd's big brother Ron was a vendor for one whole year in 1964, though the Rutzky family began its association with Sox Park in 1960 when a 12-year-old Lloyd accompanied his father, Jules, as he delivered plastic bags that cotton candy was sold in from the business he managed. Afterward, the two would "stowaway" and watch the game. Lee Cook, pictured below on September 17, 1996, sells a board of cotton candy that used bags just like they did way back when.

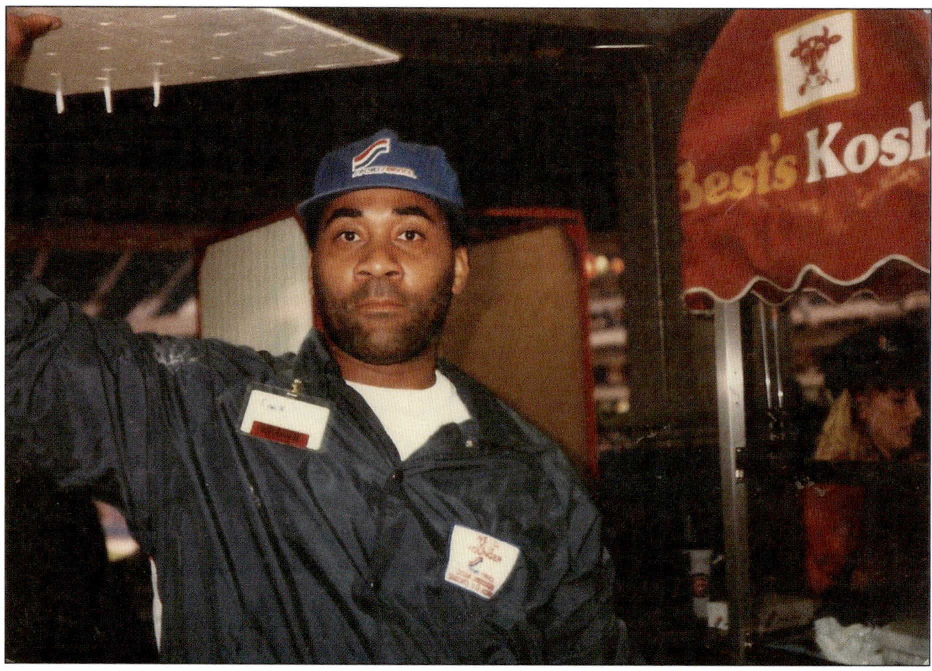

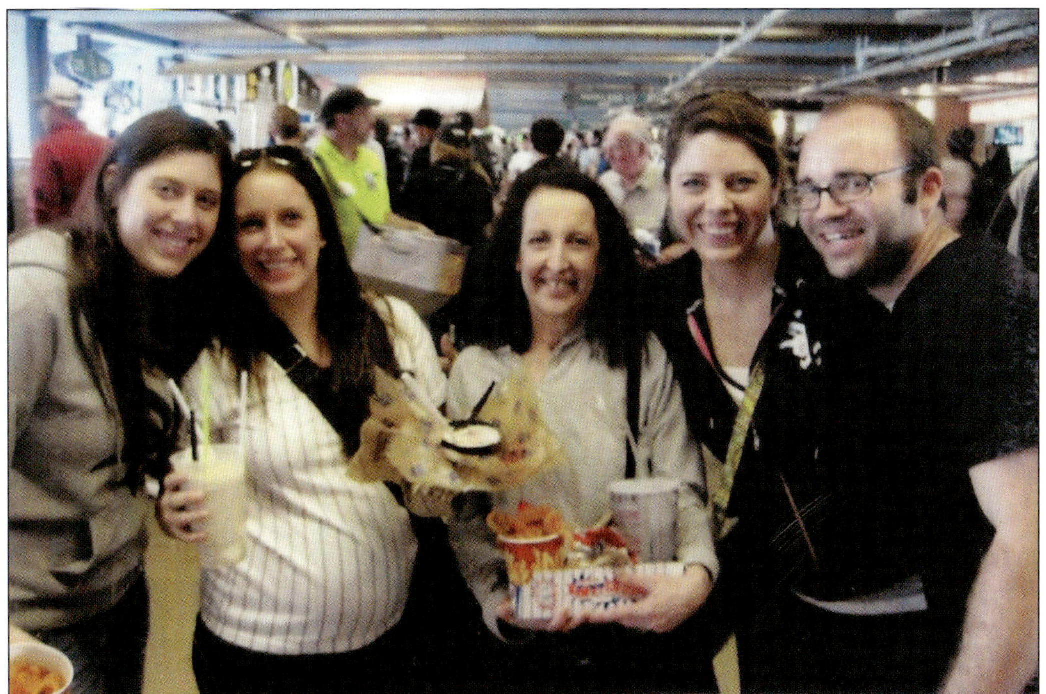

White Sox fans are "family" too. The group seen above just happens to be the real immediate kinfolk of co-author Lloyd Rutzky enjoying the park on April 15, 2012. From left to right, weighted down with ballpark yummies, are Lloyd's youngest daughter Liz, his niece Jenny, her mom (the former vending "superstar" Alise—see opposite page), and Lloyd's oldest daughter Katie with her husband, Mike Gerber. Seen back in 1977 below are other important "brothers" of Lloyd—his regulars, who would buy beer only from him. From left to right are Dale Davis, Gene Sylvester, and Greg Reinke being taken care of with another serving of brew.

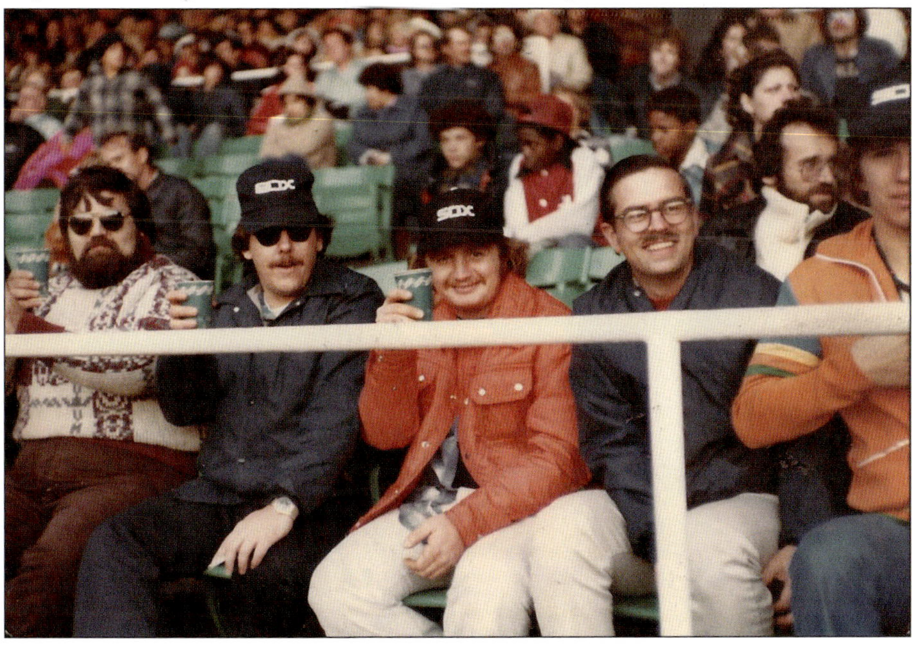

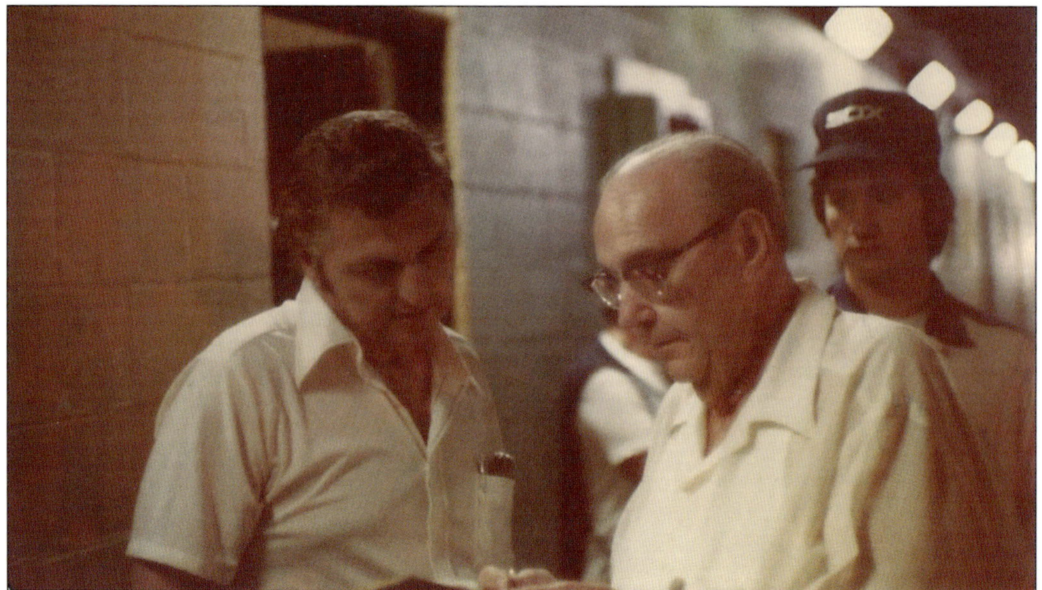

The Godfather certainly gave the phrase "the family business" a new meaning, but seen above in 1977 is the perfect example of close relations providing an honest day's work. Pat Redden (left) began 61 seasons of Comiskey Park labor in 1958, and by 1968, he was concessions manager. Here, Redden confers with commissary boss Ed McGee while "beerman" Kenny Farrell, nephew of union steward John Studnicka, observes. Before that, Redden's future mother-in-law, Mary Harper, was hired at a food stand at Comiskey in the Roaring Twenties. Then, after Mary's daughter Marie married Pat Redden, Marie and all five of their children worked there too: Pat Jr., Danny, Kevin, Mike, and Linda (Danny is pictured on page 32 of *Wrigley Field's Amazing Vendors*). Finally, Pat's parents, David and Loretta, found that their son's request to hire them at Thirty-Fifth Street and Shields Avenue was "an offer they couldn't refuse." Below, father and son Fred Richissin Sr. and Jr. share the vending life (though not the same color uniform) in the left-field stands in August 1976.

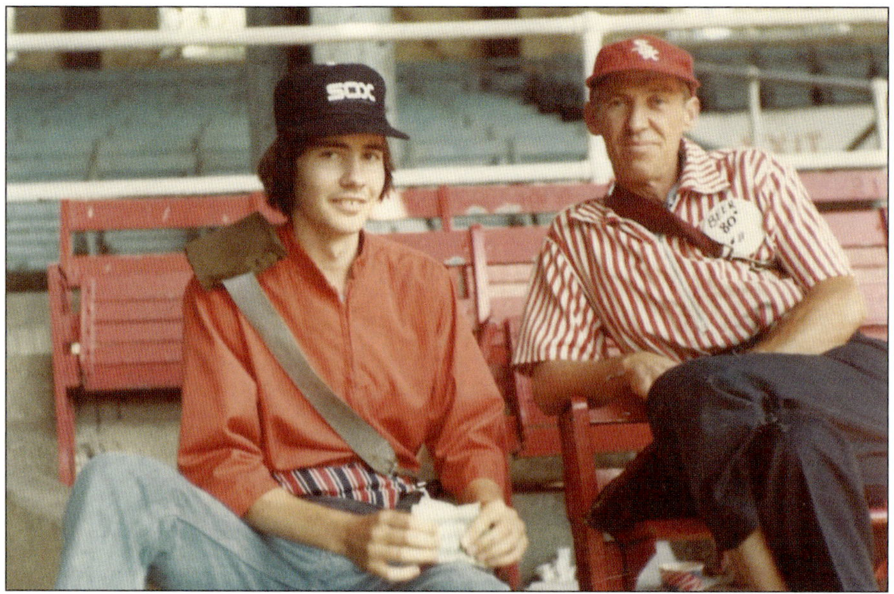

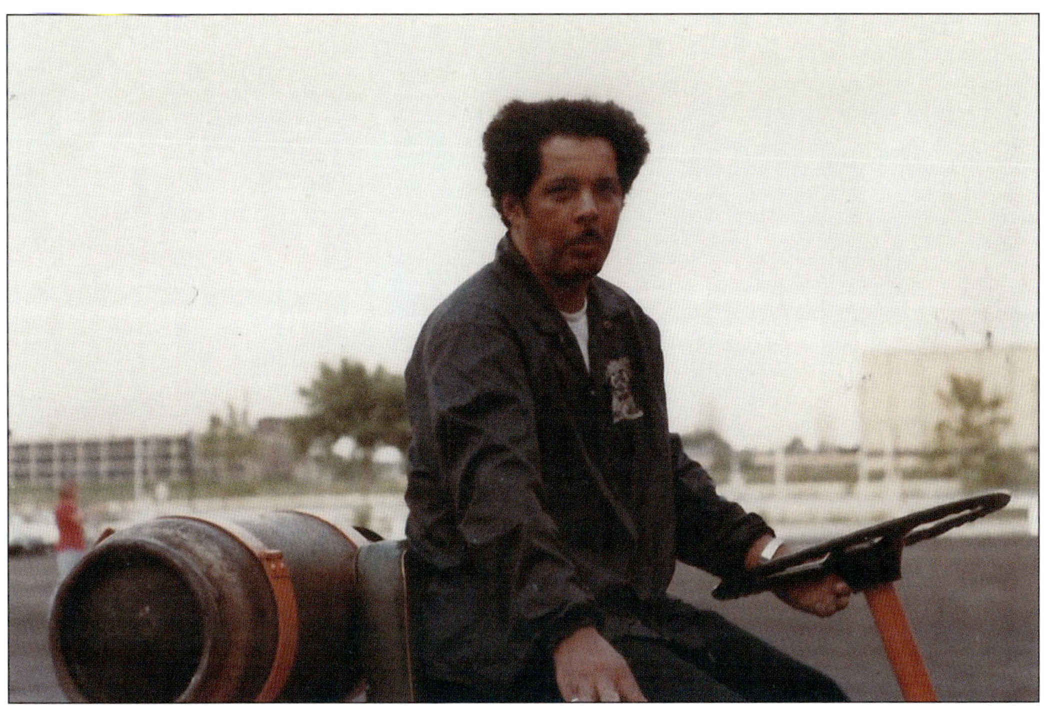

This page features the Bud David clan, with supervisor Bud, seen above working a forklift in 1977. In 1979, his wife, Joyce, ran a beer room (below left), and daughter Chrissie manned a popcorn stand (below right) that Pat Redden's wife once was in charge of.

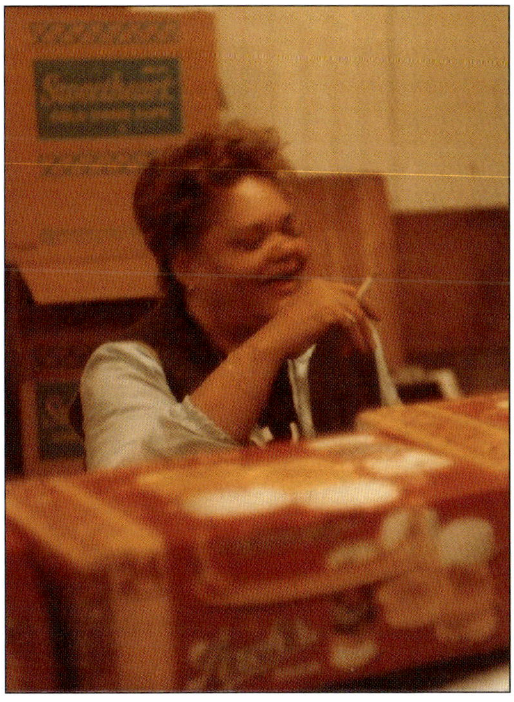

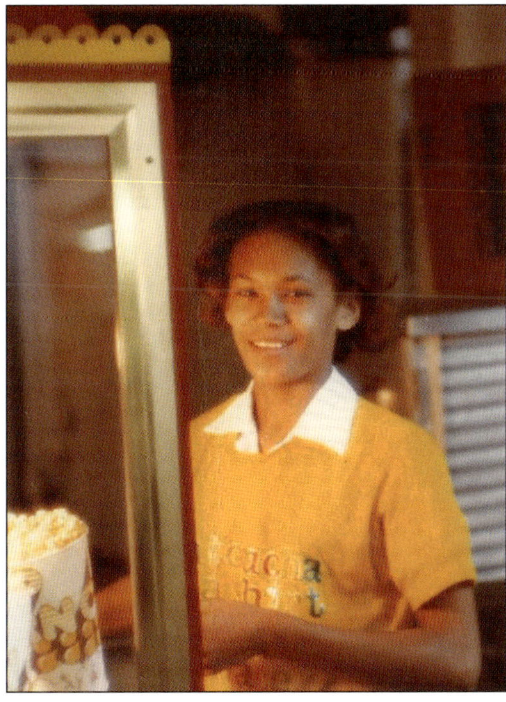

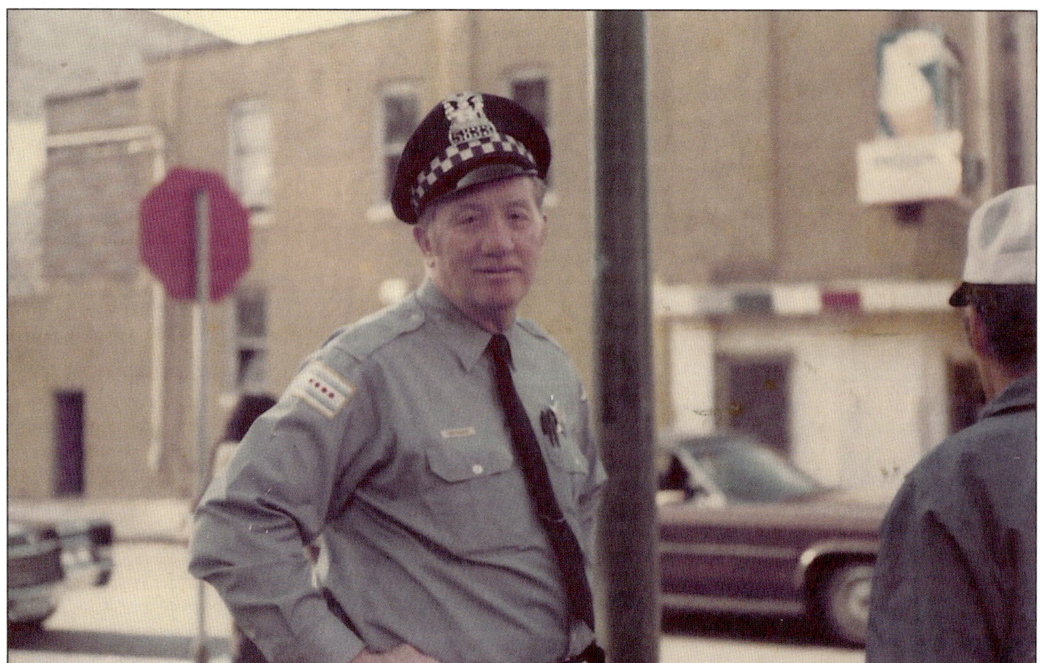

Families need somebody to protect them. These two pages feature four examples of the White Sox Park line of defense against all comers. Certainly, they have been put to the test over the many seasons of change on the South Side. Officer George Brennan, seen above in 1977 stationed at the corner of Thirty-Third and Wells Streets, a northeast checkpoint one block from White Sox Park, is just one of many of Chicago's finest keeping the peace outside. Meanwhile, the pair of "yellow jackets" seen below in 1980 was at the ready to swarm if things got out of hand, either on the field—when the occasional overexuberant fan would run out into the playing area—or into any mushrooming fracas between fans in the seating area.

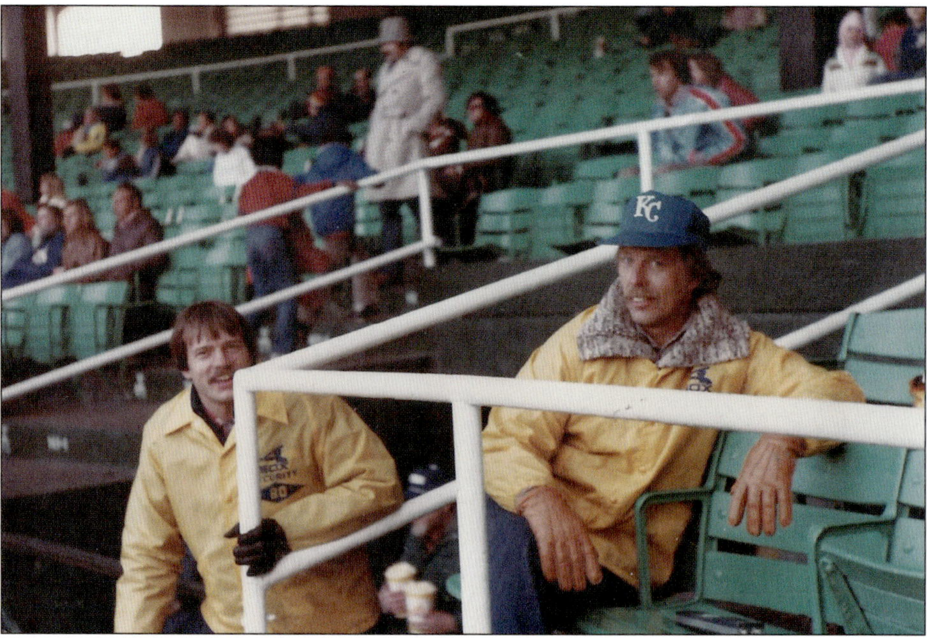

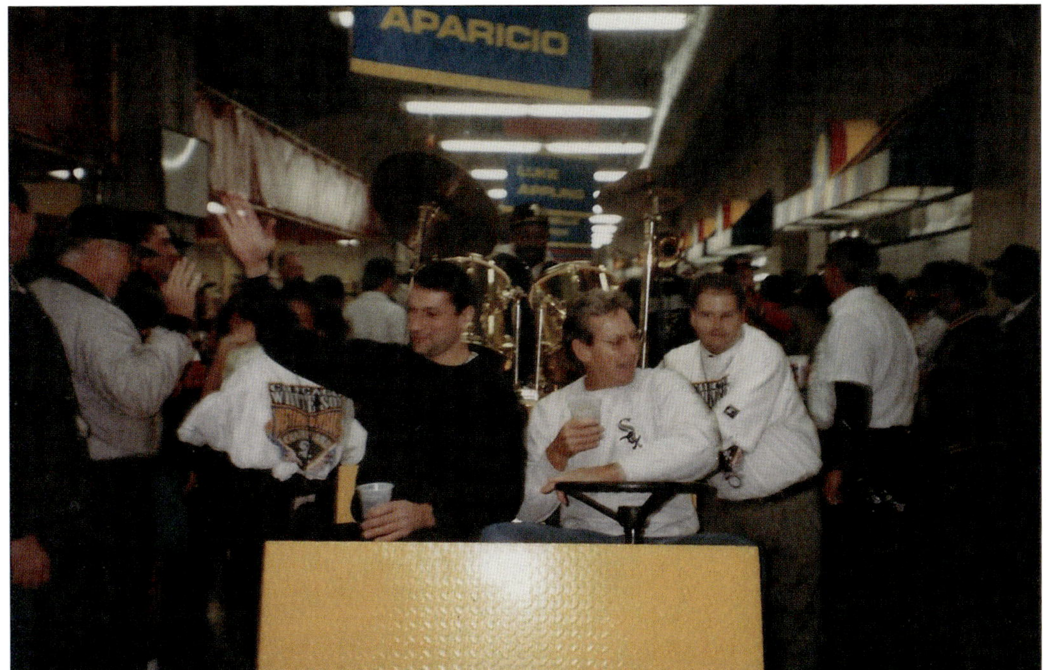

Baseball games with agitated patrons are the usual challenges the gendarmes live with. But many famed concerts at the South Side American League venue have featured incredible, hard-to-handle turnouts. August 20, 1965, was the first when the Beatles played there. The mania was repeated with Simon & Garfunkel on July 24, 1983, Michael Jackson on October 12, 1984, the Rolling Stones on September 13, 2002, and Bruce Springsteen on August 13, 2003. David Schaeffer, seen above at the steering wheel, son of Bill Veeck's former partner Rudie Schaeffer, also had plenty to deal with as head of security on September 27, 1993, the night the White Sox clinched the American League West. Mike Wargo, seen below in 1996, became the law enforcement chief after Schaefer retired.

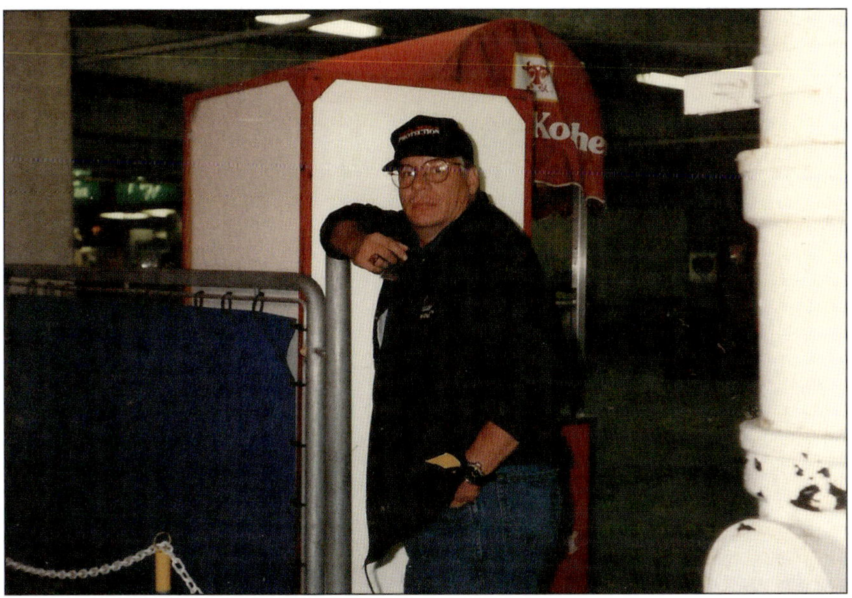

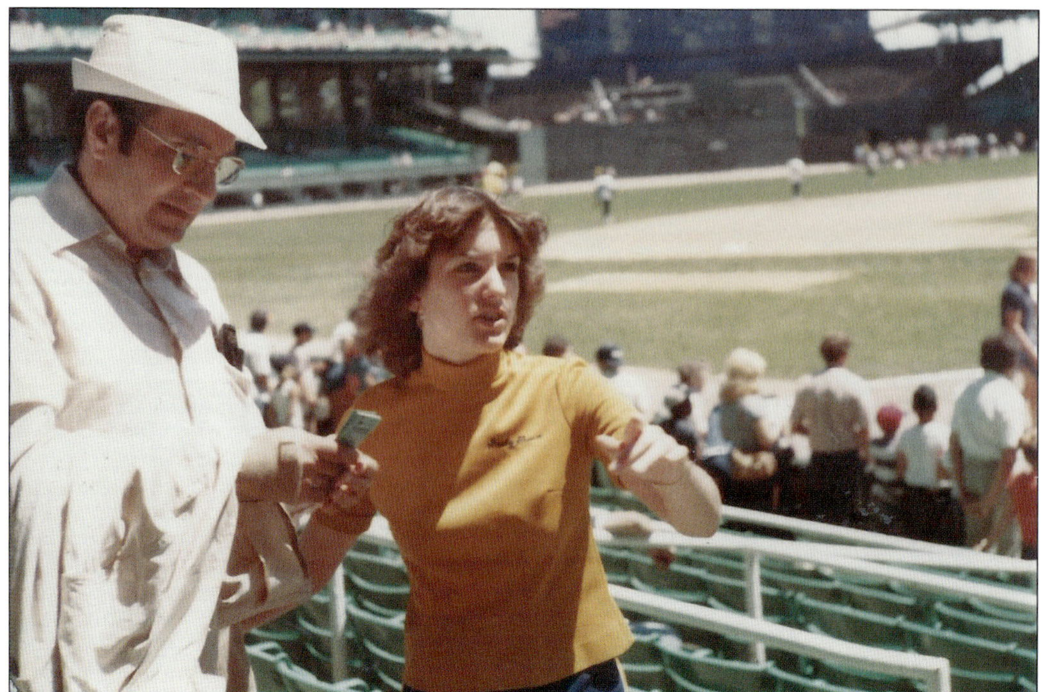

Andy Frain ushers were a very visible force at Chicago venues for over 70 years from 1924 to 1996. At virtually every sports facility, as well as other prominent locations around the city, they did their best to provide courteous crowd control. Andy T. Frain started the company after having been a vendor at Comiskey Park and provided a rather fancy-looking starting job for many young people; however, it was not a very lucrative one, as they were paid not much more than minimum wage. In 1978, Margie Qualizza (above) and Zachary Seals (below) look neat and bright at Comiskey Park.

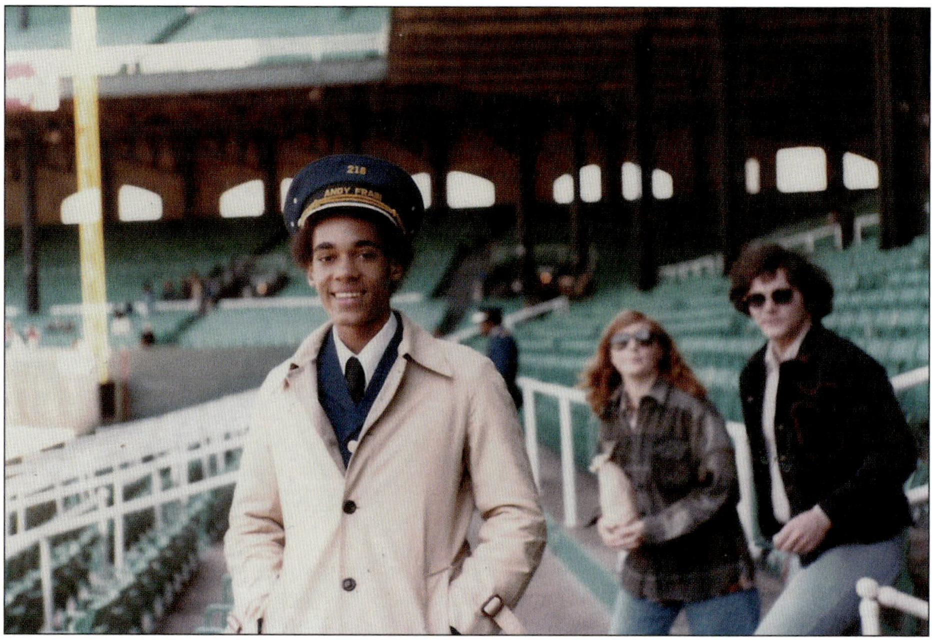

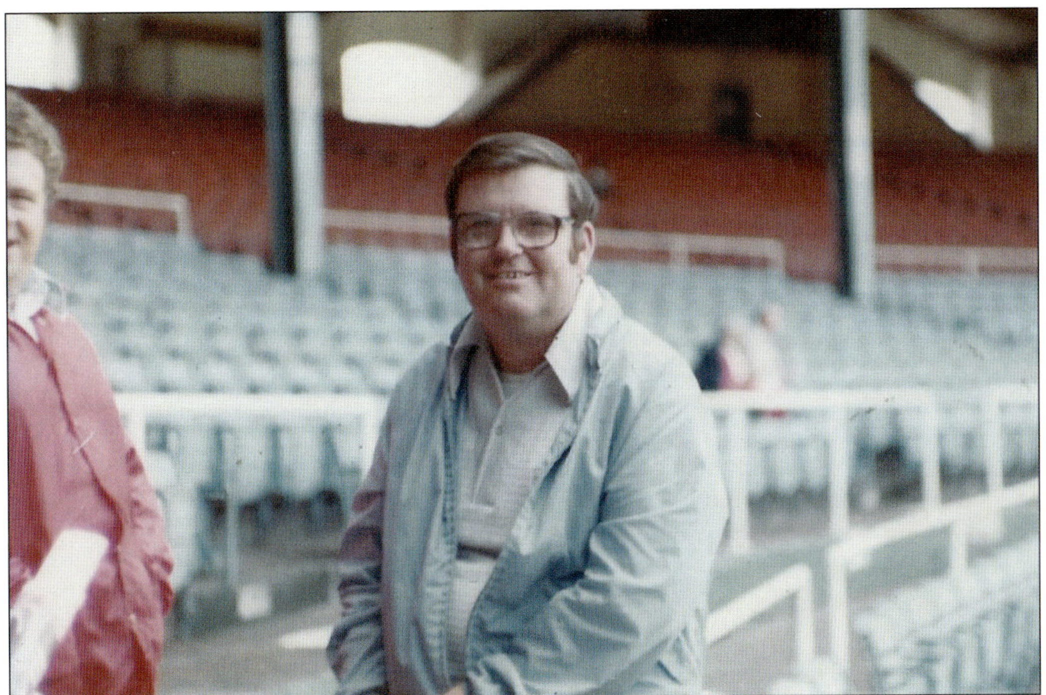

"Joe Mahoney, Joe Mahoney." Say it twice, it always sounds nice. They did, too, whenever management at Comiskey Park needed the services of its chief electrician from 1960 to 1990, everybody around the park would hear that famous plea on the intercom, usually before the game. Mahoney is smiling above in 1976 while on a break between changing bulbs and rewiring sockets. Nearly as indispensable to White Sox Park operations was Lou the Shoeshine Man, seen below second from right. Vendor Ontaria Cole (in red, white, and blue), selling peanuts, appears to be oblivious that Lou has just spotted photographer Lloyd Rutzky here in May 1978; Lou considered Rutzky to be a screwball who was always taking pictures of strangers.

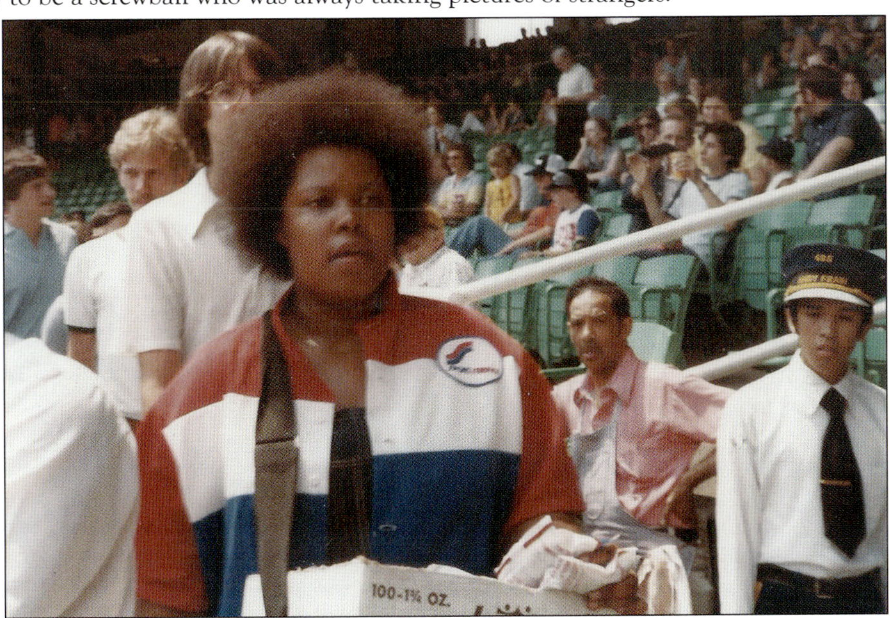

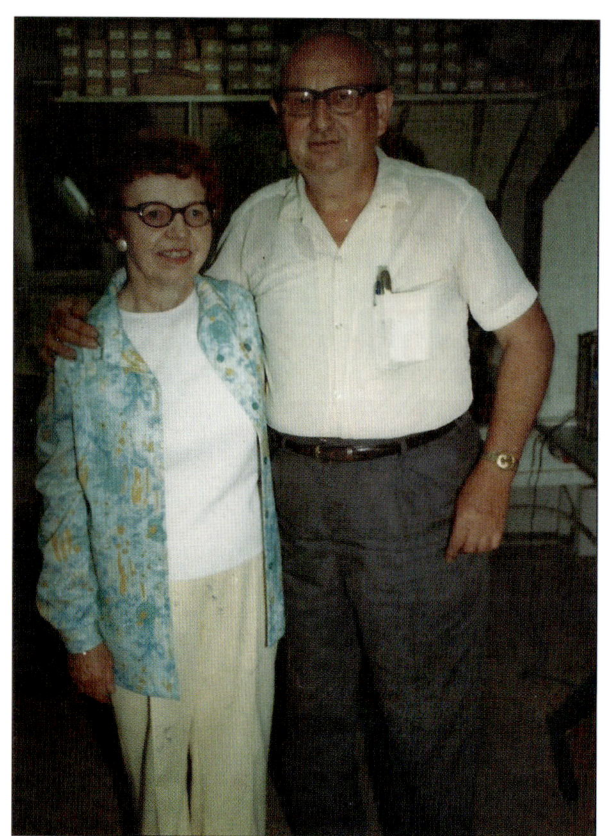

Honesty is the best policy. That is paramount to success in the ballpark, and it should be the same throughout the world. No matter how good a vendor is, they really will never succeed if they cannot trust their management team, and vice versa. Cashiers and commissary workers are the backbones that vendors rely on to make their jobs run properly—and fast. These two pages pay tribute to those most important of people. Kay and Elmer Sheridan, seen at left in 1976, and Mary Rohan Spencer, seen below in 1995 accompanied by a plainclothes security officer turning in the day's receipts, were among the very best friends a vendor had. They counted vendors' money and tabulated their earnings. (Left, courtesy of Mike Gold.)

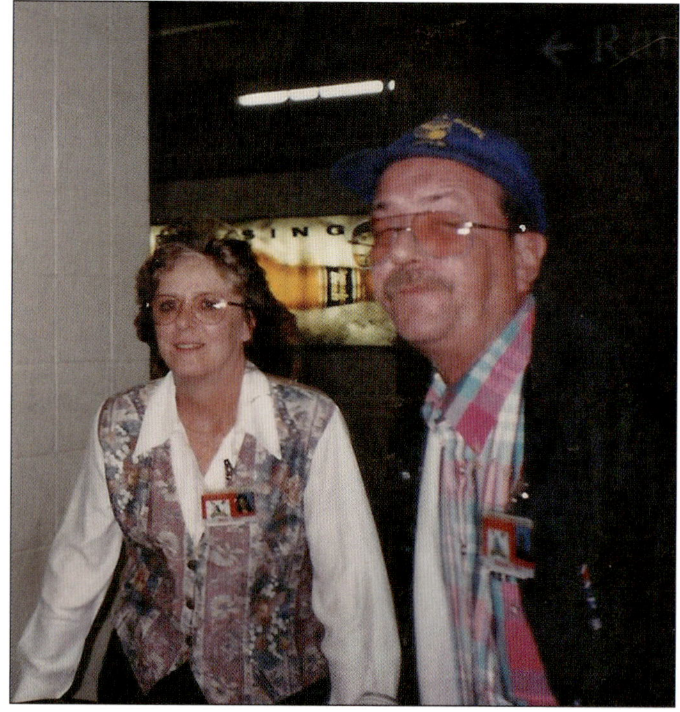

Monetary mistakes will eventually happen to every vendor. When dealing with ballpark cashiers multiple times a game, like the ones on the opposite page, vendors hope that they will return an overage, and they expect the same. It is their speed in this crucial task that makes the job a triumph if there is mutual trust. It is the same with the commissary worker who supplies the products to sell after given the proper merchandise ticket. Phyliss Bennewate, seen above in 1979, and Kim Hendricks, seen below in 1991, were among the best ever at quickly getting vendors out to sell their goods—in this case, beer. Nothing could slow down the transaction more than if either believed the other was not completely honest.

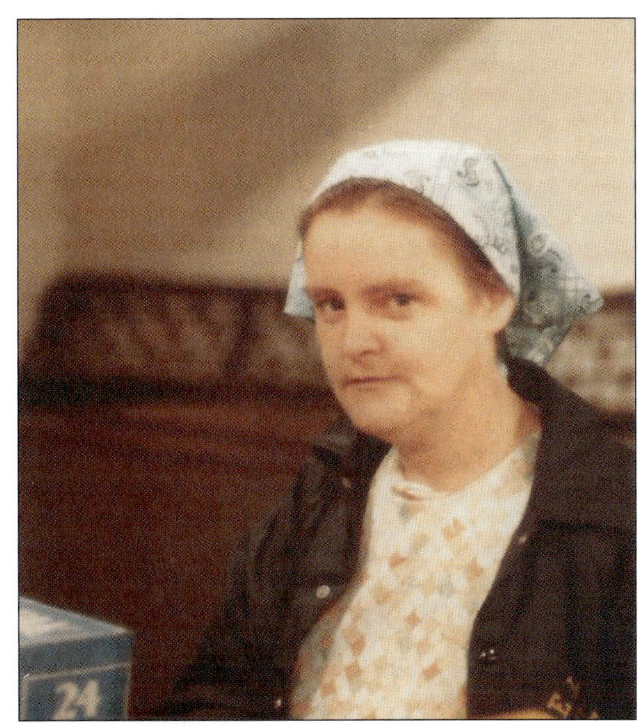

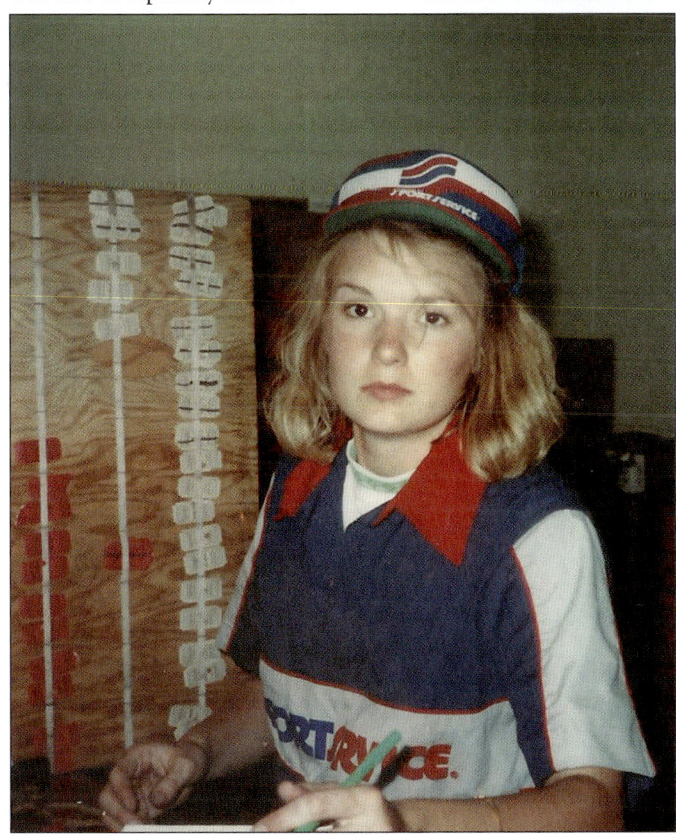

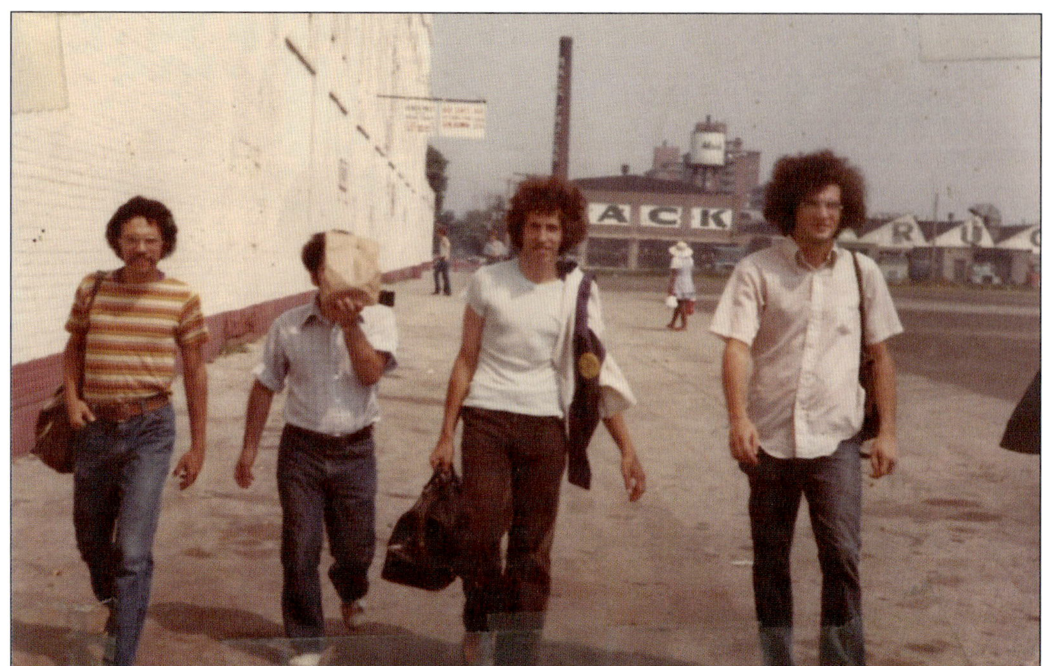

These "Magnificent Seven" glory-seeking beer slingers stride outside the Comiskey Park right-field wall in a quest for a promising showdown for vending gold. From left to right, seen above in 1975 are Jack Shifman, Paul Pechter, Lane Kaplan, and Seymour Pechter; below in 1987, Dan Martinez, his daughter Geaneen Martinez, and Lisa Jagielski have just parked their cars on the previous block. Majestically looming behind them on Thirty-Fourth and Wells Streets was the notable Chicago depot for Mack trucks. That facility—as well as the "Baseball Palace Of The World," as Comiskey Park was first christened—is now "gone with the wind."

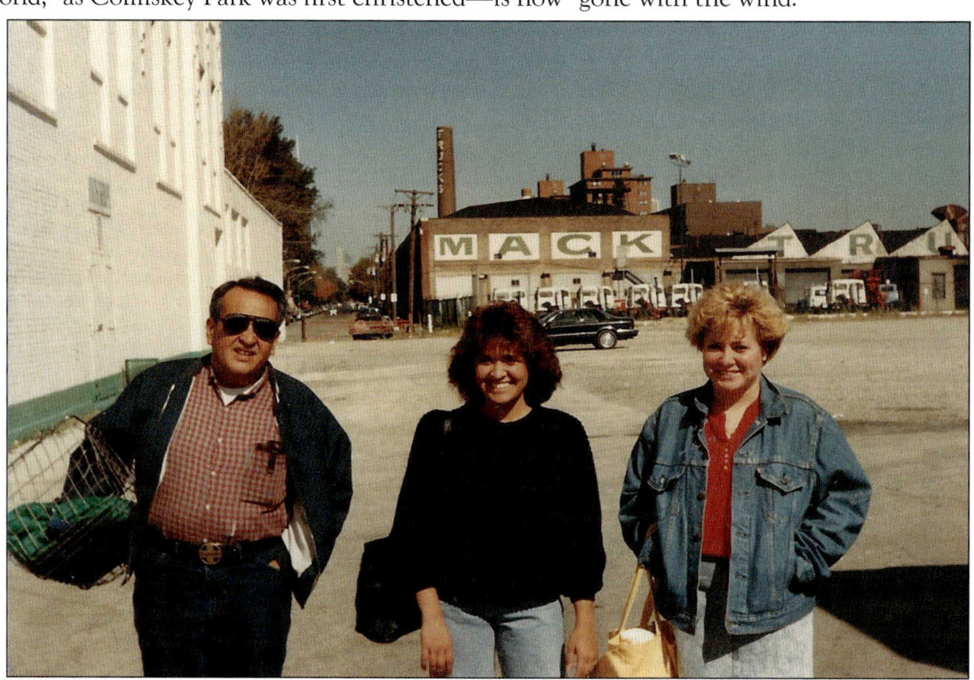

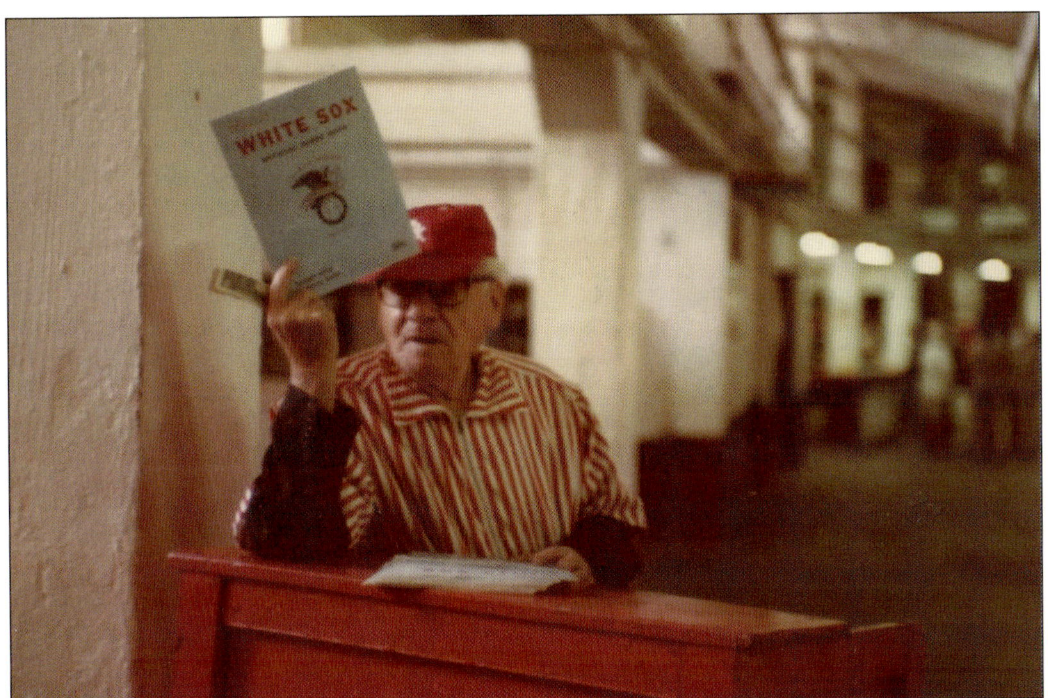

Perhaps it is an exaggeration to refer to "the loneliness of the long and distant program sellers" when speaking of the "scorecard and lineup" men—usually the old-timers—stationed at entrance gates, not having to run around, with their hustling days behind them. They can hear the roar of the crowd but never know what the fuss is all about—if they are still finding enough purchasers once the game is underway. Usually, they will be heading home by the third inning. Fans do not even talk to them much, simply putting their money down and picking up their "book" and maybe a pencil. Here, Dave Shapiro, seen above in 1975, and Bob Virgo, below in 1976, appear virtually motionless, speechless, and almost friendless, as if stranded on a desert island.

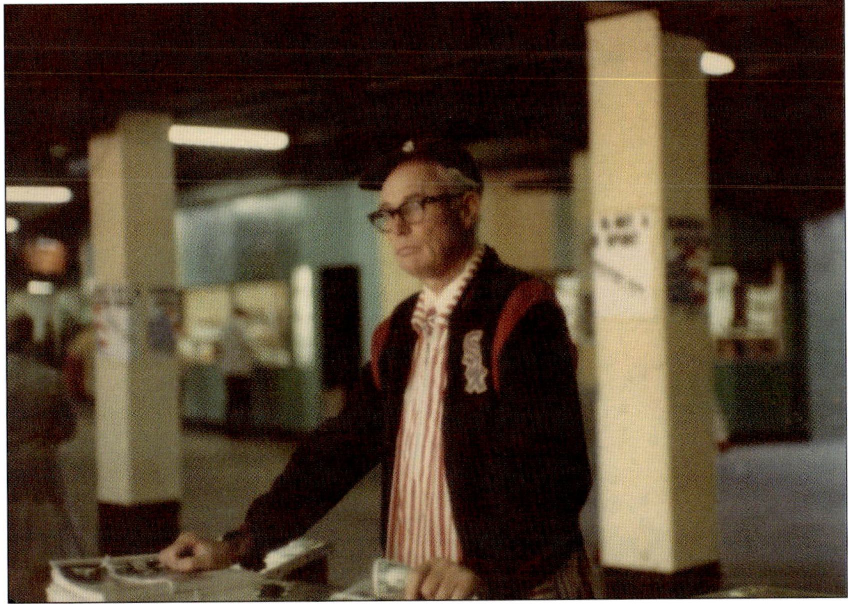

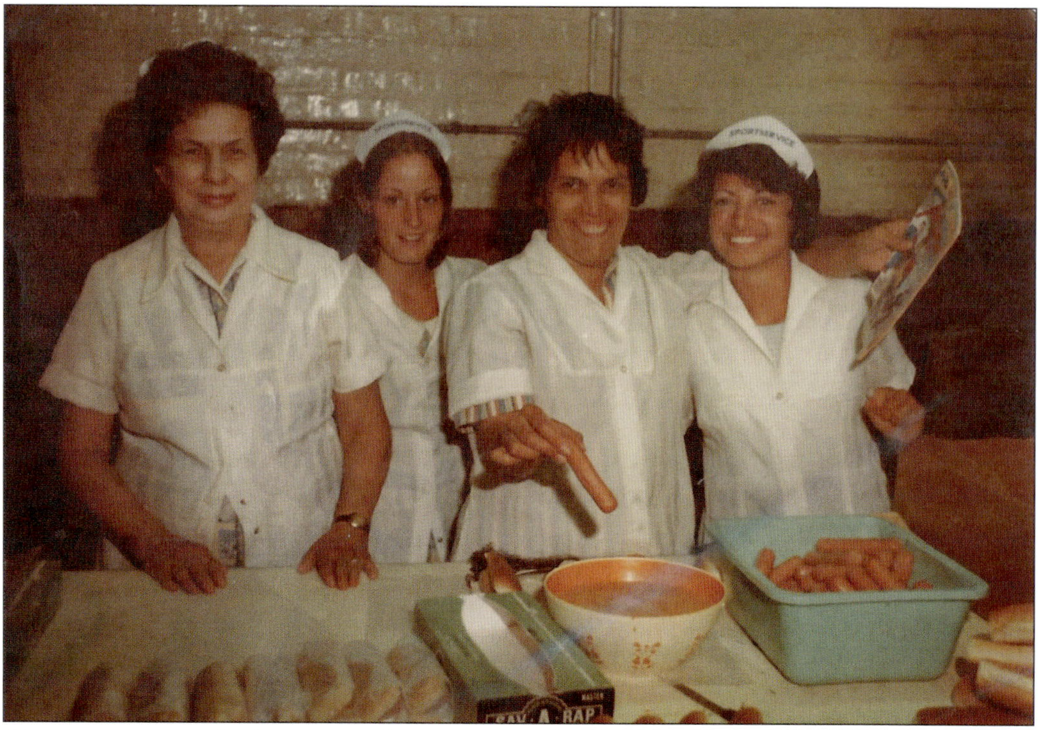

That famous song tells the crowd to "root, root, root for the home team," and it is truly appropriate for these two 1976 pictures. Ruth O'Neill is the star of both as she clowns around with her commissary crew. Affectionately, she is known as "Root-tee," and strictly for a gag, she is dunking the hotdogs into the mustard without gloves on her hands. Above with her is Carol De Santo on the right and two unidentified cookers. Below, third from left in white, she laughs along with, from left to right, Cherie Wreglesworth (who, like Root-tee, has worked at White Sox Park over 40 years), Cherie's future husband Bob Formella, John Korbel, John Ambrose, unidentified, and Tina Pappis. (Courtesy of Mike Gold.)

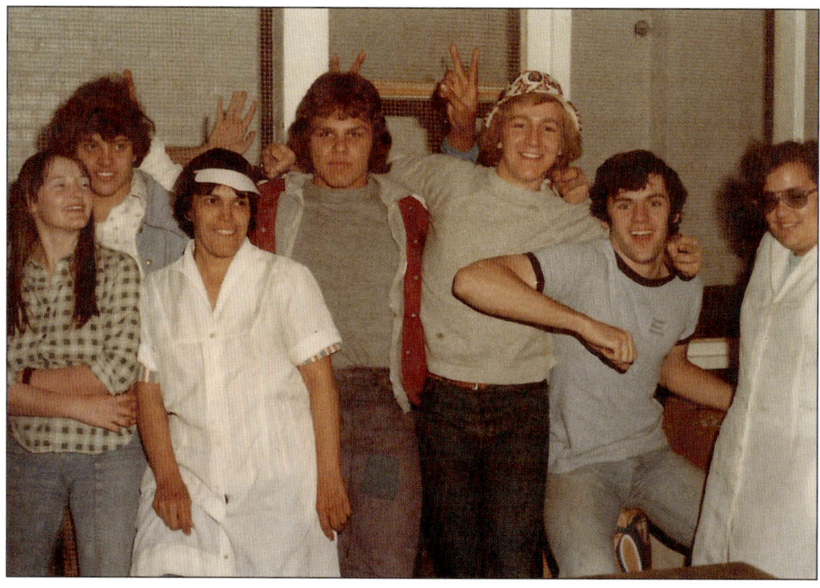

The "Breen Brood" was a fixture at White Sox Park for many years. Leo M. Breen was initially hired for the front office by Bill Veeck in 1959, eventually becoming the team's general manager and finally team president in 1969 when Arthur Allyn was the owner. Breen also worked as chief financial officer for the Cubs after leaving the Sox in 1983. Many of his eight children were Chicago vendors. John Breen, pictured at right in 1976, was Leo's first child to be employed there, and Linda, seen below in 1982 with Arnold Lipski on the left, along with sister Maryann, were known as the "Breen Queens"—a power duo on beer for quite a while. Peter Breen was another top seller and is featured on page 52 in *Wrigley Field's Amazing Vendors*.

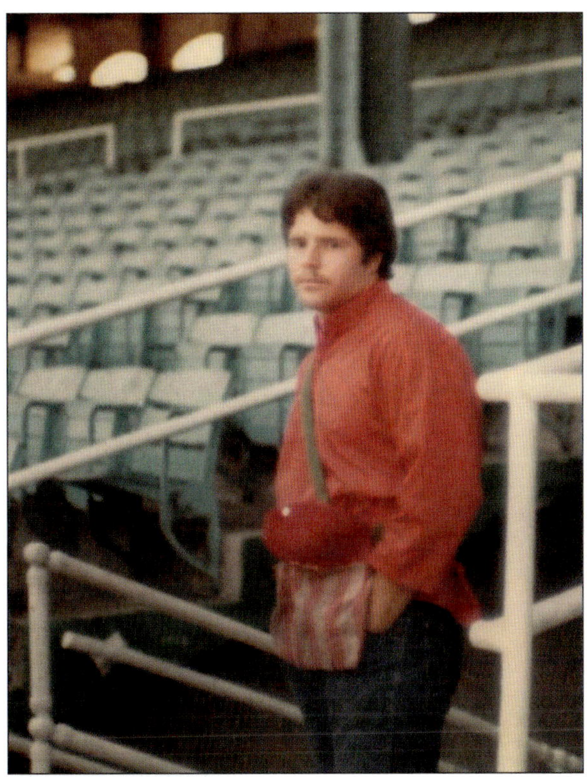

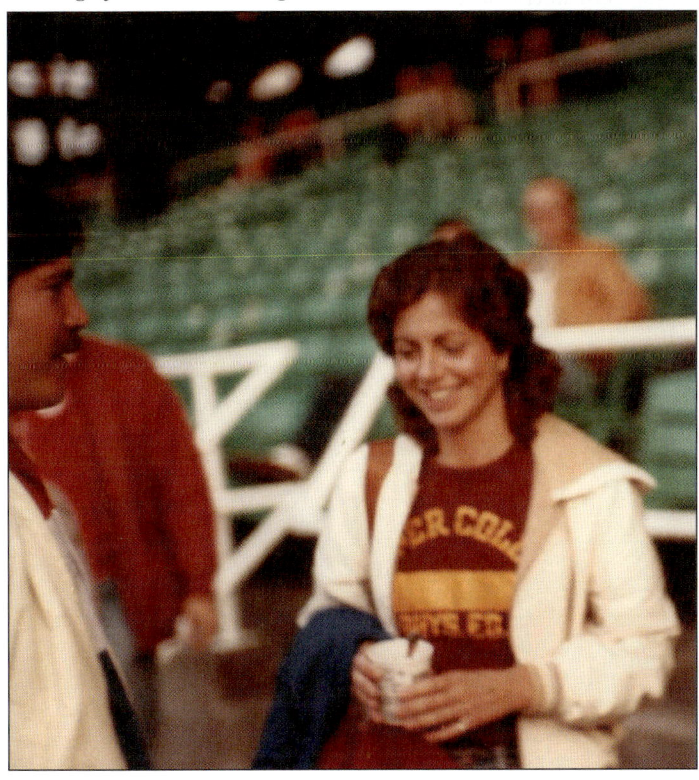

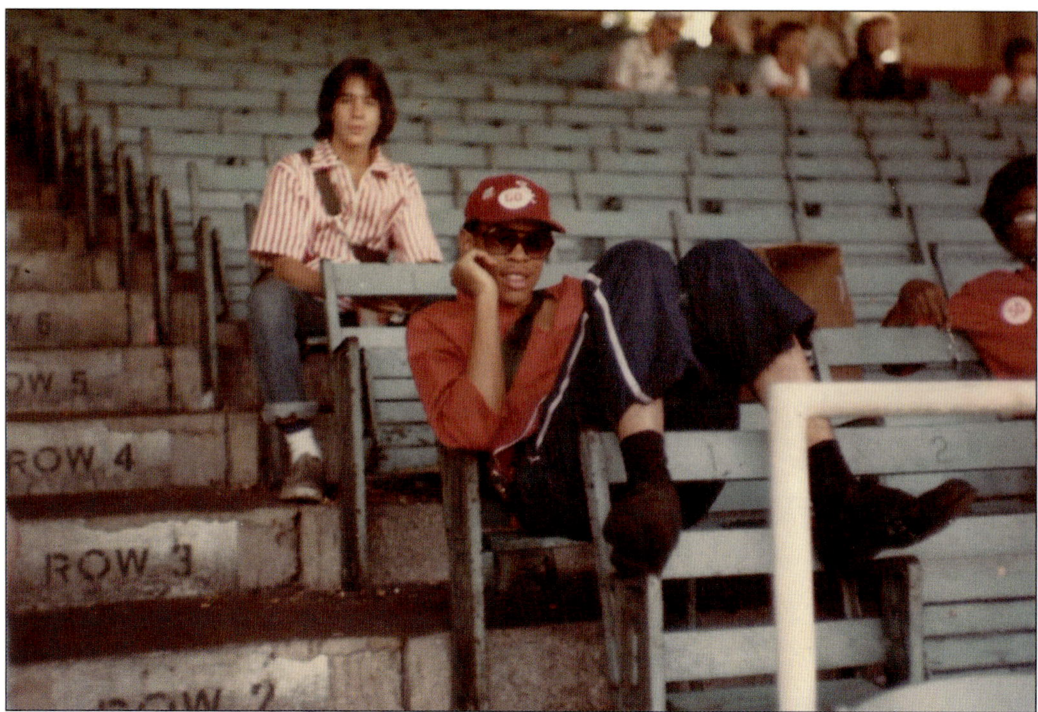

In 1976, teenagers Howard Kadet, seen above in stripes, and Charles Wheeler, wearing an orange shirt, had not yet grown into the unusual challenges of ballpark seat vending. Neither had Jim Scanner, Dave Kostka, and Mark Petrich, seen below in 1978. No other occupation consists of nonstop walking up and down steps for multiple hours without a break. They would all bide their time before "strapping up" and then go as long as they could. Lloyd Rutzky had to sit down after selling each tray of soda when he was a 17-year-old rookie in 1965. For the 1966 season, he suffered severe muscle fatigue after Opening Day and could barely walk for several weeks. Prior to subsequent campaigns, he conducted his own spring training by climbing more and more stairs.

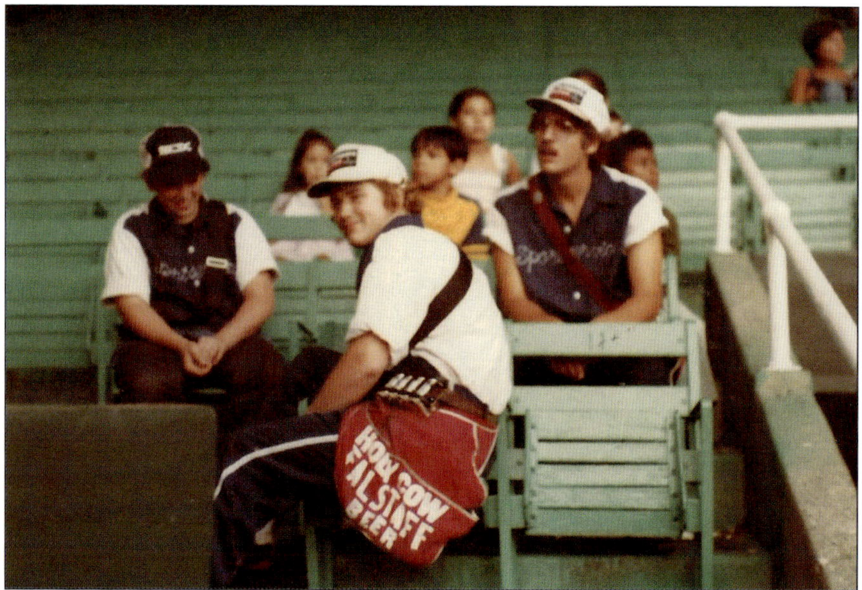

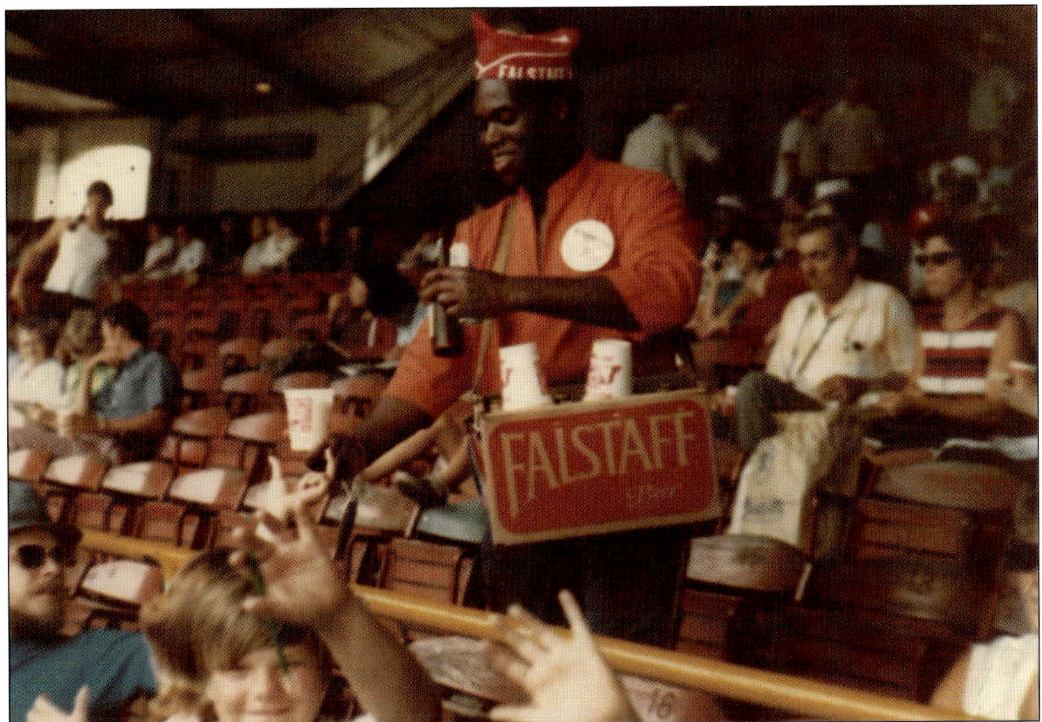

Mel Mormon was unique in ballpark history. Seen above selling beer in 1975 and laughing with the apparently unamused Kevin Anderson in 1979 below, he soon left his job vending at White Sox Park for another job—with White Sox Park ground crew. After working the seats for 10 years, he decided he liked the atmosphere there but wanted to "get back to nature." He also got to work with the renowned Roger Bossard, the head of the ground crew lovingly nicknamed "the Sodfather." Roger started in "the field" in 1967 working for his father Gene Bossard, and ascended to the throne of ground crew chief after his dad retired in 1983. He patented a drainage system he invented when the Sox moved across the street to their new park in 1991.

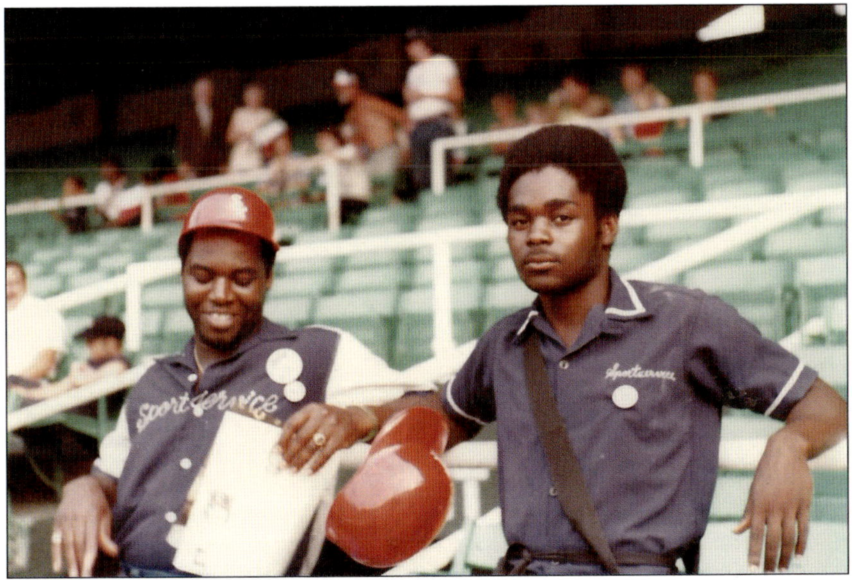

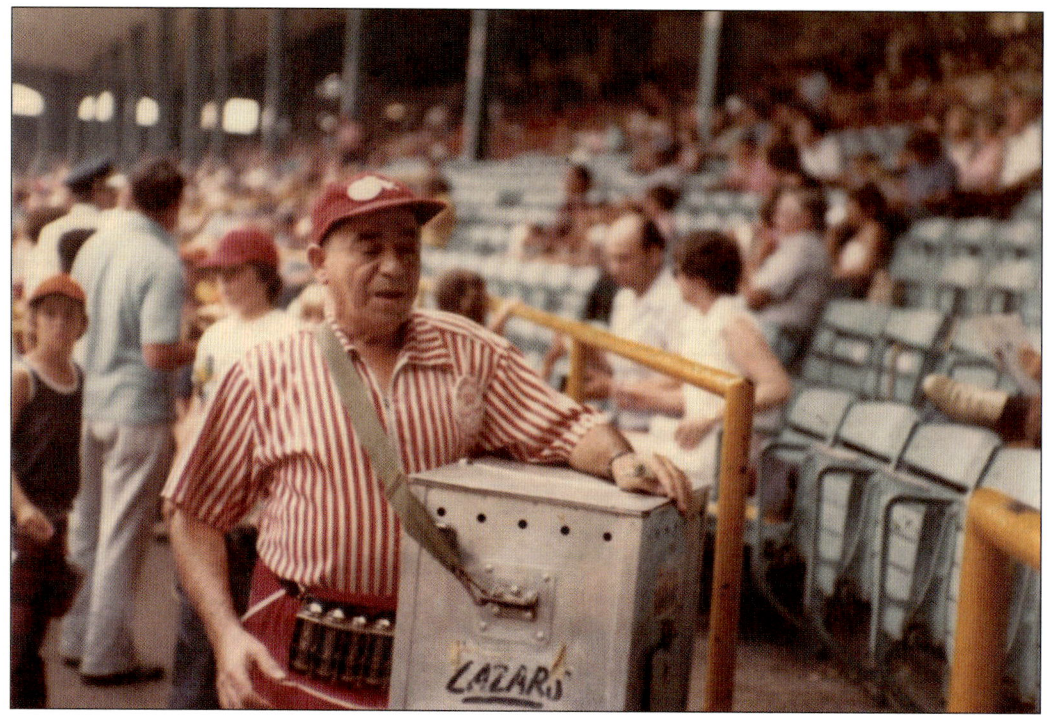

In 1975, George Rizzo (above) sold hot dogs at White Sox Park for 60¢. He was pictured on the cover of *Wrigley Field's Amazing Vendors*. Twenty-nine years later in 2004, Les Medoff (below) sold them for $4. In 2004, beer was $5.50; the last time it was 60¢ was 1972. By 2018, a can of Budweiser at White Sox Park was $9. Fans often remark that they have a hard time adjusting to such high costs for refreshments, though others feel that if they have to pay $50 or more for admission, the price of a beer and a hot dog is pretty much in the same ballpark. (Below, courtesy of Dave Levenson.)

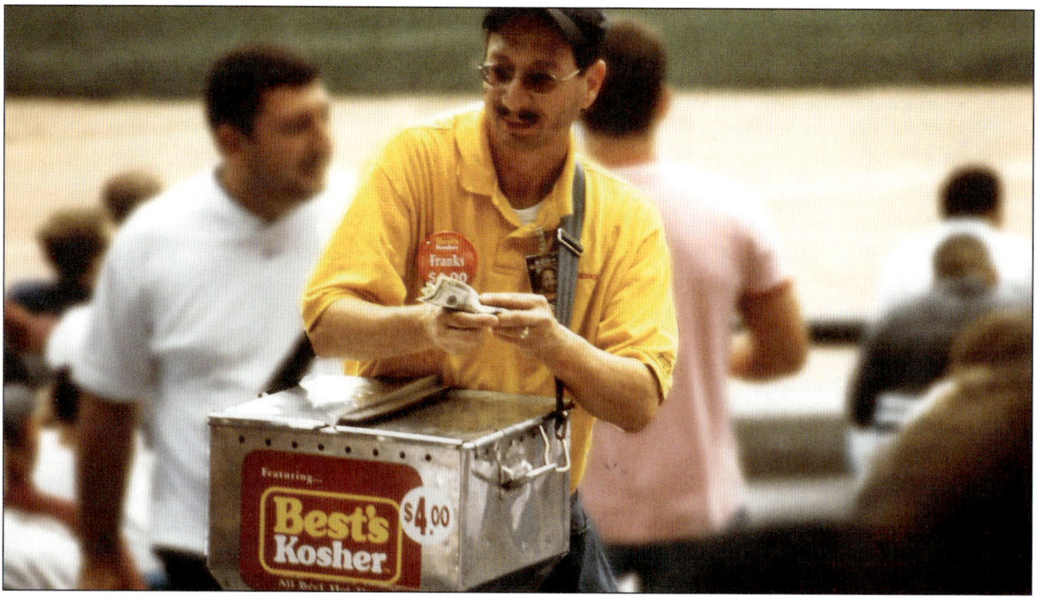

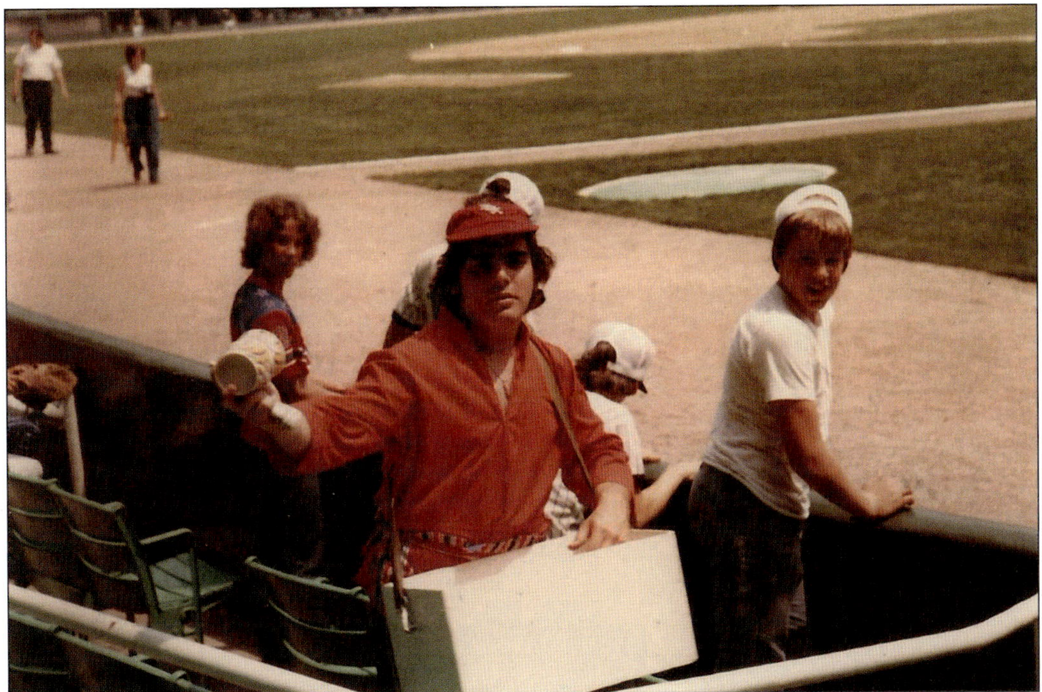

Hey, who's hungry now? In vending terms, the "hungry" ones are those who work harder than the competition. They start earliest, finish latest, and show up even on days that are predicted to be lean pickings. Michael Halperin, seen above in 1978, ranked among the all-time "grubs" and was proud of it. Halperin is selling ice cream here, but he would always squeeze every last dime out of whatever item he was assigned. Leah Mooshil, seen below at right in 1991, on the other hand, demonstrates what most people do when they are hungry—they eat, as many employees usually did before games. Mike Gold (waving) was always starving and known to consume mass quantities of just about anything.

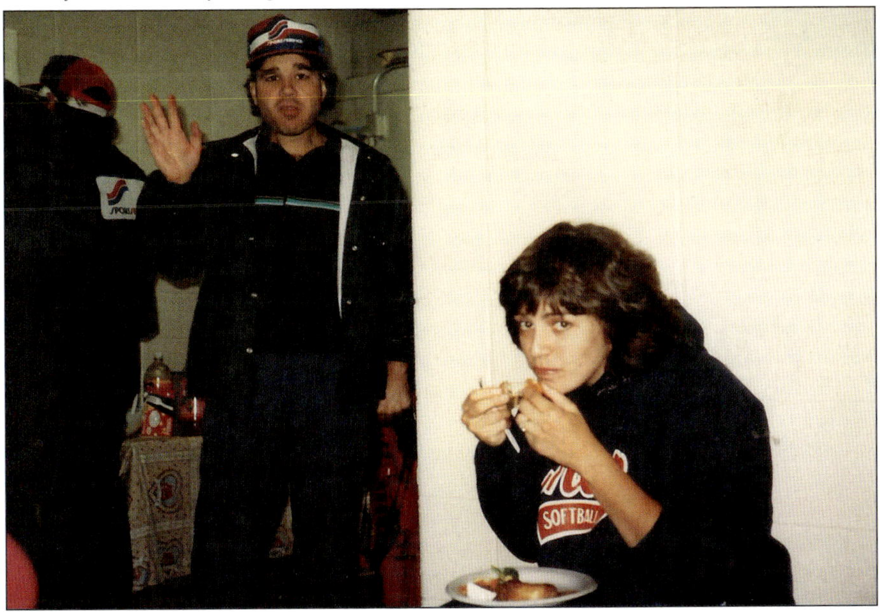

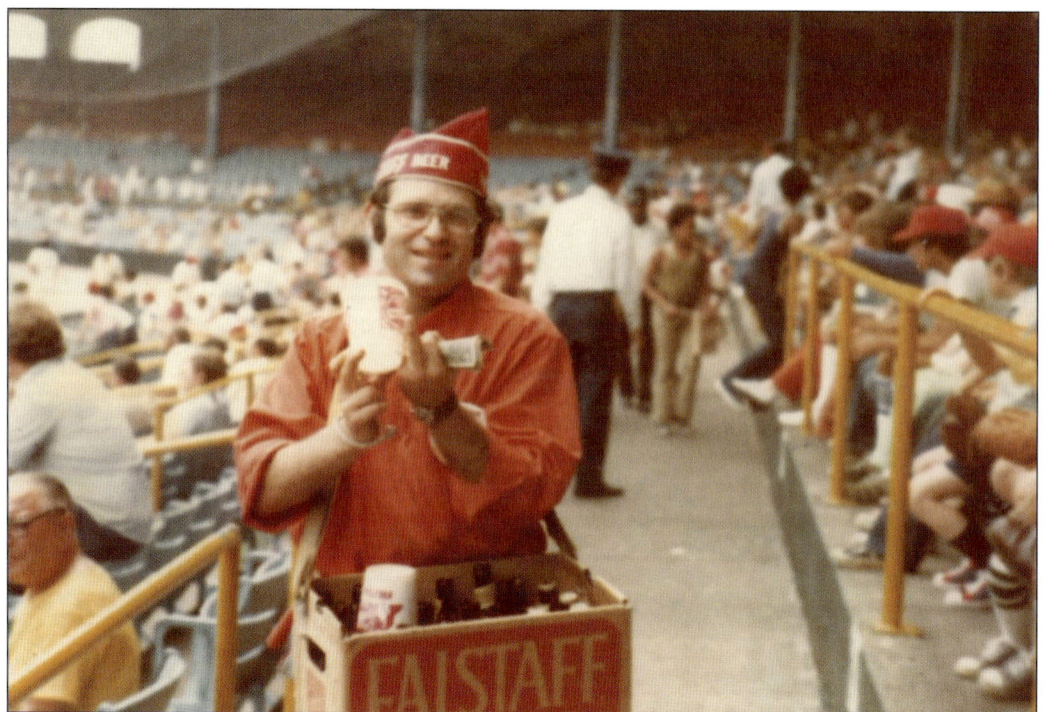

Chicago vendors use straps, but around the world, there are plenty of locations where straps are forsaken. The debate rages in the vending community on which method is better, but vendors in the Windy City say, "no, absolutely not—our way is the right way." On these two pages are four advocates of the "belt." Don Gerstein, seen above in 1975, demonstrates how a beerman, with two free hands, can hold his money securely and maneuver his cups while not blocking the aisle by having to put his case on the ground to make a sale. Hot dog man Dan Ferrone, below in 1975, is able to doff his hat to get a customer's attention. Without their belts, they could not do it.

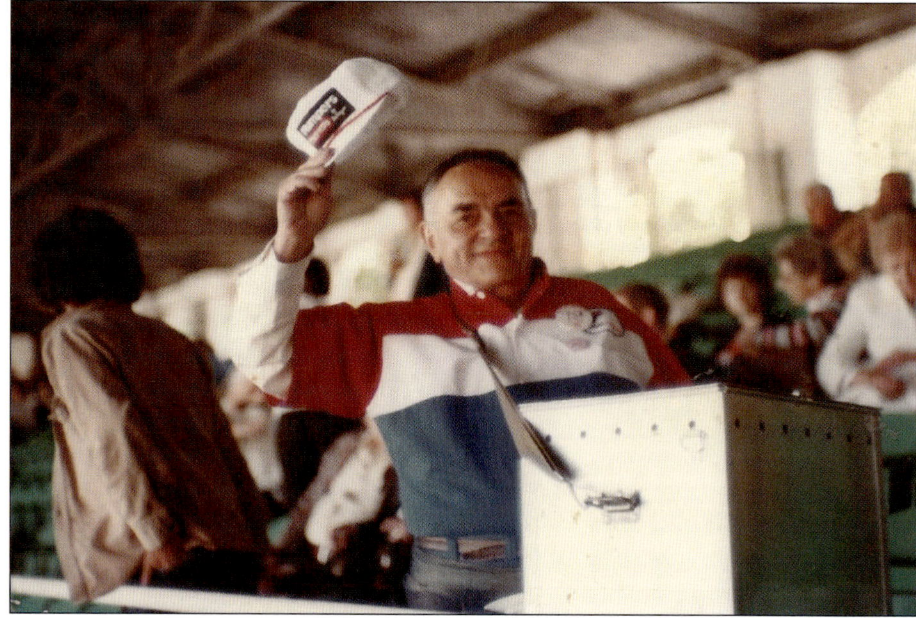

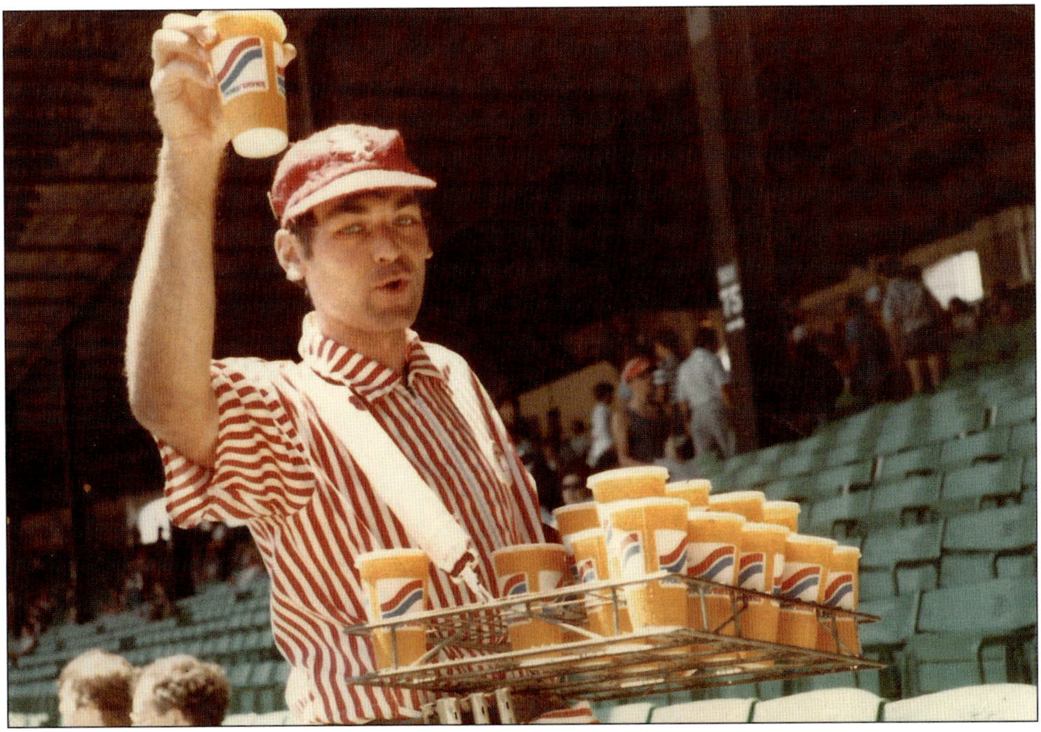

Pictured here are two more vending-strap users. Like those on the opposite page, they show why they believe that utilizing a belt to hold their products is far more efficient than having to hold their trays with both hands, or—can you believe it—balance it on top of their head. Both Al Chiss, seen above in 1978 peddling pop, and peanut man Arthur Bailey, at right in 1996, can both advertise their items by holding them high for all to see. They can also count their money while they walk, pass their goodies to customers, and make change, and keep anything from spilling or falling. The main thing, though, is they never have to waste valuable time constantly picking up their goods and putting them down.

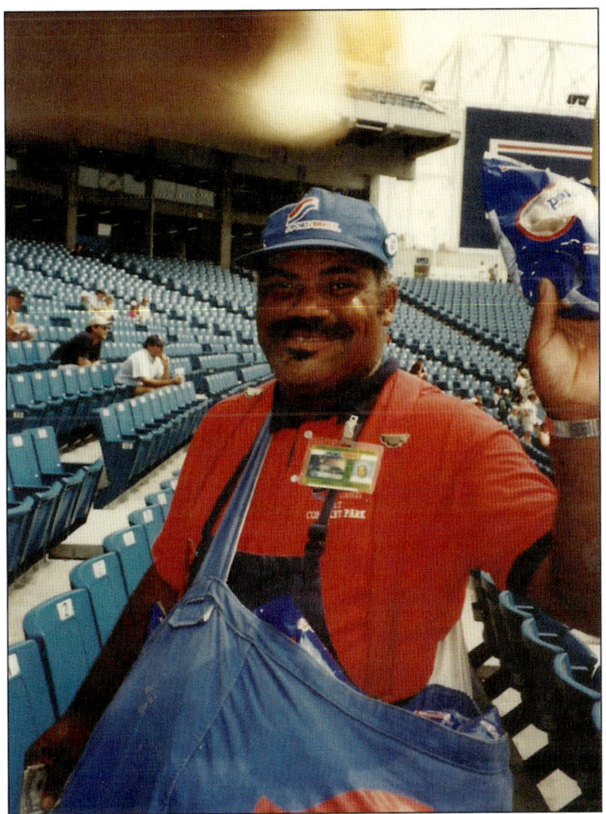

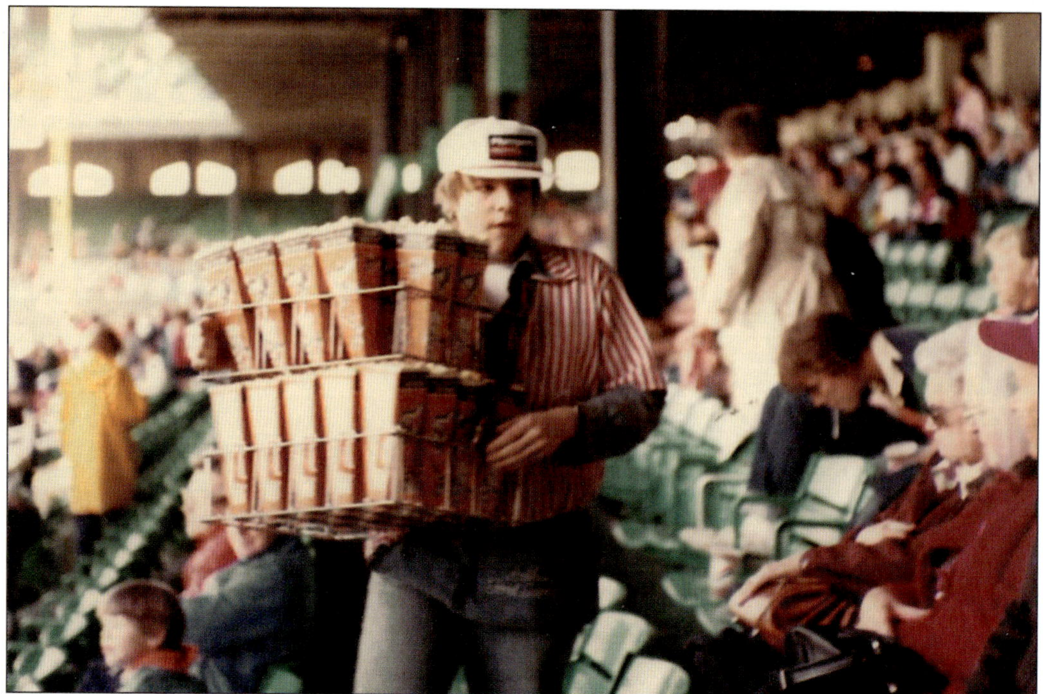

Seen here are the "Brothers Sorn," both selling double loads of what some vendors called "Corn in the Horn," because after the salty, buttery treat was consumed, the container could be used as a megaphone to shout "Go-Go-Sox," or yell for more popcorn. Observe the older Sorn, Eric (above), in May 1979 and the younger Keith (below) a couple months later. In the brief interim between these pictures, not only had the color of the popcorn boxes changed, but so had the style of their uniforms.

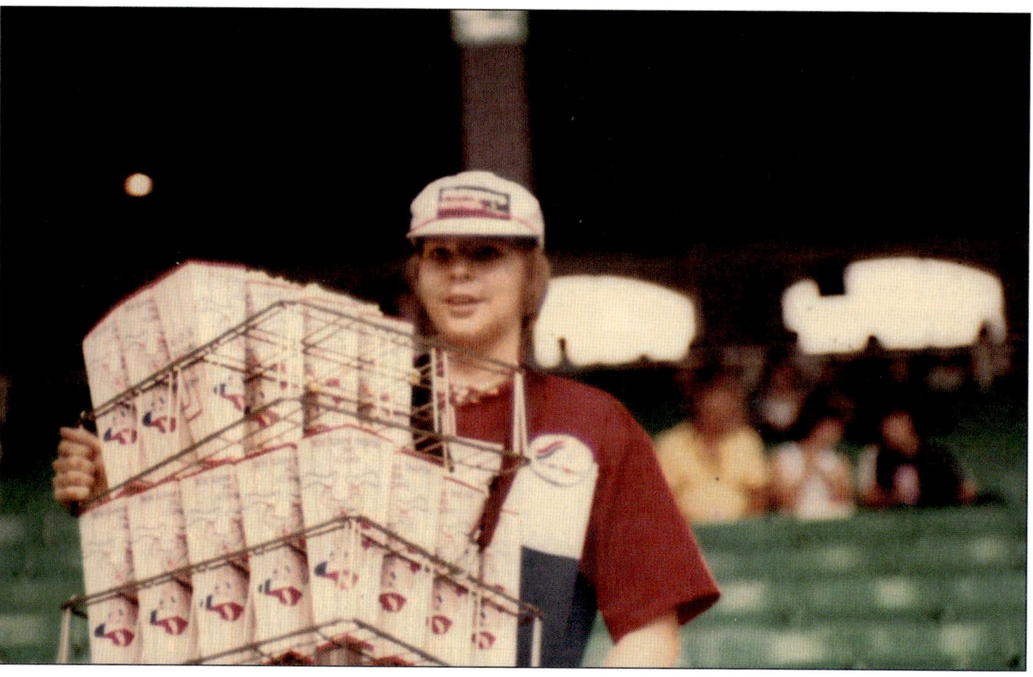

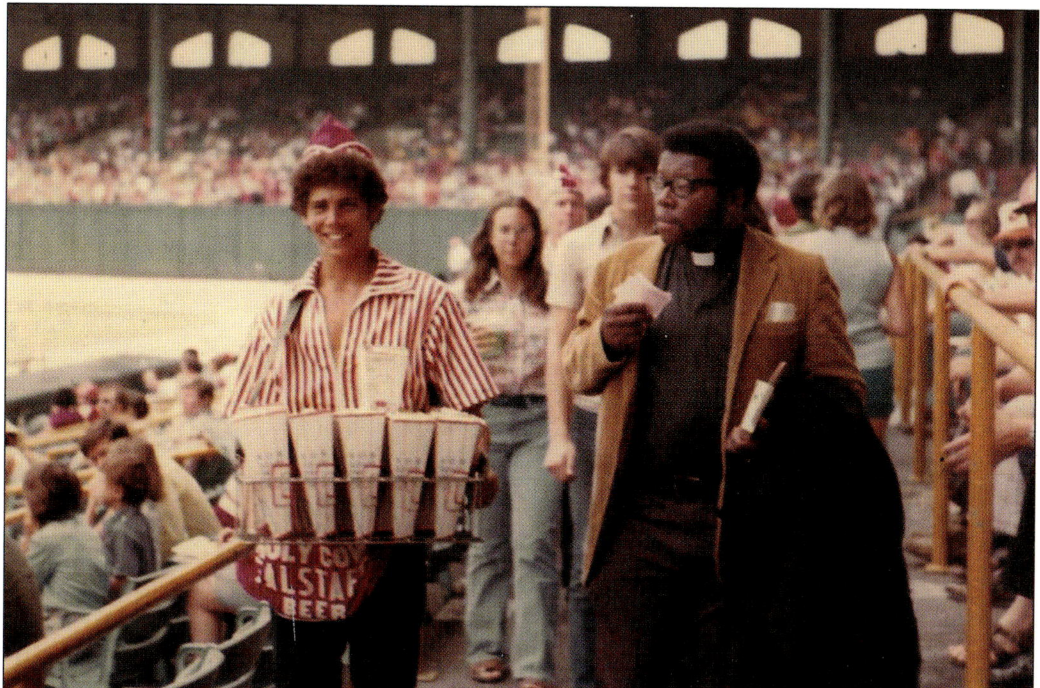

Scott Weber (left) sells popcorn in 1975, although his apron clearly reads, "Holy Cow, Falstaff Beer." Contributing to the possible confusion is that strolling alongside Scott on his daily vending pilgrimage appears to be a clergyman seemingly oblivious to his "horns of plenty."

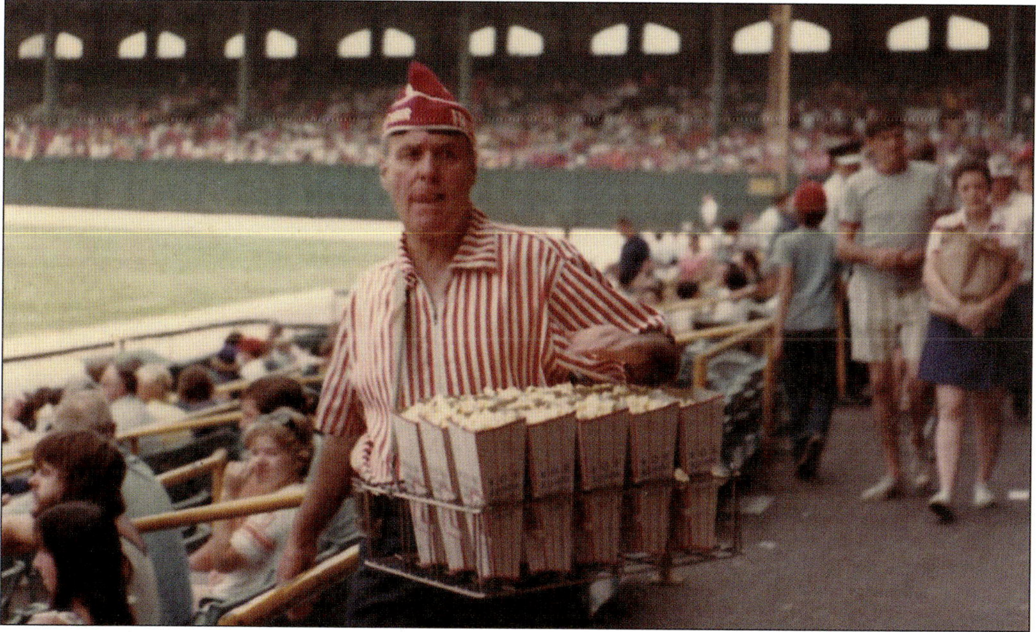

Vending veteran Jimmy Winters is seen here in 1975 peddling popcorn in the twilight of a six-decade career after numerous years of selling beer. Winters claimed to have worked as a young teenager at the first World Series at Comiskey Park in 1917, in which the White Sox defeated the New York Giants four games to two.

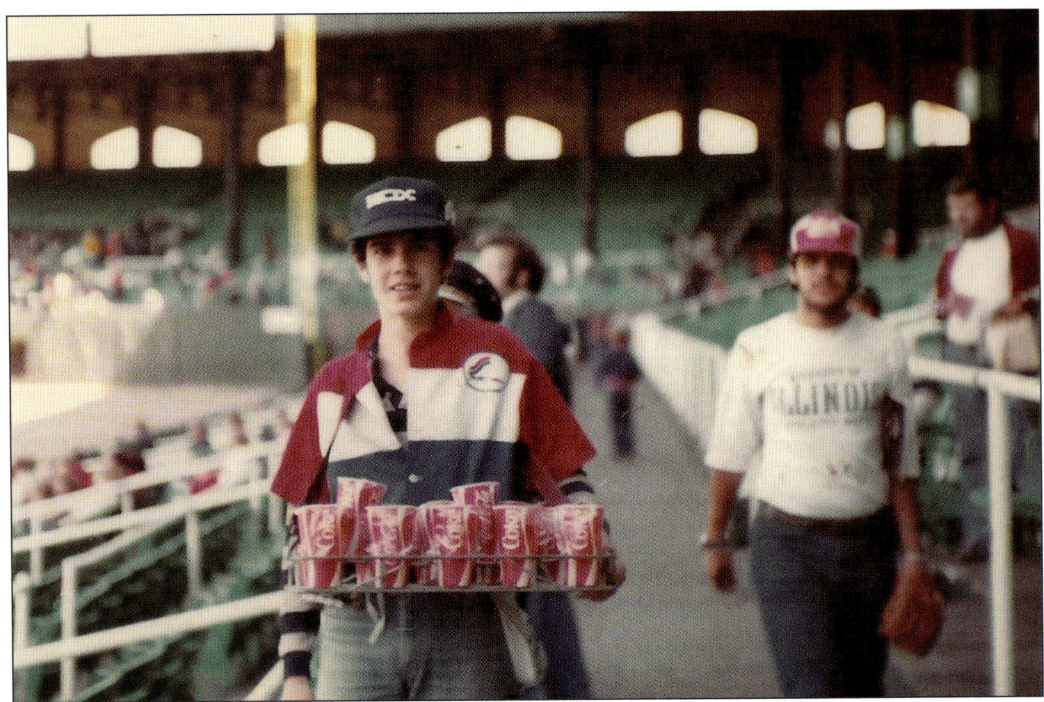

Here, two young men sell Coke along the first base line on the same mid-September afternoon in 1979, yet they have on different uniforms with different hats. George Alpogianis (above) and Bruce Cooper (below) were fortunate they were not pop vendors just a couple years earlier, because with every tray of soda, the vendors were compelled to sell with their 15 Cokes either 5 orange drinks or lemonades, which found few takers. Finally, after endless years of futile attempts to force those unpopular beverages on a reluctant clientele, the concessionaire gave in to the realities of soft drink tastes and discontinued this policy.

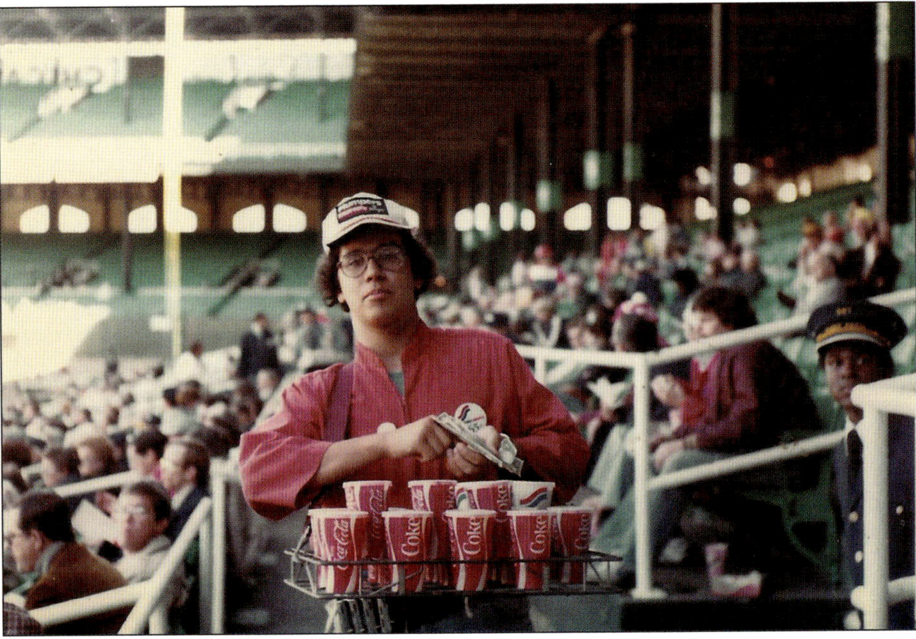

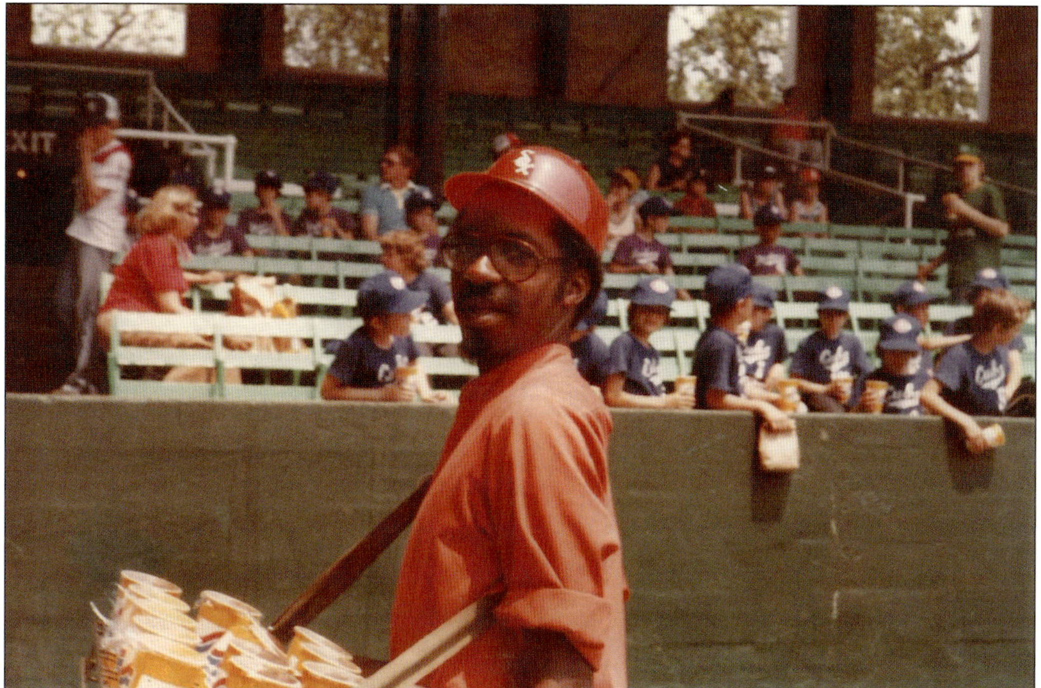

For those vendors selling kid-friendly items, Little League days were the games they hoped for. Henry Grant, pictured above in May 1978, heads for the left-field outfield with his tray of pop. It appears that the Cubs have invaded the White Sox Park seats, but it is apparently the Cubs junior team carrying lunch bags. Randy Stoler, seen below in May 1979, is still selling a lot of pop despite the fact that the pre-game parade of budding ballplayers has eroded most of his customer base.

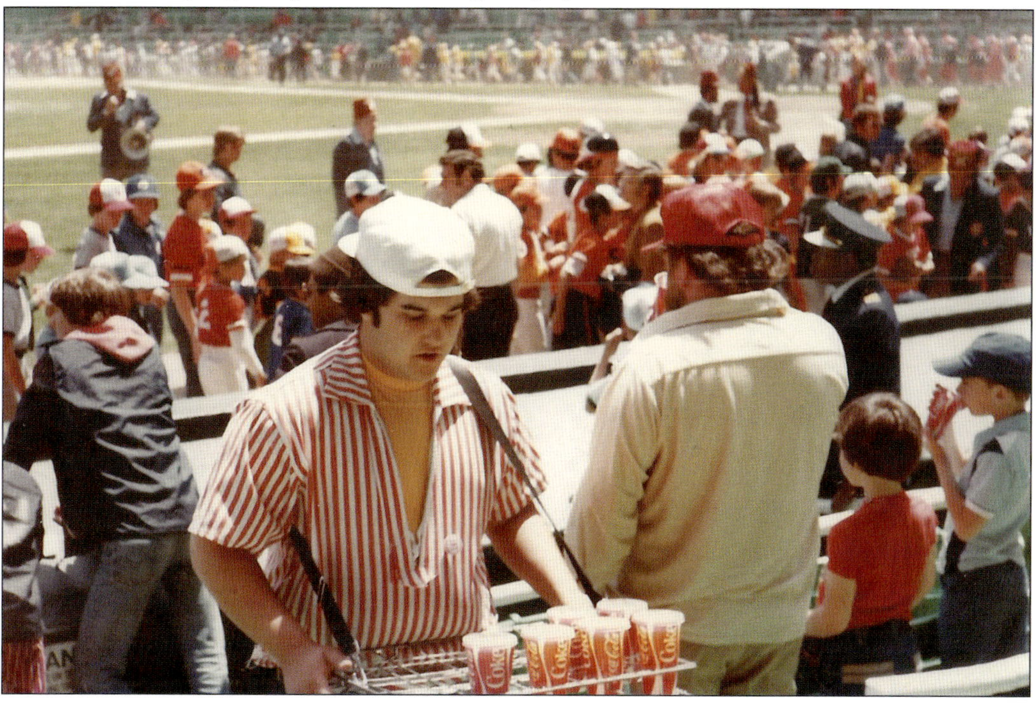

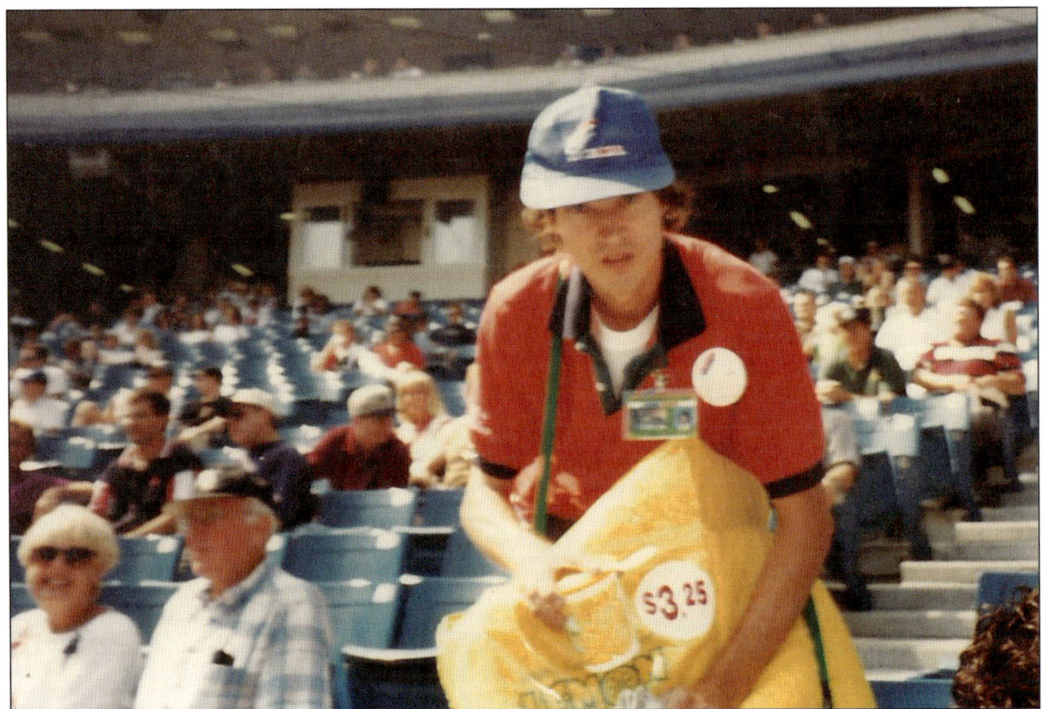

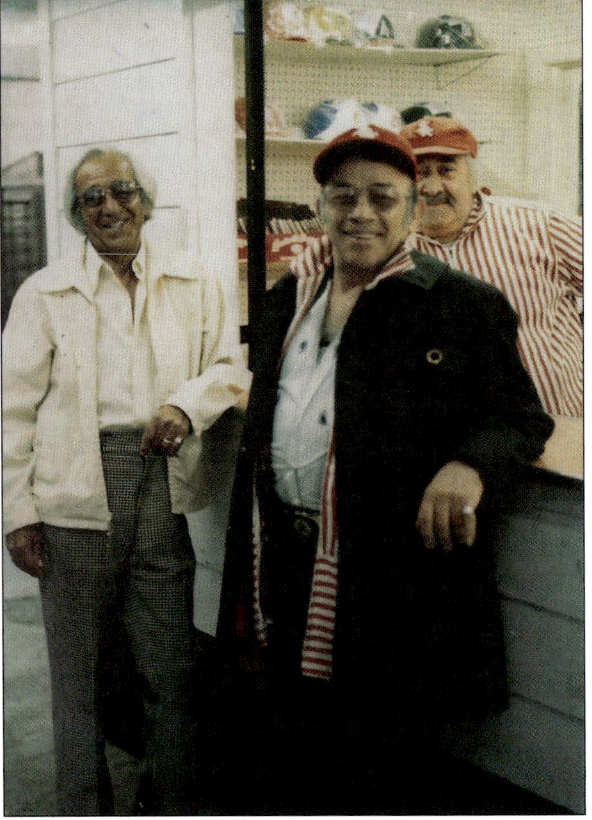

Selling lemon chill could make one feel like they had superpowers. Though most of the games are at night with a predominantly adult crowd not exactly craving a kid's item like this frozen treat, on a sunny Sunday with temperatures in the 90s, it can be like providing oxygen to somebody who is drowning. Tom Kirk seems on the verge of collapse from working so hard in this photograph taken on August 25, 1996.

Carmen LaPapa (left) was like a visiting dignitary at Comiskey Park in 1976. He was the union steward at the nearby International Amphitheater, which stood from 1934 to 1999; it held a Beatles concert on September 5, 1964, as well as the infamous 1968 Democratic Convention. His tour guide is the assistant steward, Nick "Cappy" Caputo. Tony Randazzo is in the background.

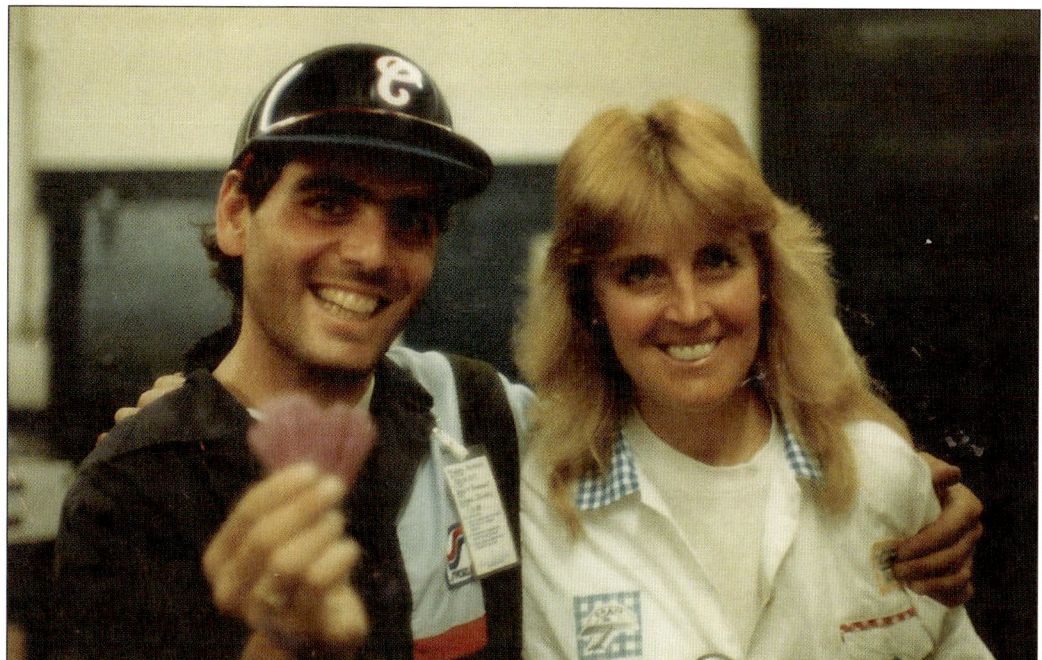

On June 12, 1988, Mike Halperin and Cindy Fosco, among the fiercest of adversaries vying for "high person" on beer every single game (that is who sells the most—not who is the most inebriated), have come together to smile and forget.

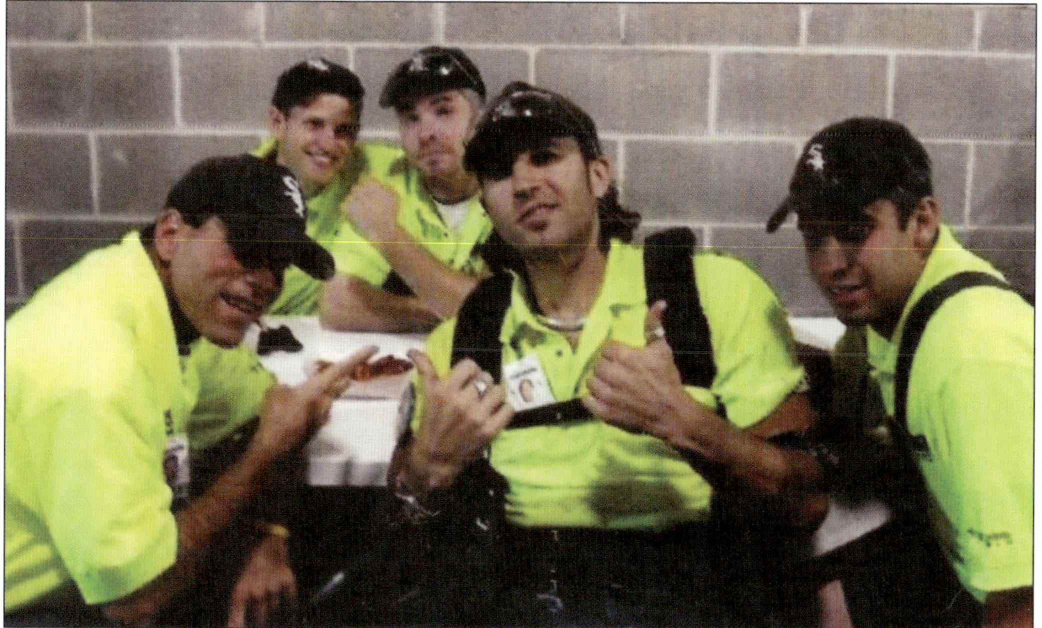

It was an incredibly water-logged weekend that saw these five green-shirted guys waiting to work a delayed doubleheader on September 14, 2008. From left to right, Darin Kopac, Jared Ralsky, Joe Cavise, Adam Carter, and Mark Carman sit at an employees' area picnic table. Carman was just moonlighting here from his new WGN radio broadcasting job and did post-game WGN White Sox shows in 2018. (Courtesy of Adam Carter.)

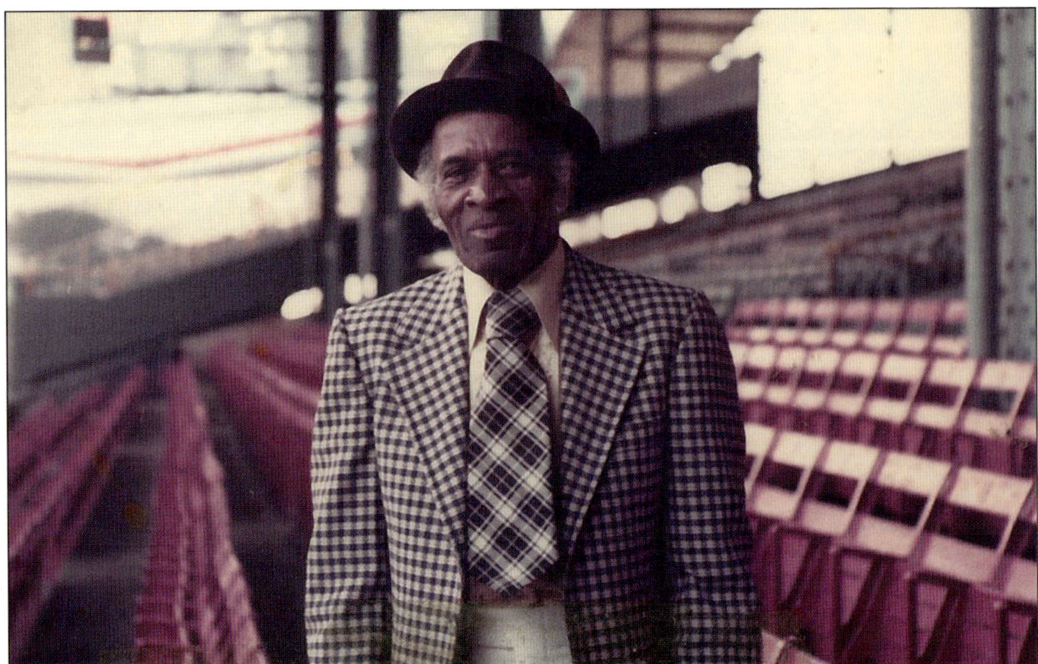

"Clothes makes the vending man," as the saying goes, and here were two esteemed men responsible for costuming the vendors. Charlie Porter is seen above in 1975 in the right-field stands directly above the two-floor "uniform room." Below in 1985, Dave Parker stands inside that historical landmark. Both men needed enormous amounts of patience to wait and wait for the vending men to get changed after each game so they could go home. Many a night also featured extra innings of self-control for Charlie and Dave, as vendors frequently were treated to lengthy exhibitions of Lloyd Rutzky taking his frustrations out after his White Sox suffered a defeat, symbolically horsewhipping a table with his belt to thrash out his anger.

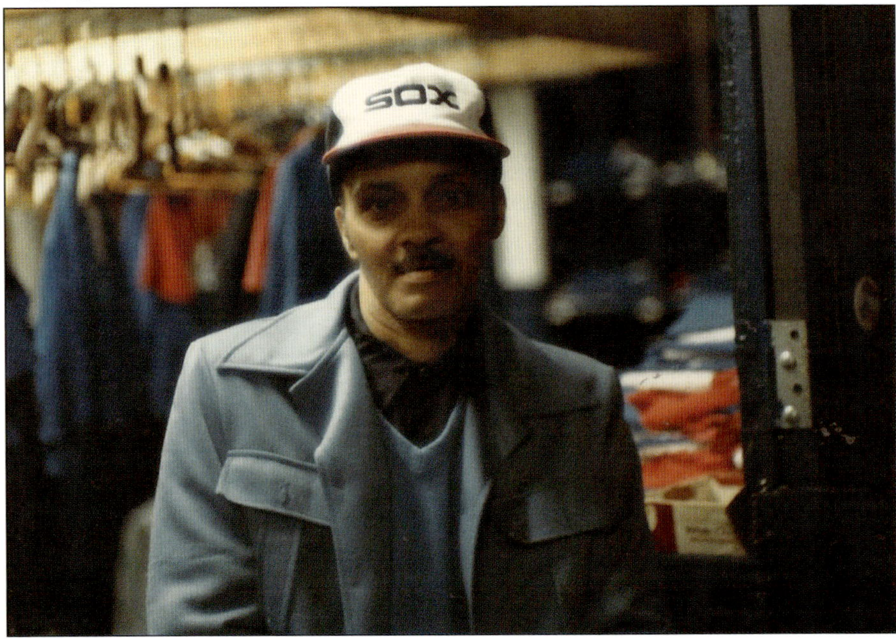

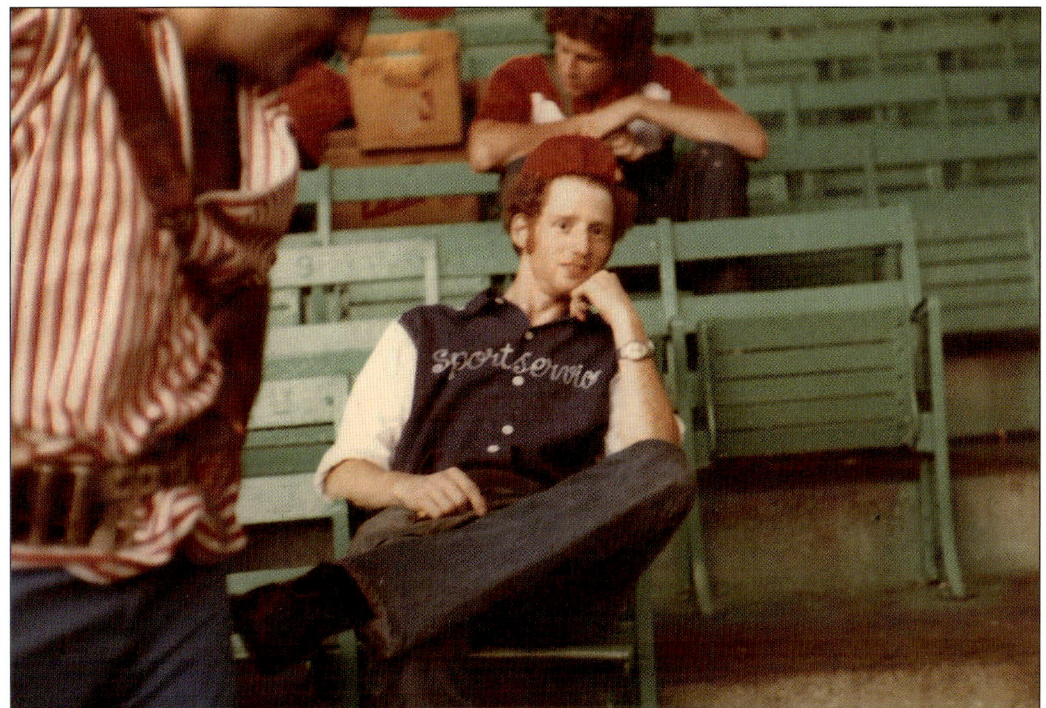

Gary Tuch, seen above, remembers the August 6, 1976, night at Sox Park and called it "Ten Flew over the Cuckoo's Nest." Lloyd Rutzky was incredibly incensed after the Sox were swept in a lengthy doubleheader by Kansas City, leading to a very inspired double horsewhip incited by taunts from his Cubs fan co-workers, such as Tuch. Meanwhile, clothes man Charlie Porter, with his warnings about "no hosswhuppin' tonight" ignored, had endured more than he could take after seeing that Marty "the Barber" Portnoy was giving a post-whip haircut to Morrie Rosenblatt. He locked everybody in, and they used a bat to smash a hole in the door. The next day, steward John Studnicka, seen below with son Jimmy Studnicka at the 3B shoeshine stand, confided he would have broken the door too.

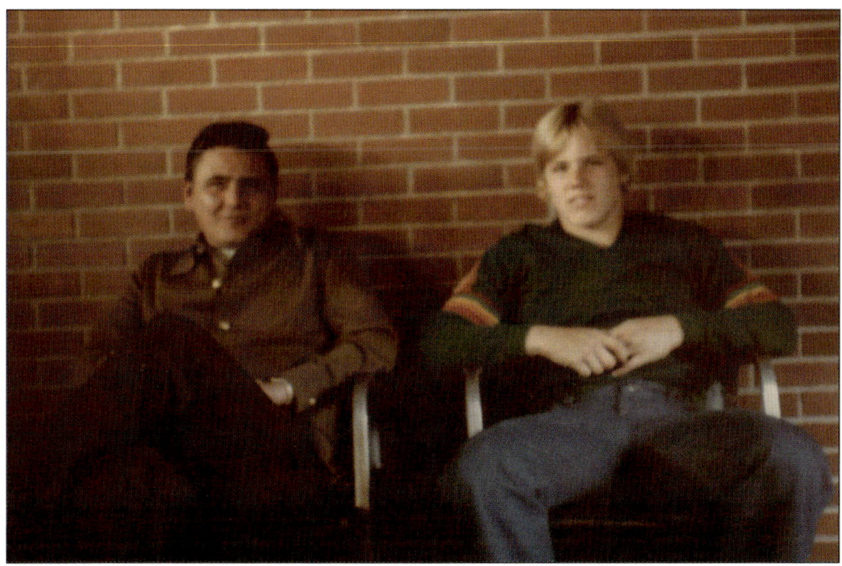

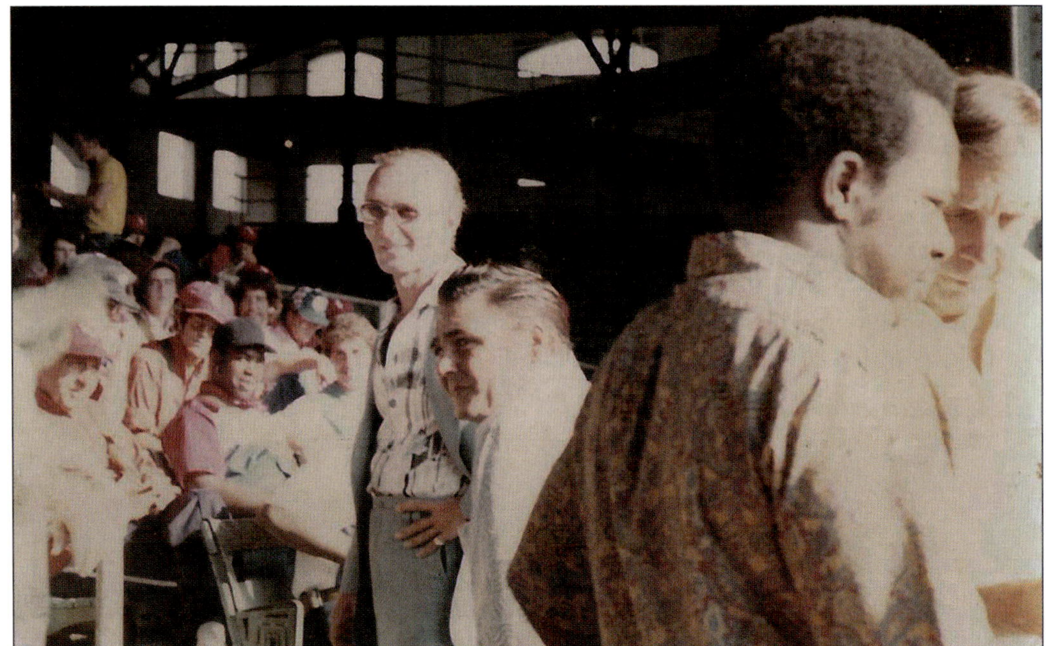

Union president Nick LaPapa and White Sox union steward John Studnicka are seen at center above in the right-field stands on the night of August 2, 1977. It was nearly one year to the day after 10 very boisterous vendors were forced to make the "Great Escape" from the uniform room after being locked in. Led by Lloyd Rutzky, who had found a bat stored in the room, they smashed through the door with some helpful swings by fellow incarcerates Morrie Rosenblatt, Marty Portnoy, Arnold Lipski, Abe Rapuch, Neal Halter, Marv Mitofsky, Ken Dolin, Eric Eckstrum, and former vendor Gary Isaacson, and climbed out to freedom. LaPapa, after a plea for leniency from Studnicka for the young "breakers," ultimately decided the 10 were innocent.

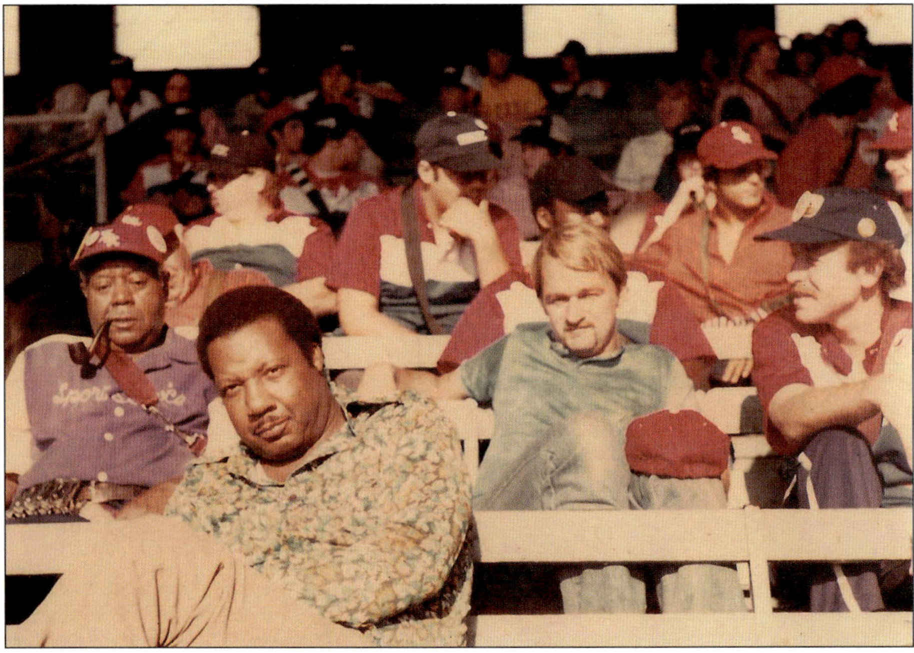

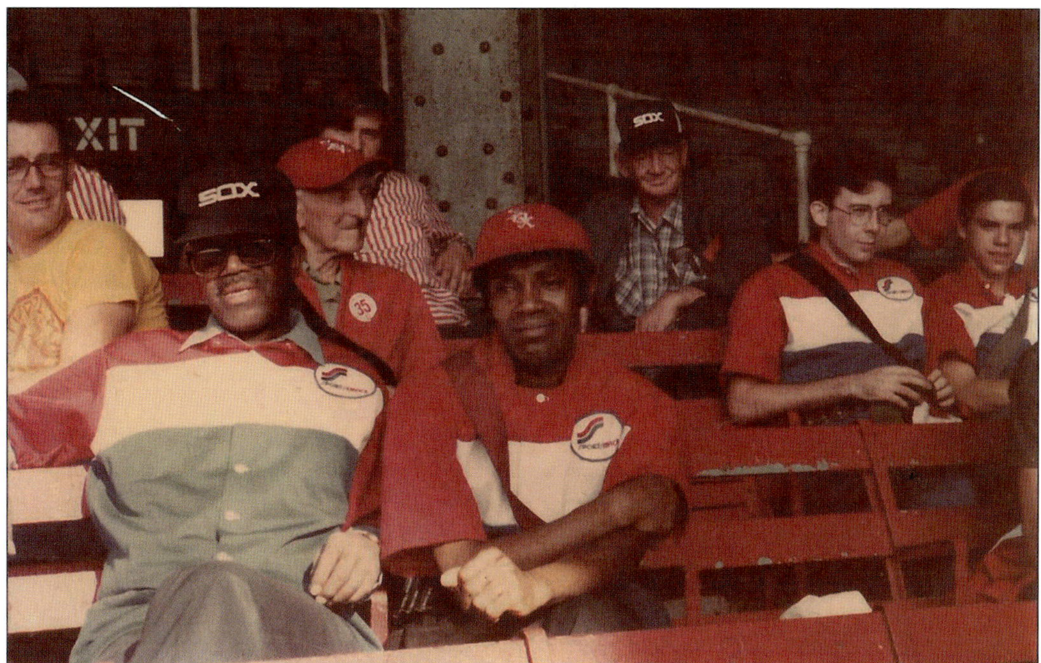

A rare summer union meeting is seen on these two pages. Then called Local 236, but known in the 2000s as Local One, the usual procedure was for monthly gatherings from October to April when there were no ball games to work. During the season, labor issues would be handled by union stewards. In the image above, however, on August 2, 1977, union president Nick LaPapa addressed the problems members were having with rowdy fans. Among those pictured are Bernie Lasinsky, Mel Mormon, Mark Reiner, Irving Newer, Greg Cola, Millard McCoy, Jim Gwisdala, Dave Klemp, John W. Rogers Jr., and Gary Shulman.

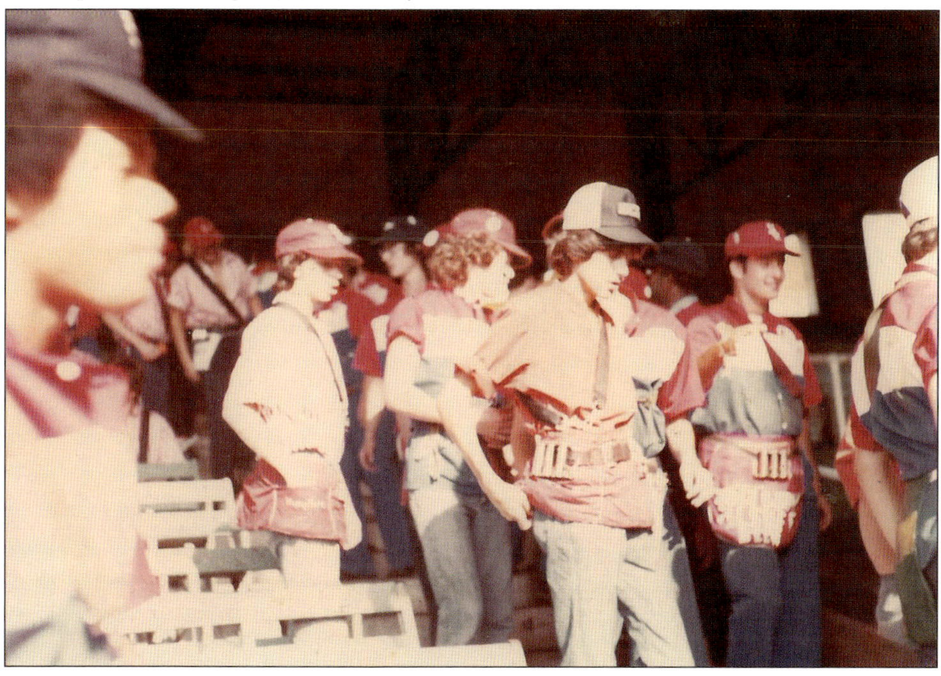

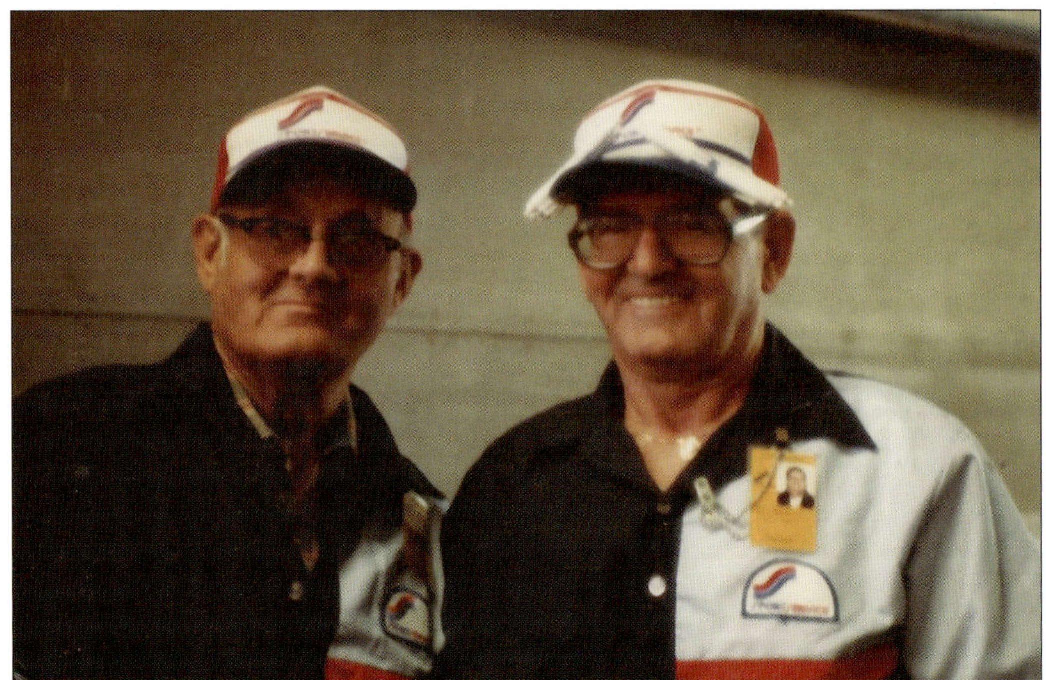

Chuck Berry sang it best in "Johnny B. Goode"—this trio of Johns has certainly been "goode" for the vendor's union. John Moscato, seen above at left in 1986, was a vice president of Local 236, which has protected vendor's interests for over 70 years. Moscato had been famous before that as the chief Andy Frain usher at Gate Seven at Comiskey Park. John Segvich (above right), a former US Army sergeant, was assistant steward for many years at both Chicago ballparks before becoming chief at Wrigley Field from 1995 to 2000. After Segvich retired, the new steward on the north side was John Studnicka Jr., pictured below in 1991; his father, John Sr., had the same post at Comiskey Park from 1973 until his untimely death in 1987.

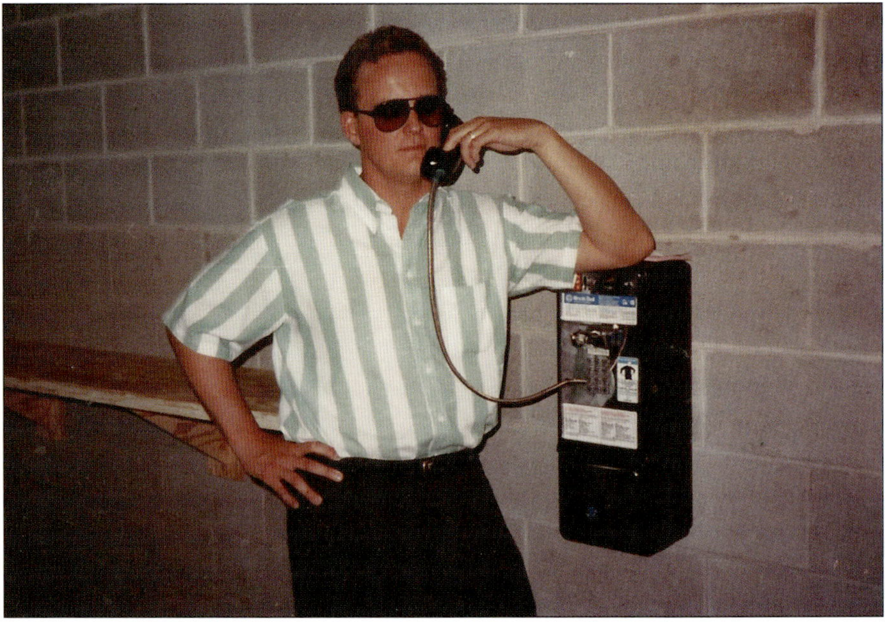

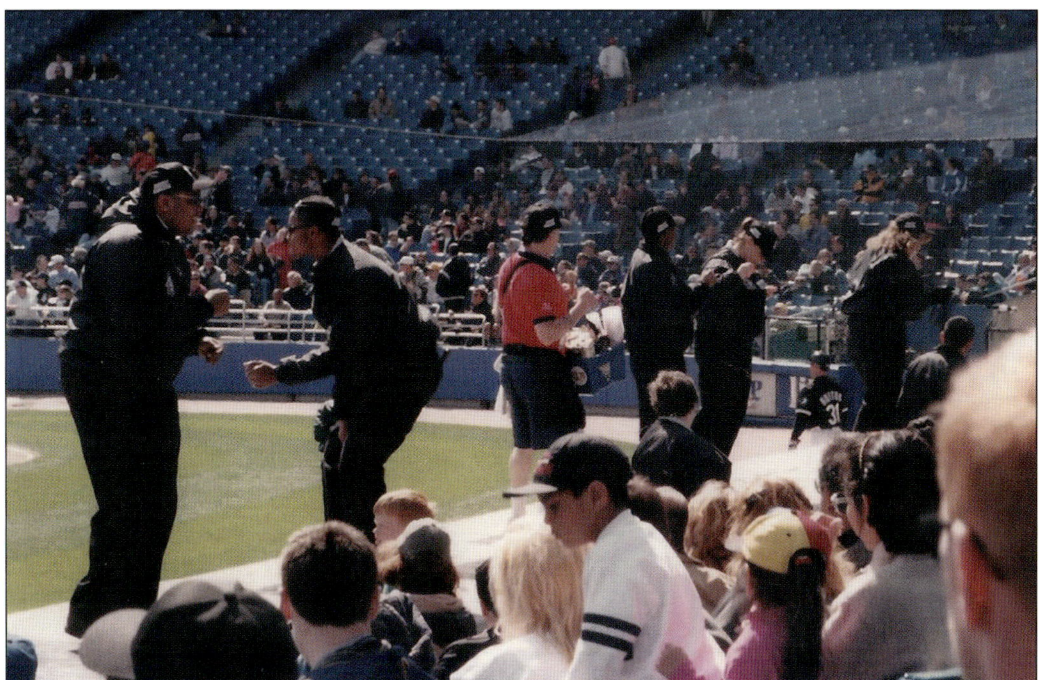

Above, these ballpark workers were all "Stayin' Alive, Stayin' Alive" in April 1999. That Bee Gees hit was part of the opening act that year for the Dugout Dancers. Trying to heat up "Disco Inferno" excitement for fans here was Lloyd Rutzky in his flaming-red vending shirt (center), commissary cashier Helen Tomczuk (far right), and four very "Hot Stuff" ushers. The "Dy-No-Mite" employee chorus line wowed the crowd between innings, but their show closed in September—the "Suspicion" was, due to an overdose of "Boogie, Oogie, Oogie." That led two of their biggest hot dog men fans, Randy Antlept (of the rock group Public i) and Dave Gaborek to lament "How Can You Mend a Broken Heart?" as seen below in 1982.

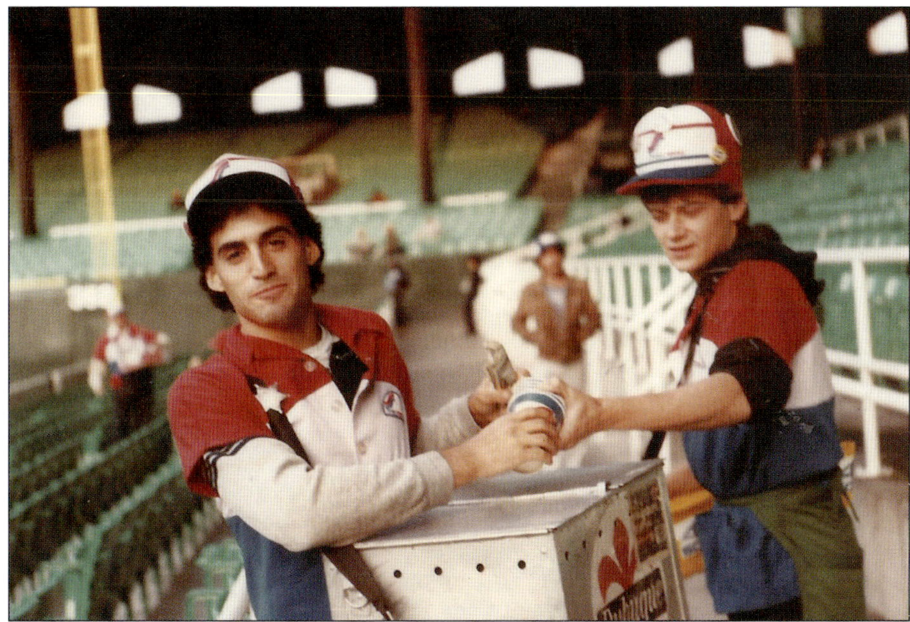

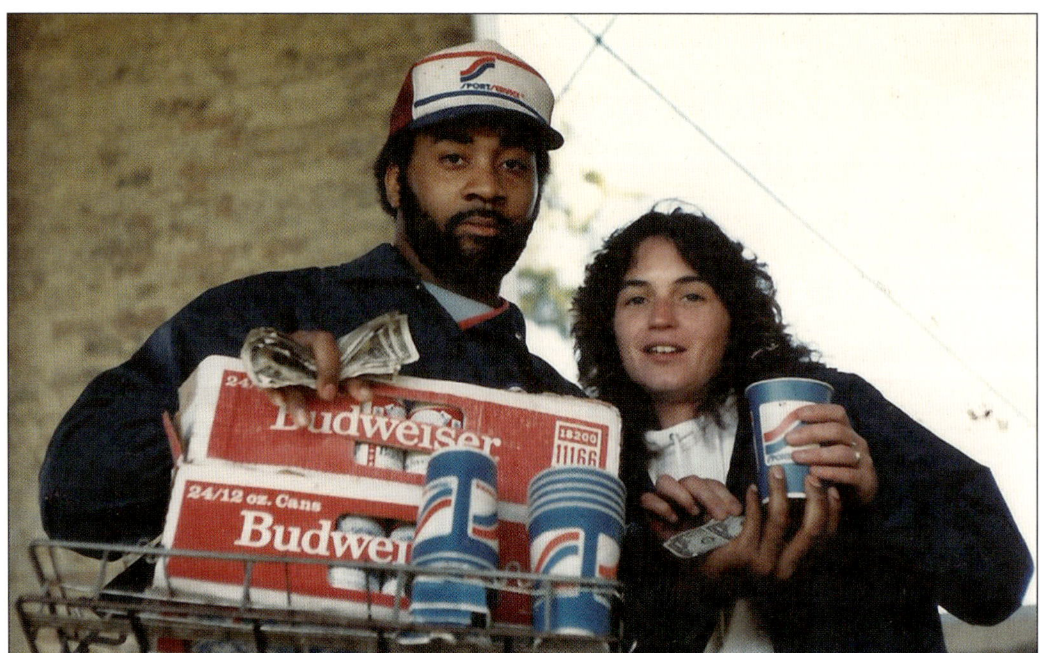

Lee Cook (above) and Bob Hill (below) have double loads of Budweiser on October 6, 1985. They seem to be pretty cool with their jobs; however, it was not always that way selling beer in cans. The day the switch was made from refrigerated bottles to cans on Opening Day 1978 caused more than mere pandemonium. One vendor, Brandon Medow, called it "Can-demonium!" There had been no training given to the workers on properly opening the pop tops, and beer showers were inadvertently given to fans all day. Vendors' fingers could barely function afterward, and the empties were strewn all around the park. A few guys tried to beat the system by just handing out beer by the case. The next day, new strict rules would forbid that.

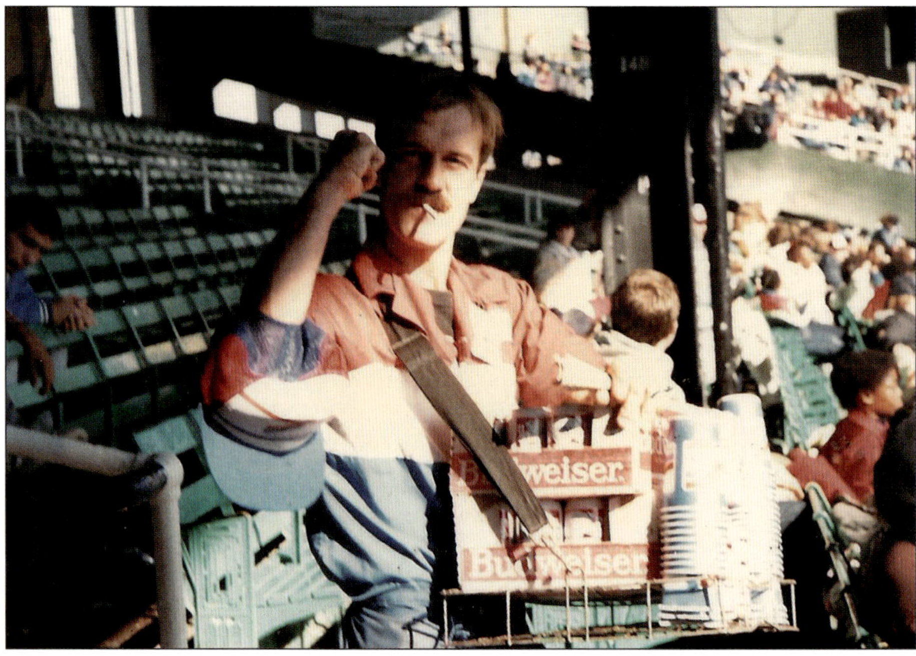

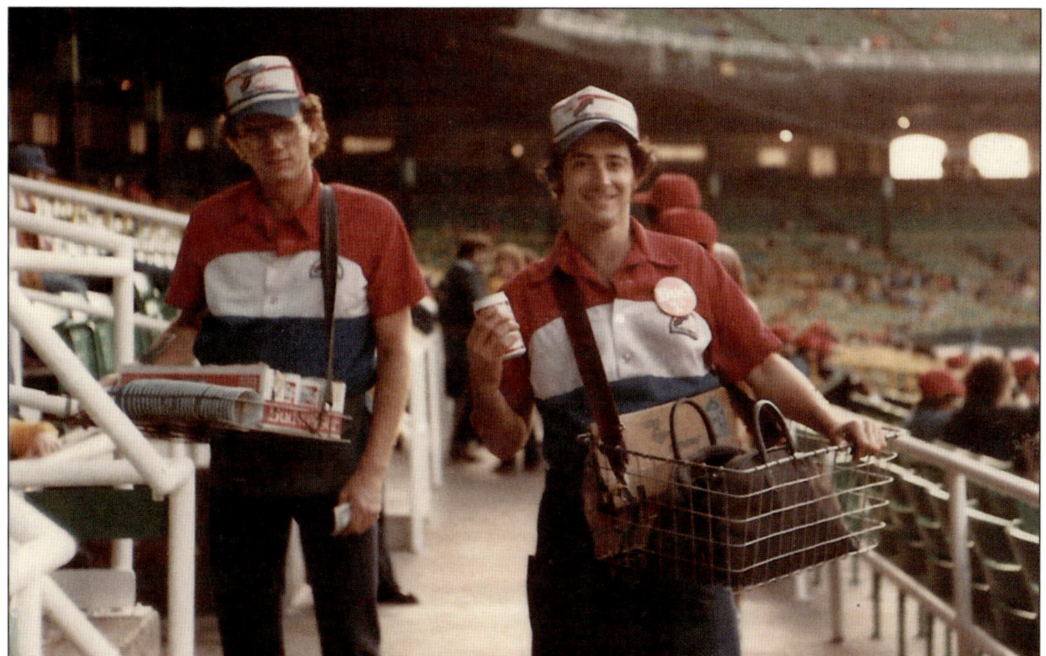

The opening of the can-beer era at White Sox Park brought with it a "carrier crisis." With bottles, vendors merely strapped on the box they came in. Those cases were sturdy enough to hold the weight of the cargo through the rigors of stair climbing, while the cups fit easily on top. Cans came in much smaller cases with no place to attach a belt or put cups, so there was a scramble to retrieve old empty bottle cases to squeeze in the aluminum 24 packs. Others discovered that a pop tray would work, like Eugene Frankowski, seen above left in 1982, who found his, but those could not be bought in a store. Lloyd Rutzky (above right) was the first to purchase a bicycle basket. Corey Goldstein, pictured below in 1985, also bought one. Others tried laundry baskets or dish trays.

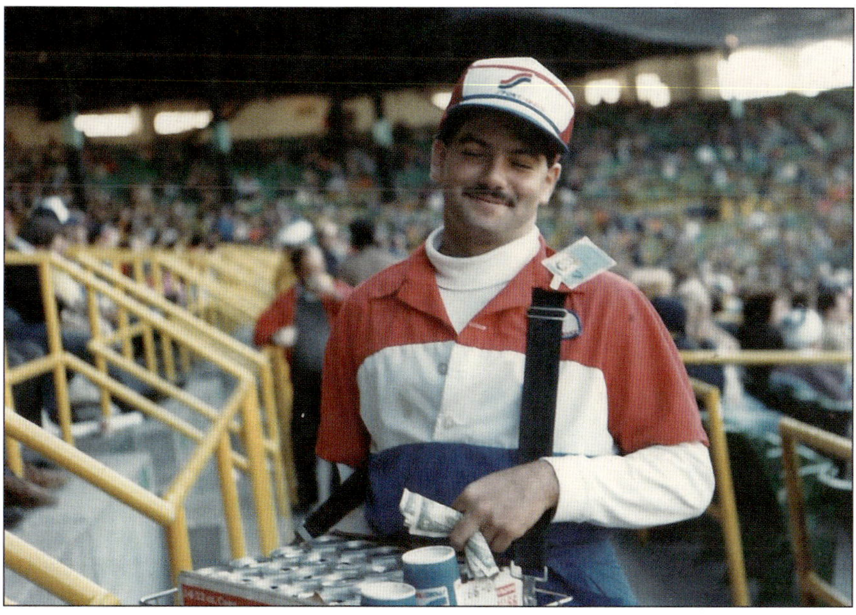

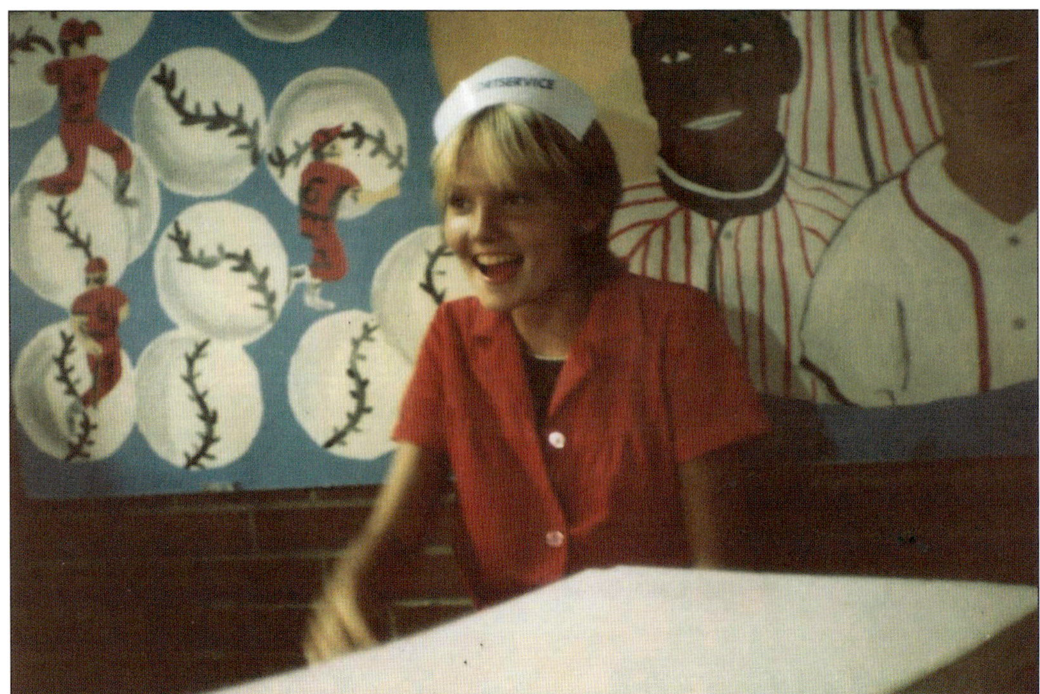

The walls behind these young women working the "portables" under the stands offer a glimpse of rare artistic treasures. Portables are movable stations where a number of items are sold. Denise Buck, seen above in August 1977, sells her wares with images of baseballs and a smiling pair of ballplayers over her shoulders. Meanwhile, Sharon Pesha, seen below in May 1978, appears to be in danger of being grabbed by a mysterious figure. These paintings were the work of youthful White Sox fans who were encouraged by then-owner Bill Veeck to glorify the drab concourse walls with baseball scenes—a masterstroke by the mastermind of so many innovations.

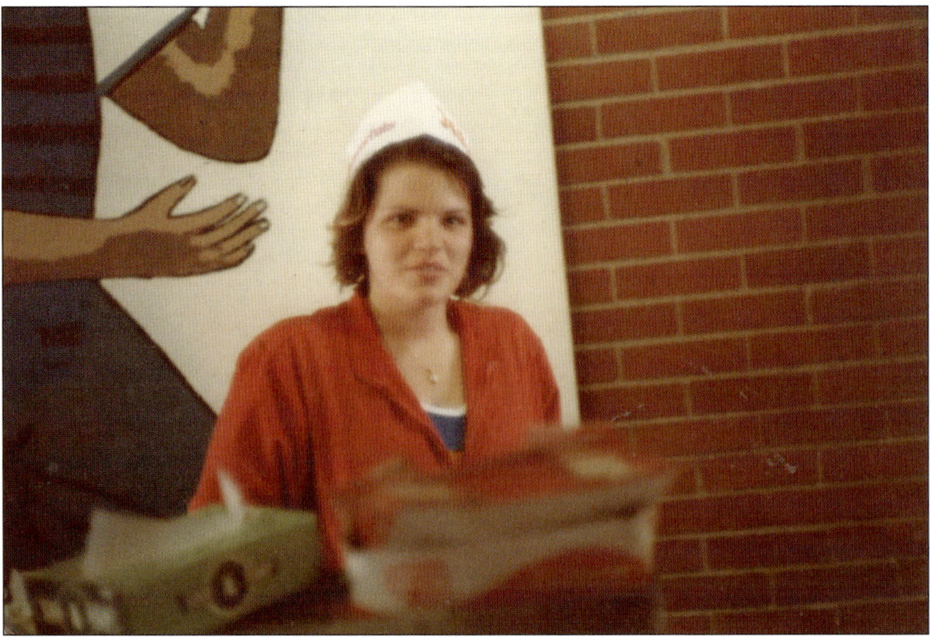

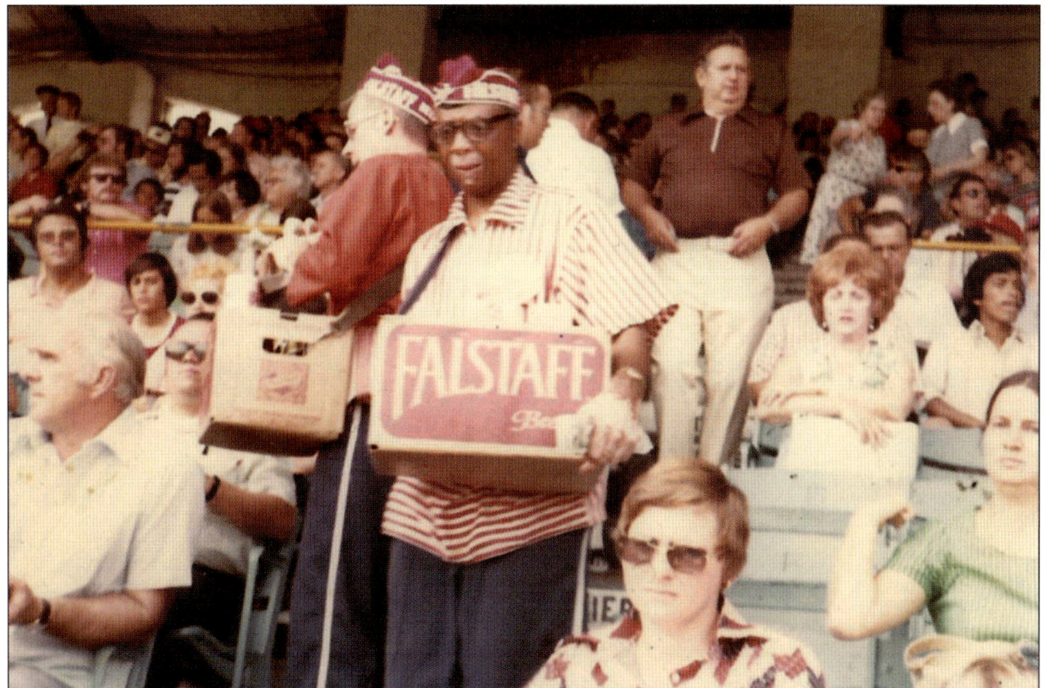

For a vendor to truly succeed, they need the proper attitude, which means not minding the inevitability of fans walking every which way around them and bumping into them. Looking up and around for the little ones is the most important thing. Saying "excuse me" and "I'm sorry" continuously with utmost sincerity for even the slightest bodily contact can be incredibly effective. Still, a fan can complain to management if they feel a worker was wantonly careless, and at the very least, that employee will either lose a little moneymaking time explaining their side of the encounter, or their job. Above, Ed Carney (left) and Woodrow Walker, and below, Mike Gold, jostle their way through the crowded aisles in 1975, knowing how careful they must be.

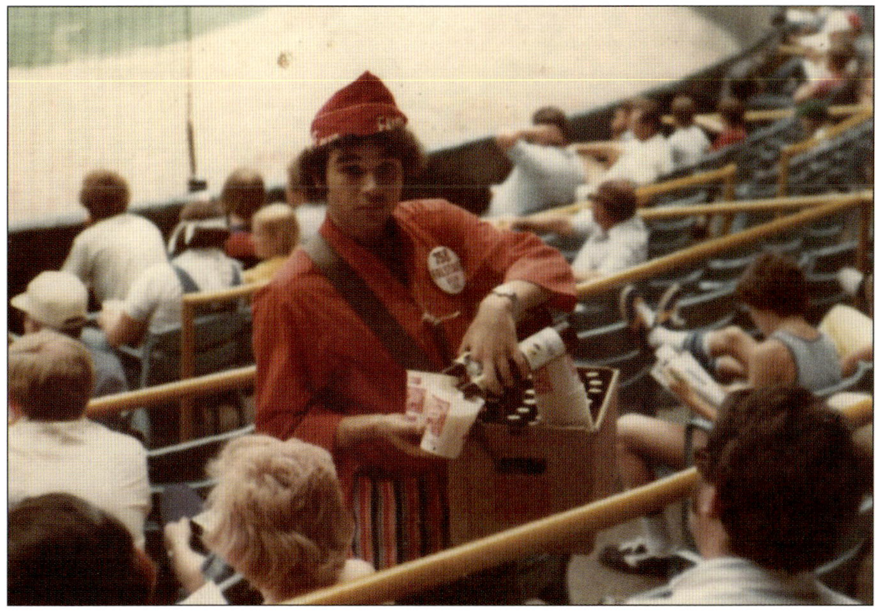

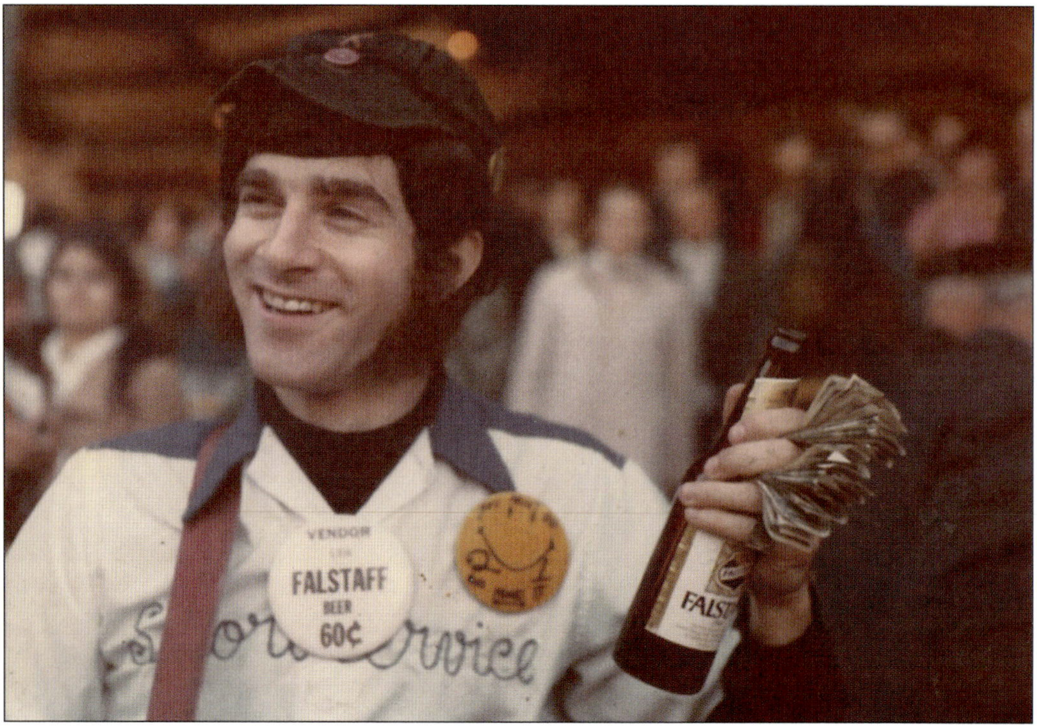

Fans are always coming up to vendors and saying hello. They know them because they have been seeing them for years, and because of their ID badges, they even know their names. Therefore, it is pretty embarrassing when the workers really have no idea who they are. Roger Sosner, seen above in 1972, sees hundreds of thousands of faces each season, but can he remember them all? Below in 1977, Scott Weber (in stripes), Ron Kohn (in red, white, and blue), and David Levenstam (lower right) are experiencing just such an encounter. Kohn was even pointing at one of his "public" and struggling to recall who this person is.

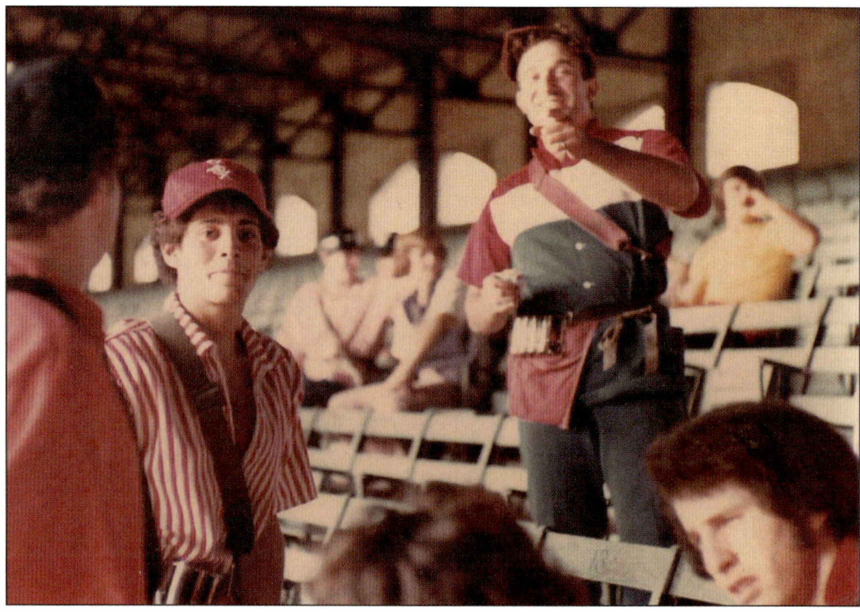

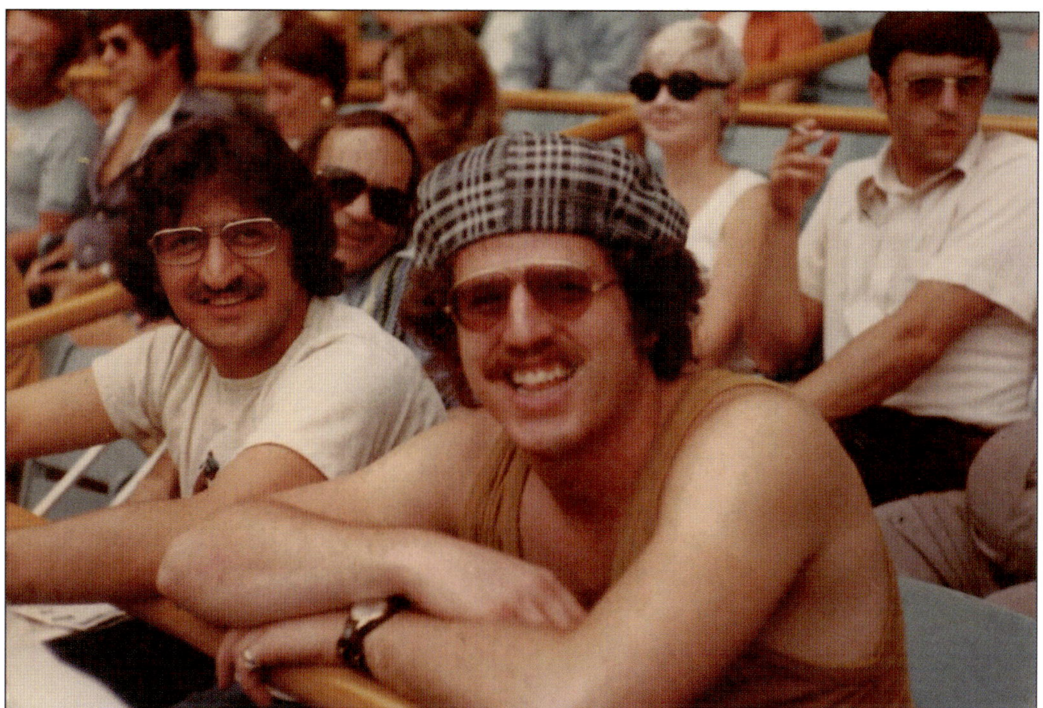

Everybody at the game loves to catch a foul ball—unless it is a foul ball to the face. Those in the park must be constantly on the alert for a screaming line drive that could be a cool souvenir if they make a clean play, or a risk of a casualty if they are not prepared. Above in 1975, sitting dangerously close behind the plate, are fans Phil Immergluck (left) and Ted Schwartz. Immergluck had plenty of experience in dodging flying baseballs, having been a vendor himself as a teenager. Gary Bernstein, seen below in 1979, was at a somewhat safer distance in the right-field corner. His metal hot dog box, in fact, could be used as a shield if he had enough time to duck. However, here he's looking the other way and might never know what hit him.

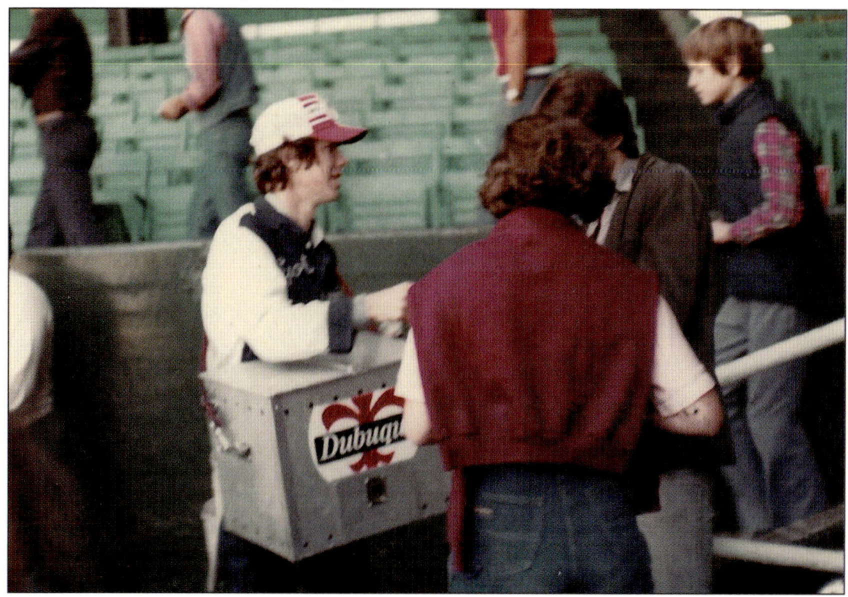

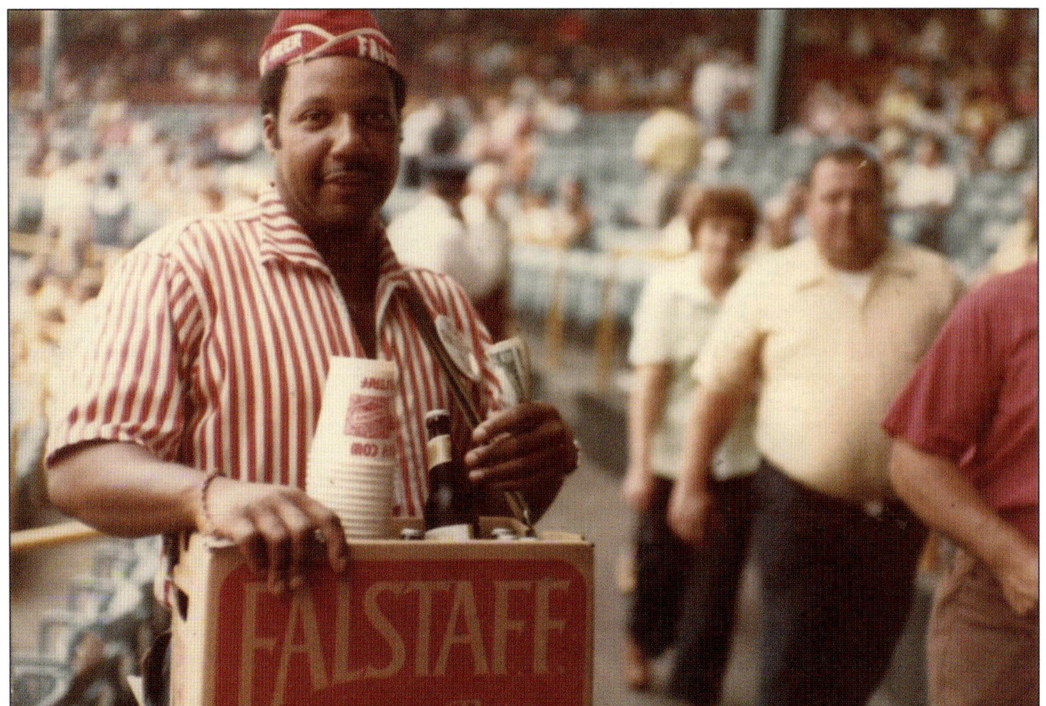

Beer vending has changed mightily over the years at White Sox Park, especially with the quantum leap from bottles to cans in 1978. However, one problem was the same: "Firebrew." That's actually the method that one of the beers at the park advertised as making it special, though being proud of a word denoting heat does not seem very smart when trying to sell "cold ones." On these two pages, this party of five could offer quite a tale of woe on the subject. It meant that the brew they had been given to sell was warm, many times due to selling out the previous day and the cooler not being restocked in time to get the suds to the desired temperature. It should be icy so it could stay properly chilled while vendors walked the aisles searching for drinkers. In 1975, Millard McCoy (above) and Dan Martinez (below), seen with bottles of Falstaff, are coming and going. McCoy, with a full load (note his supply of cups), looks like his beverages will satisfy fans' thirst for the moment. Martinez's case, though, is about empty and "heating up."

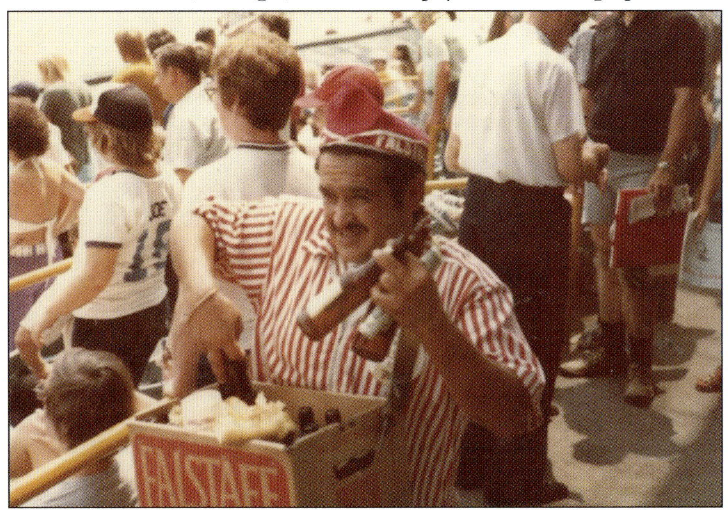

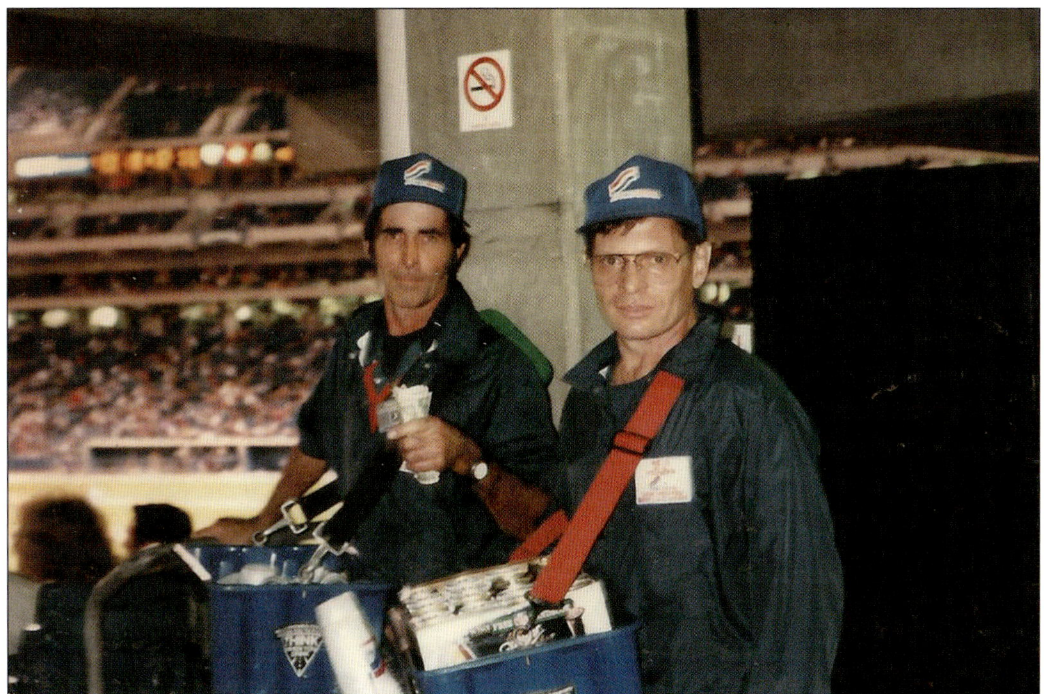

Before 1978, vendors sold beer in bottles from the corrugated cases they came in, so ice could not be used, as the drippings would rot out the container. Kurt Klingbeil and Don Kraus, seen above in 1997, and Stacey Eaton, below in 2004, have cans of Miller. The cardboard cases were put in hardened plastic shells, making it safer to use ice. Still, if one vendor whispered "fire" to another, a fan was not going to get the quenching refreshment they desired. (Below, courtesy of Dave Levenson.)

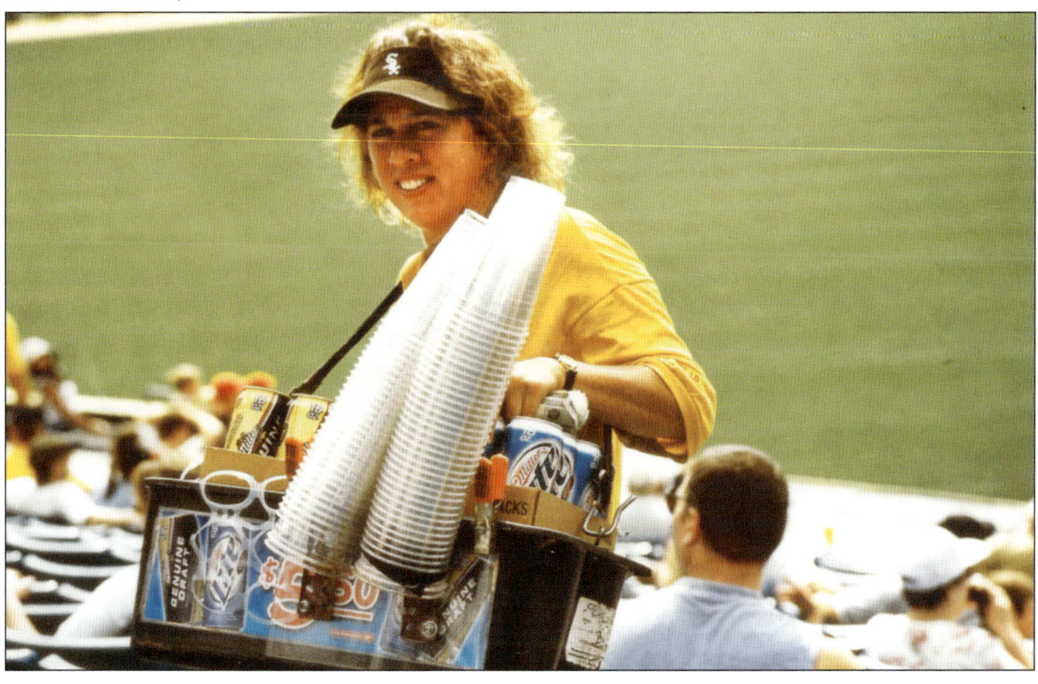

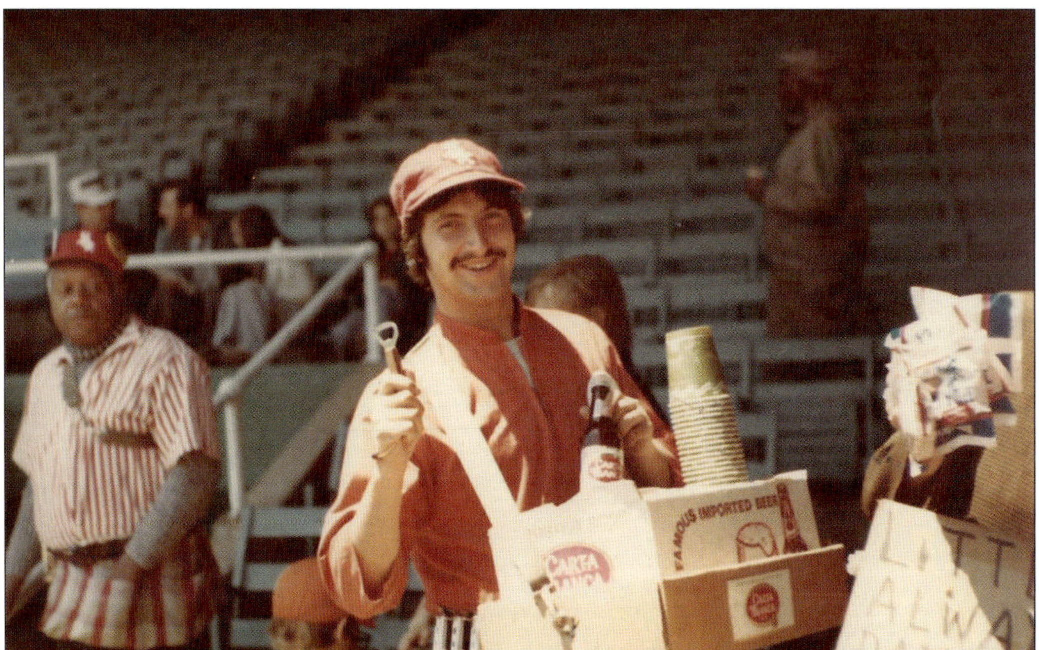

For most seasons, Comiskey Park's vendors only sold one brand of beer. Hamm's "from the land of sky blue waters" was the new regular beer in 1976 after five years of Falstaff. However, along with Hamm's, Sox Park introduced a specialty beer, Carta Blanca, for a dime more, that a few rookie beermen had problems selling. A lot of fans did not know it was a higher price and even punched some "Blanca boys" because they thought they were being overcharged. Future Arizona restauranteur Arlen Korer (above) smiles bravely that year with his load of the "expensive" beverage. Two years later, as seen below in 1978, Arlen's grin was genuine because not only had the Carta Blanca experiment ended, but he had befriended the boss's (union steward's) daughter, Diana Studnicka.

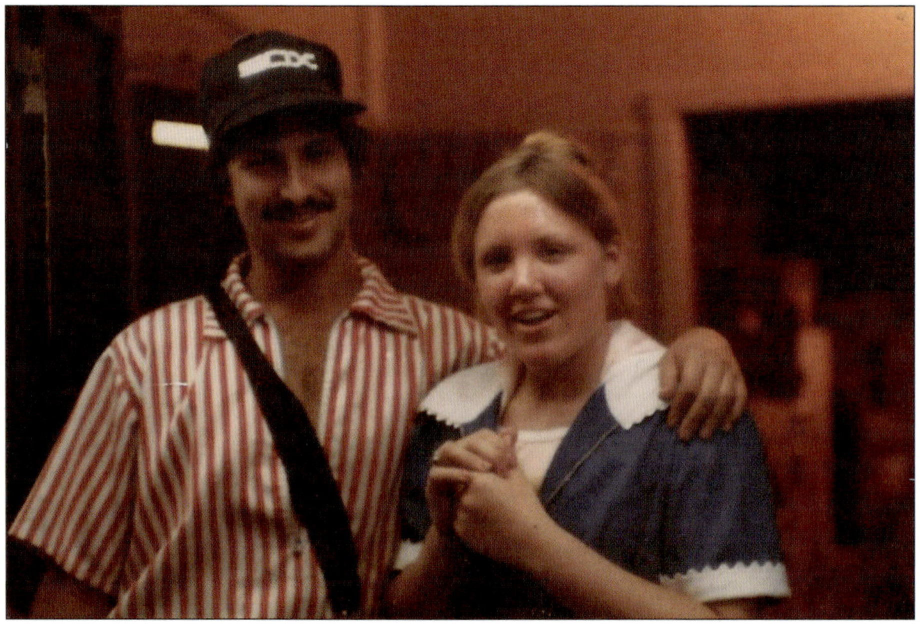

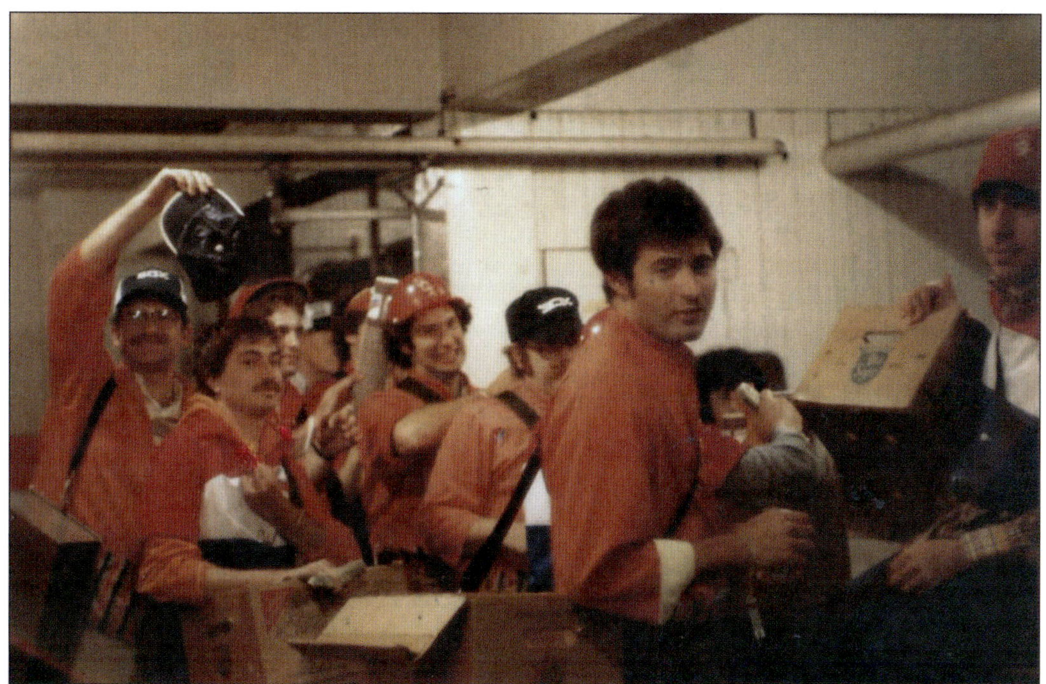

The wild and crazy guys seen above in 1980 were very eager to go out and vend. The three previous seasons, beermen either sold Stroh's or Schlitz. Stroh's was the top seller of the two, but only about one-fourth of the vendors could get that assignment per game, so everybody could only have a "Stroh's day" once out of every four—no exceptions. However, when the 1980s began, for two years the very popular Old Style was exclusively being offered, which greatly pleased (from left to right) Michael Ginsburg, Fred Batko, Gary Newman, Eli Lawrence, Dave Ashkanazy, Ron Pollakov, and Steve Drexler. Below, back in 1975, it was just a one-beer system—Falstaff—and Ira Levin (foreground) finds a customer who knew this was his only choice.

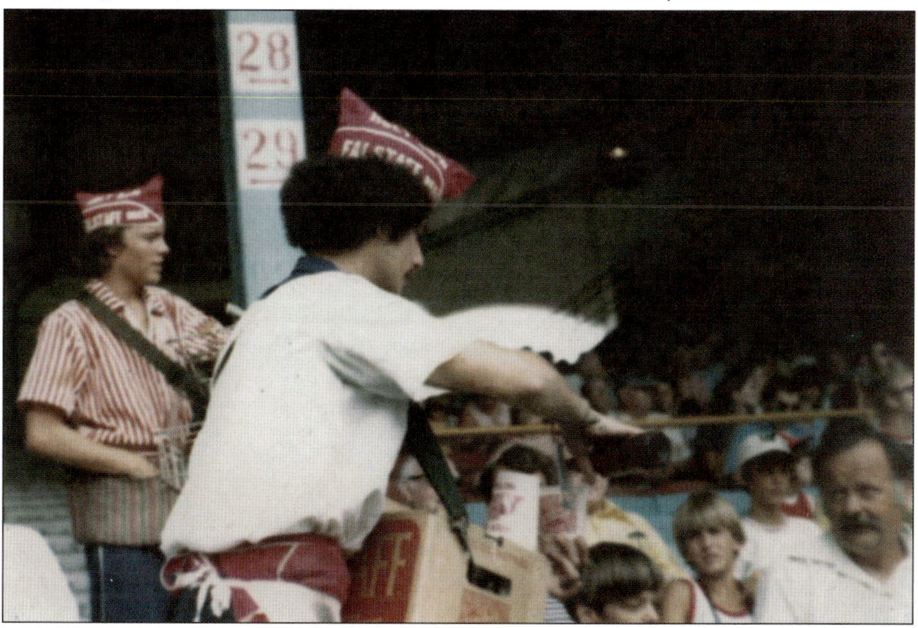

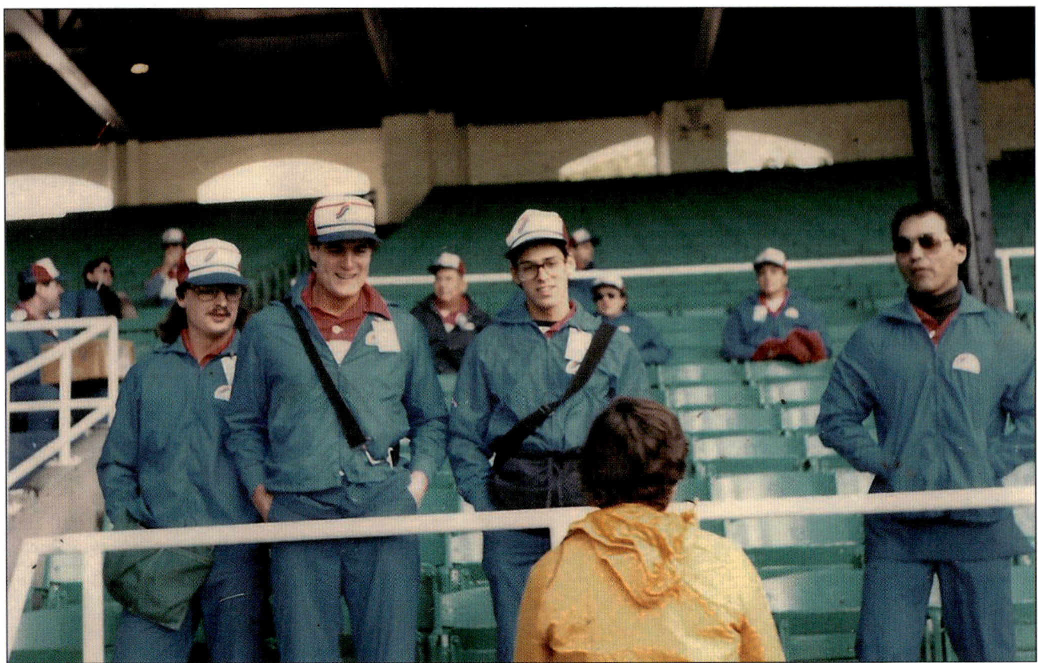

Behold the four upright gents above, from left to right, Bo Daley, Frank Bellizzi, Michael Kofsky, and Suk Graham on October 6, 1985. Below, in 1986, are two seated Romanek brothers, Scott (left) and Daron, with Jay Mages in the background. They were also living under a beer monarchy at Comiskey Park. Budweiser, "the King of Beers," now ruled the roost and had since 1982. However, Budweiser's reign would soon end because former White Sox announcer Harry Caray, having headed north to broadcast Cubs games in 1982, began doing ads in 1986 proclaiming "Cub Fan—Bud Man," as it was also vended at Wrigley Field. In 1987, the throne on the South Side belonged to Miller.

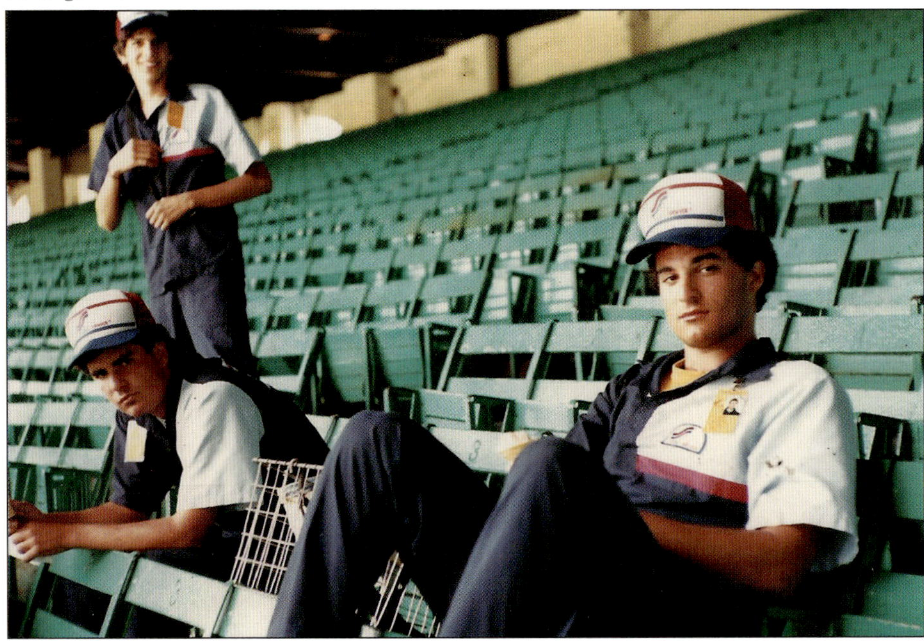

Vendors are free to start selling as soon as they get their assignments from the union steward, which is usually more than an hour before game time; yet not everybody takes out their product that early to make each minute count. Many want to save their energy until most of the fans have arrived. However, a few, like Joe Aleman, seen at right in 1989, and Steve Czyzniejewski, below in 1999, were among those with enough boundless strength to "go the distance" and probably outdo those who chose to come off the bench with fresh legs. Don Grabowski (above left) usually decided to be one of the latecomers.

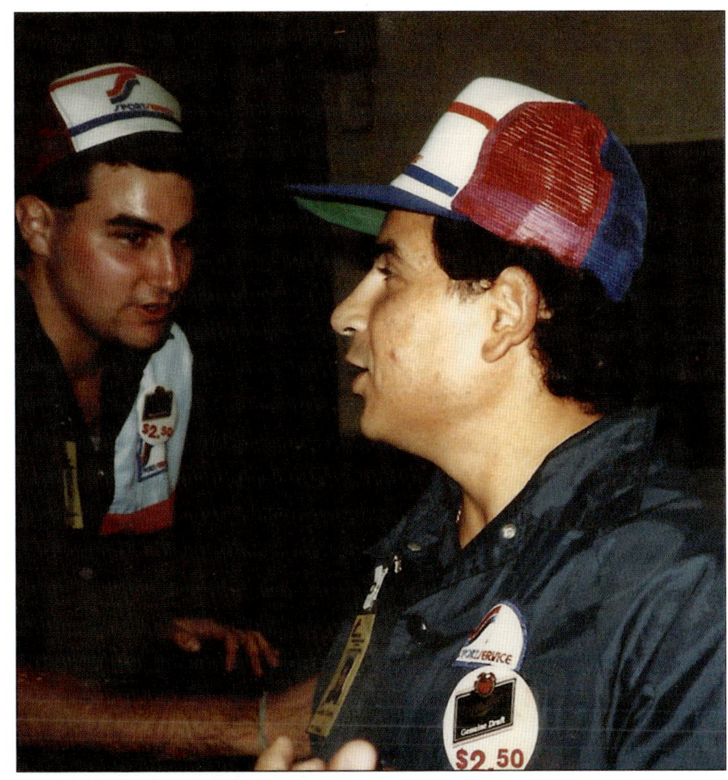

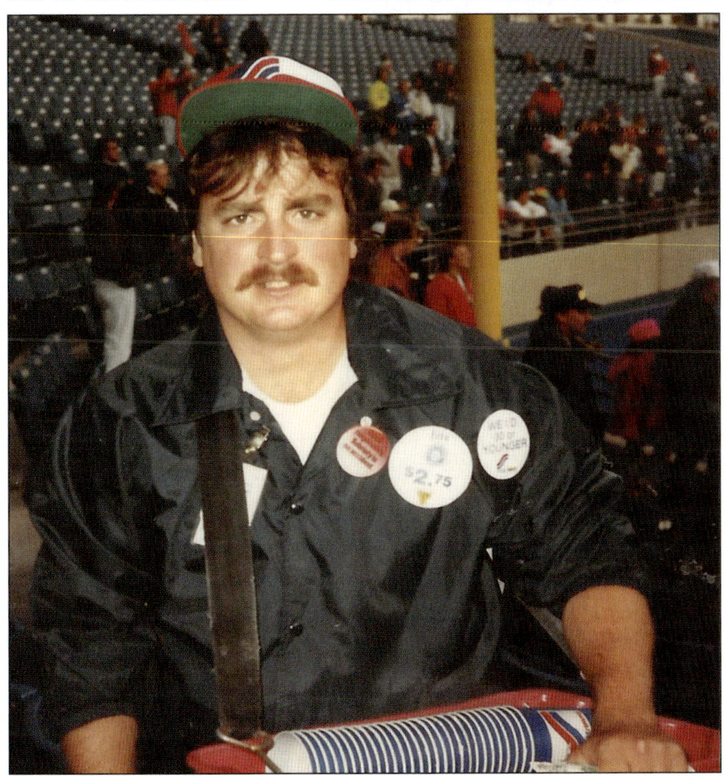

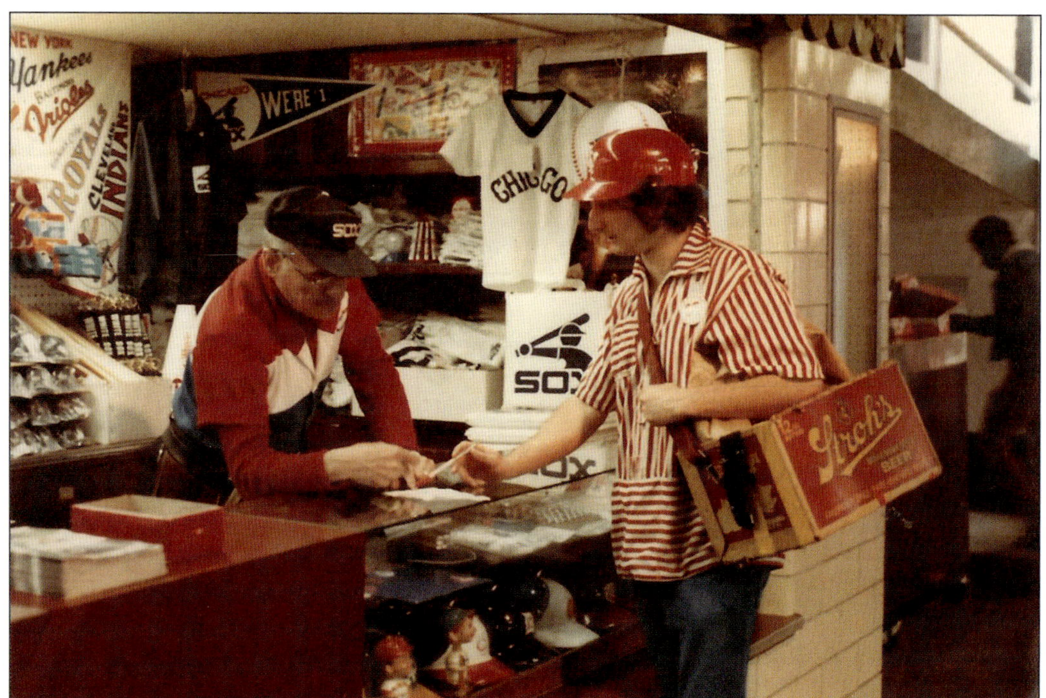

Souvenir stands are for the fans, of course, but to a lot of vendors, they were a favored hangout to talk baseball and other sports. Located across from Lou the Shoeshine Man's place and the Dugout Cafe on the third-base line was where one could often find "Boston" John Kurpiel (left) and Lloyd Rutzky, seen above in 1978. The pennant races, statistics, and which Chicago team was better were subjects always up for debate. A little bit farther down near left field, seen below in 1980, the highly opinionated Melvin Berman (right) would be at his spot selling memorabilia while Henry Wakefield (left) would frequently throw his two cents in with a predictable rant and rave. (Above, courtesy of Mike Gold).

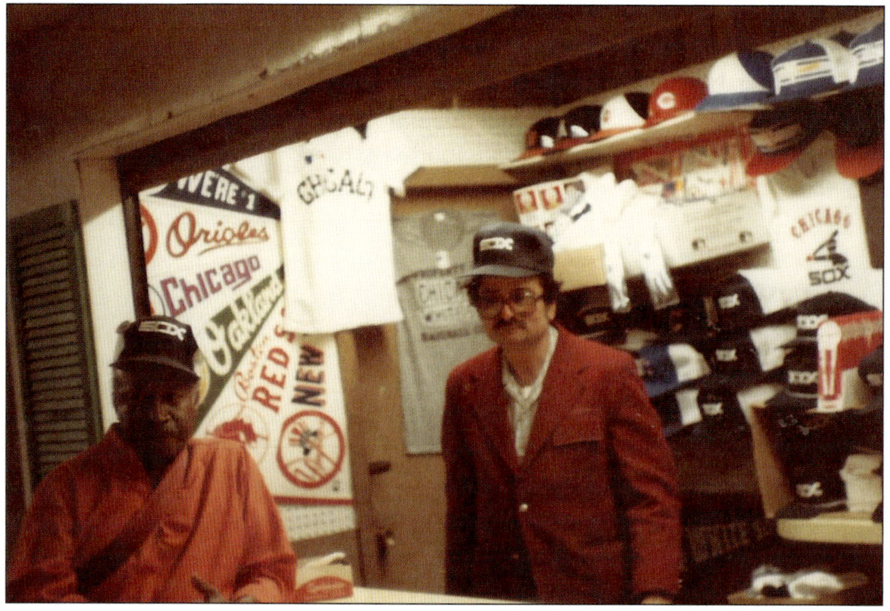

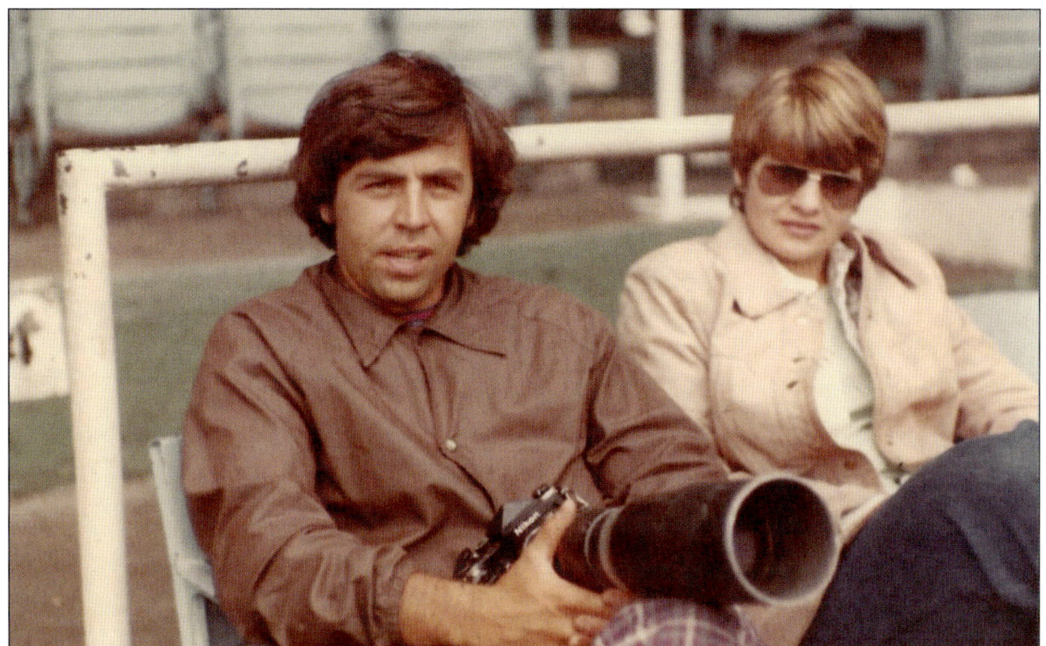

Lloyd Rutzky took his pictures for fun, but the two photojournalists seen on this page were real pros. Bob Langer, seen above in 1976, began a frame-worthy newspaper career in 1959 as a copyboy for the *Chicago Tribune*. He snapped up a job at the *Chicago Sun-Times* from 1965 to 1983 and back-tracked to the *Tribune* to shutter the last 15 years in his portfolio, taking countless thousands of pictures all over the world, including of the Olympic games. But his main beat was the teams of the Windy City. That fancy looking camera he is flashing won him over 100 awards. The young lady sitting next to Langer, though, had no idea who he was, as he would frequently grab any empty seat to get his job done and then be on his way. Barb Urbanic, a White Sox team photographer seen below in 1977, poses nicely for her amateur competitor.

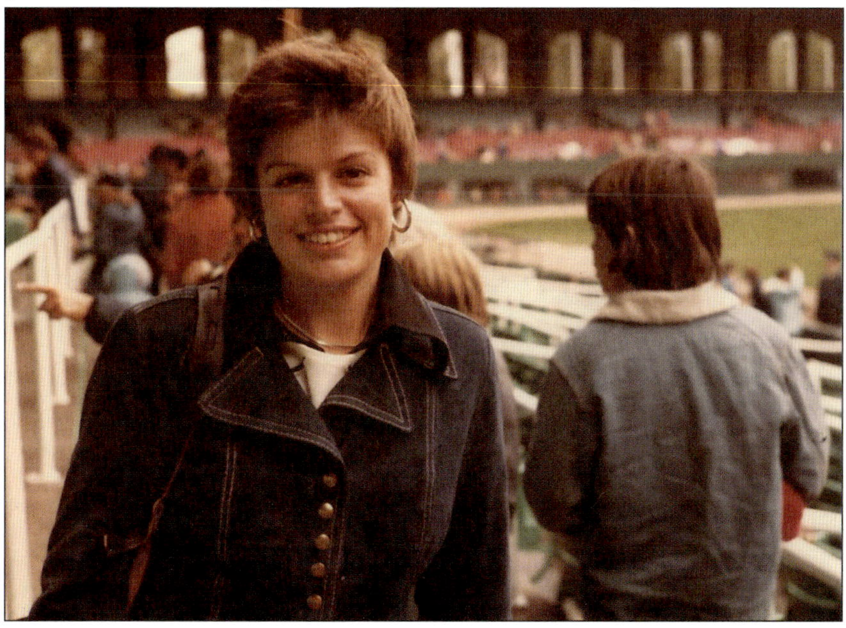

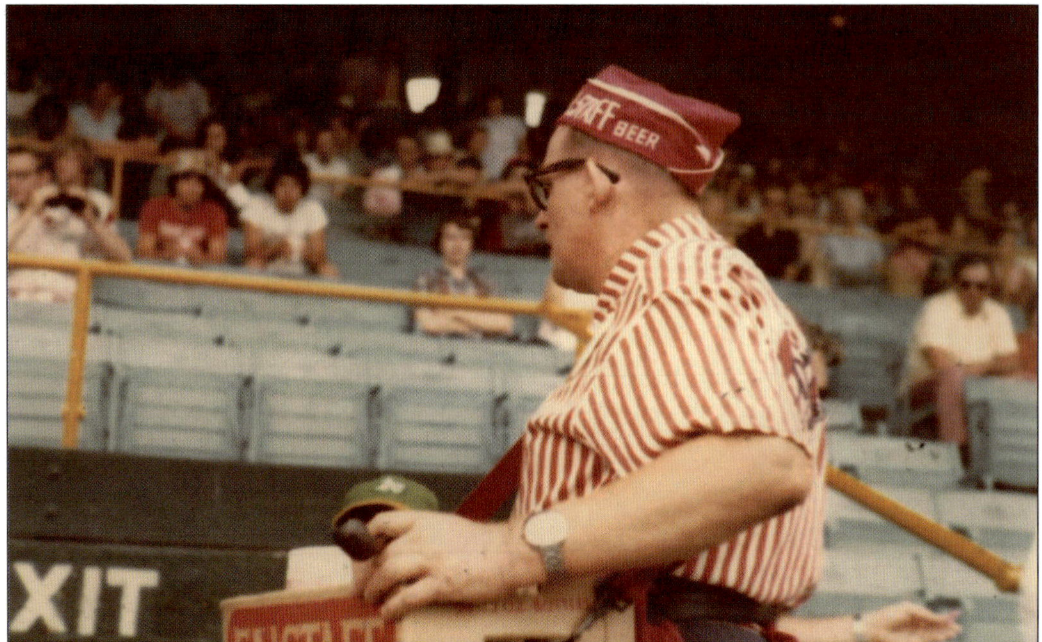

Not everybody gets enshrined in this book's chapter four, The Legends. Just like other Halls of Fame, there is a process of debate and analysis among vending historians before the consensus is that they have "the right stuff" for such an honor. Harry Reichen, seen above in 1975, certainly would be on a lot of voter's ballots, with his virtually indecipherable babbling on a plethora of topics, all the while this "Pipeman" sucks his trademark mouthpiece, here in his left hand for just a second as he cries out "beer!" Bob Kletnick, below right in 1985, is another candidate, viewed with commissary worker Karen Green; he could be informing her of the location of every single street in Chicago or listing the entire major league baseball schedule (with scores) for the last 25 years.

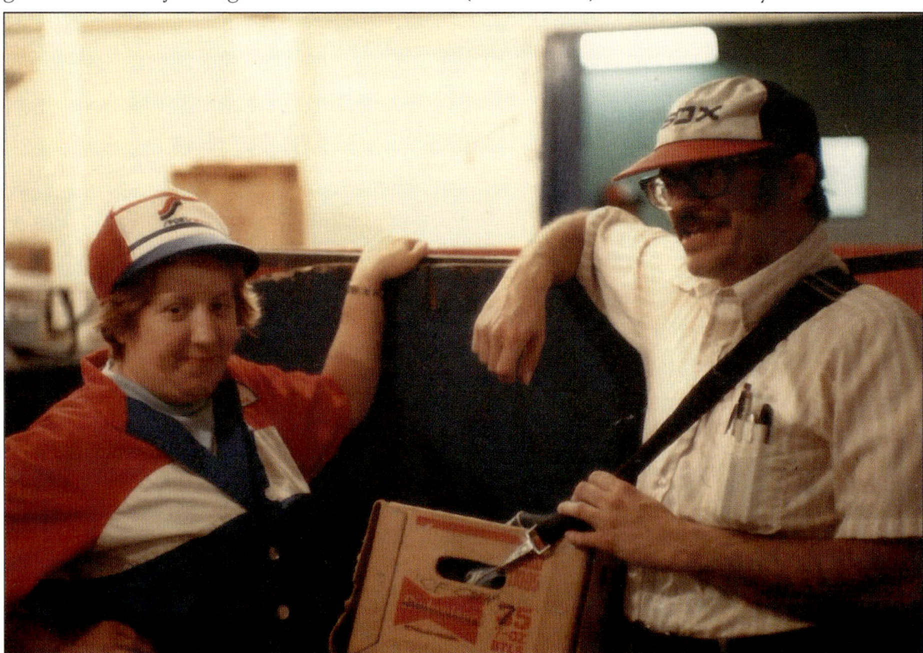

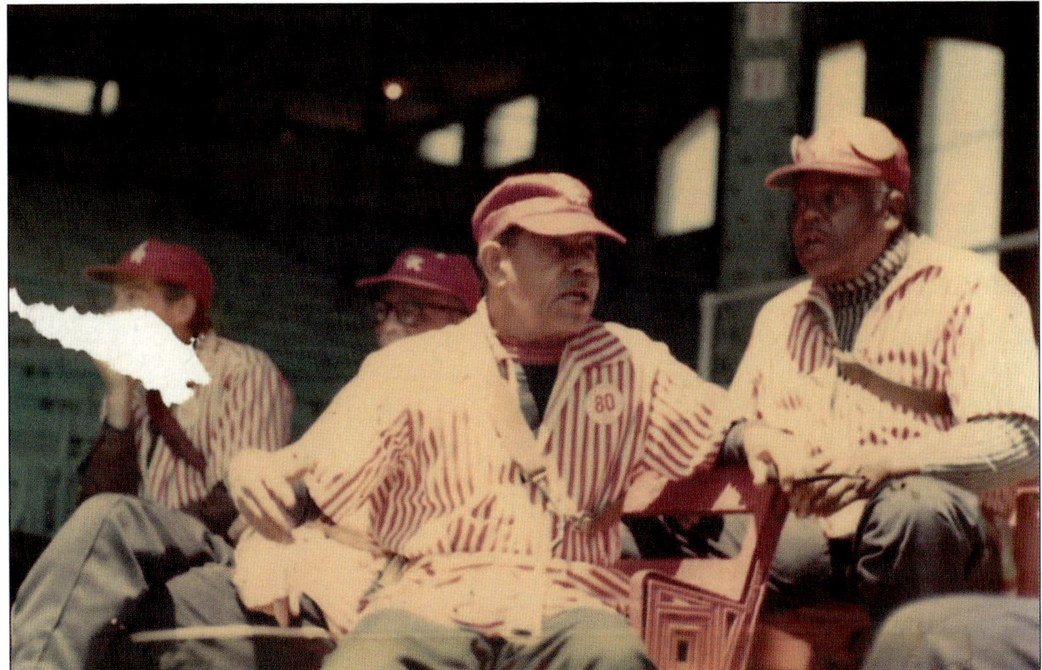

There are no guarantees or fringe benefits. Above, Fred Richissin, Woodrow Wilson Walker, Lawrence McCullough, and Greg Cola, and below, Al Rutka, Frank LeDuc, and Jimmy Bendas in 1976 had all been in the vending game a long time when these pictures were taken. Like everybody else selling at White Sox Park, they were considered "day of game employees." Nobody had a contract, they did not get any salary, and there was no such thing as a "sick day." They showed up, worked as hard as they could, and were rewarded with good commissions. If they didn't like it, they could go get a "real job." But they did like it—and they would be back tomorrow.

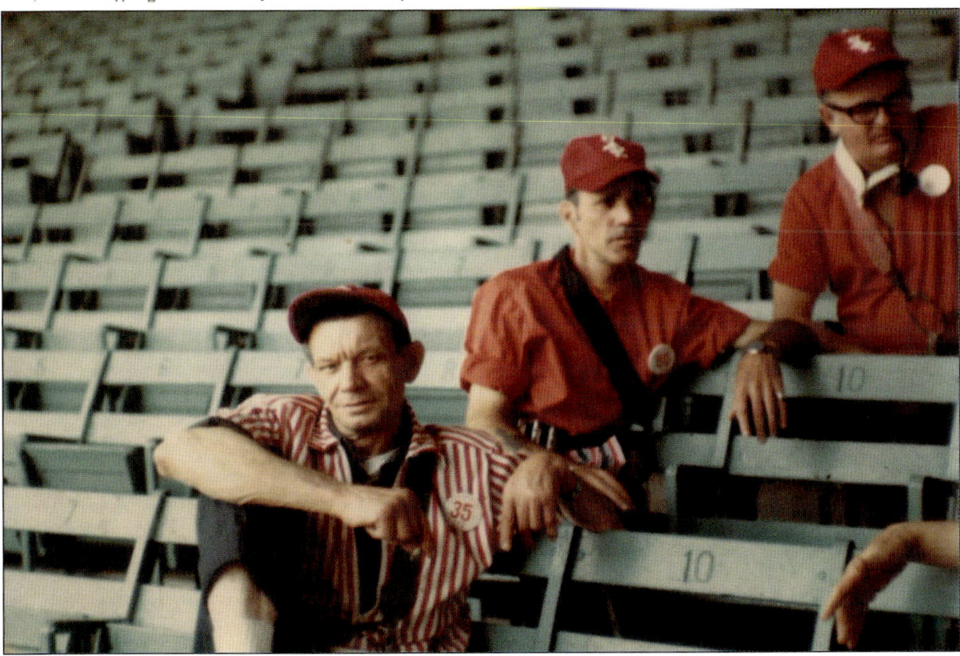

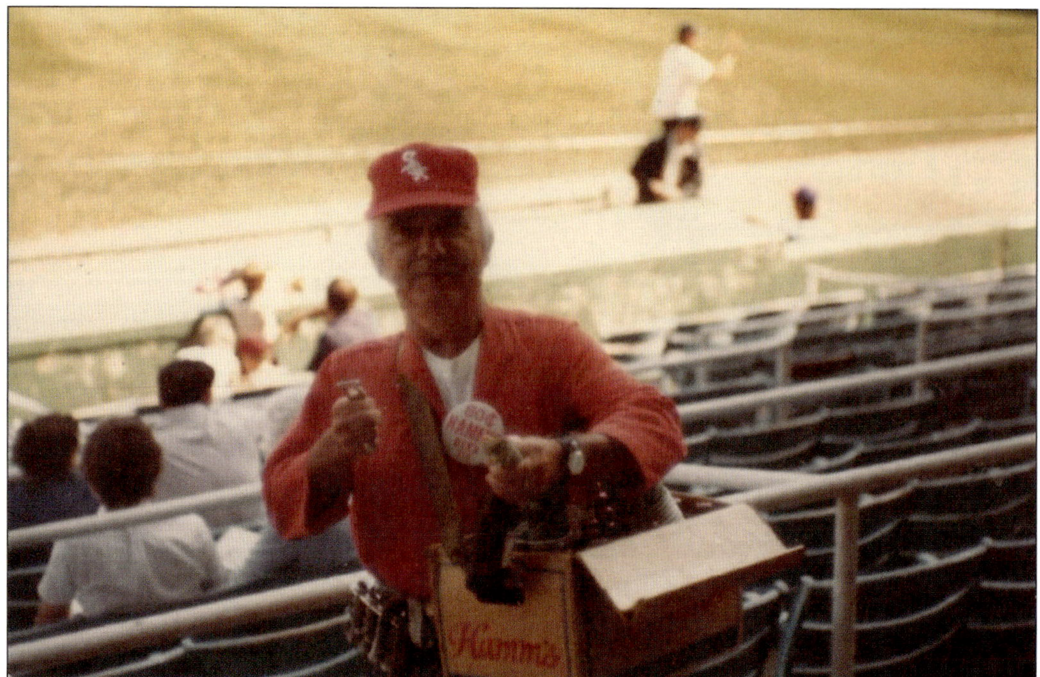

The four beer vendors on these two pages dreaded rain delays. They disrupt brisk sales while the crowd jams the aisles running for cover. It is falsely assumed by most spectators that ballpark peddlers love these stoppages, as it gives them more time to do business, yet nothing could be further from the truth because during the waiting, the demand for all products dwindles to a pittance as the crowd develops a wait-and-see attitude about spending money, if they even stay. Joe Zbacnik (above) and Nicholas Cotter (below) are both sporting three-barrel Johnson fare-box changers on their hips, eager to make good "coin" that game, yet those sunny skies could darken at any time to drown their hopes.

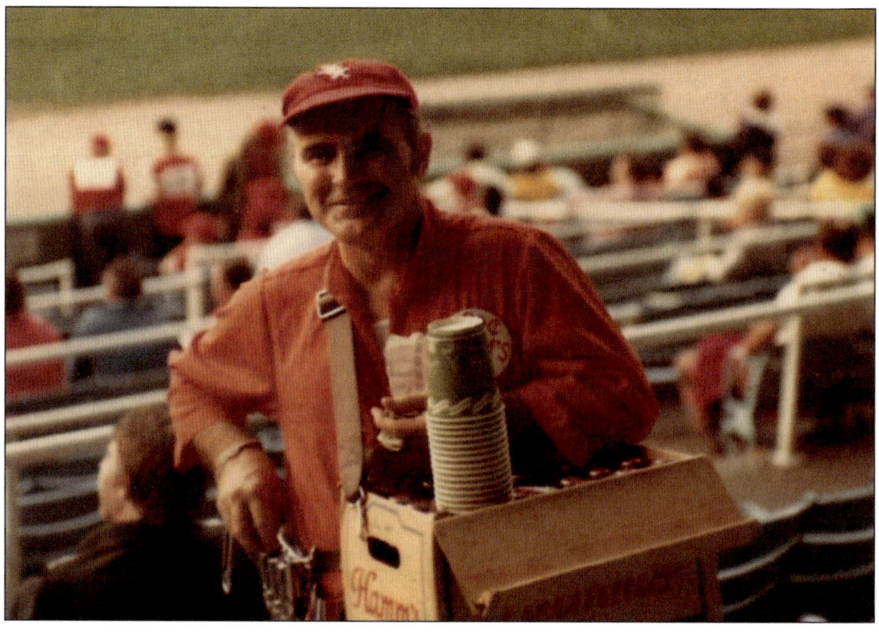

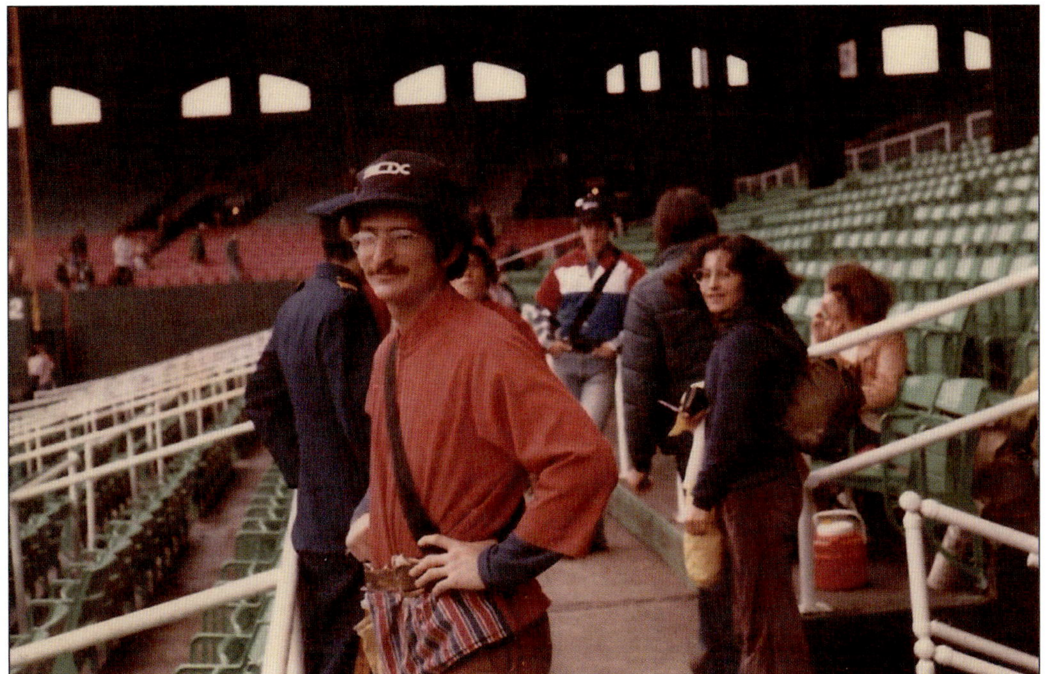

No one can be sure about weather forecasts or precipitation percentages. Many times, vendors travel long distances to the park to hear those heartbreaking words, "game canceled." Fans, too, deliberate whether they will "get it in" or if they should go. These beermen, Henry Davis (above) and Jeff Levenstam (below), have to deal with uncertainties like this almost every day of the season. Could it be another case of fans perpetually asking them, "When will the game start?" (As if they would know.) These two have yet to take the plunge into working, knowing that once they go out, they might be compelled to stay, no matter how poor sales are, as if trapped on a sinking ship.

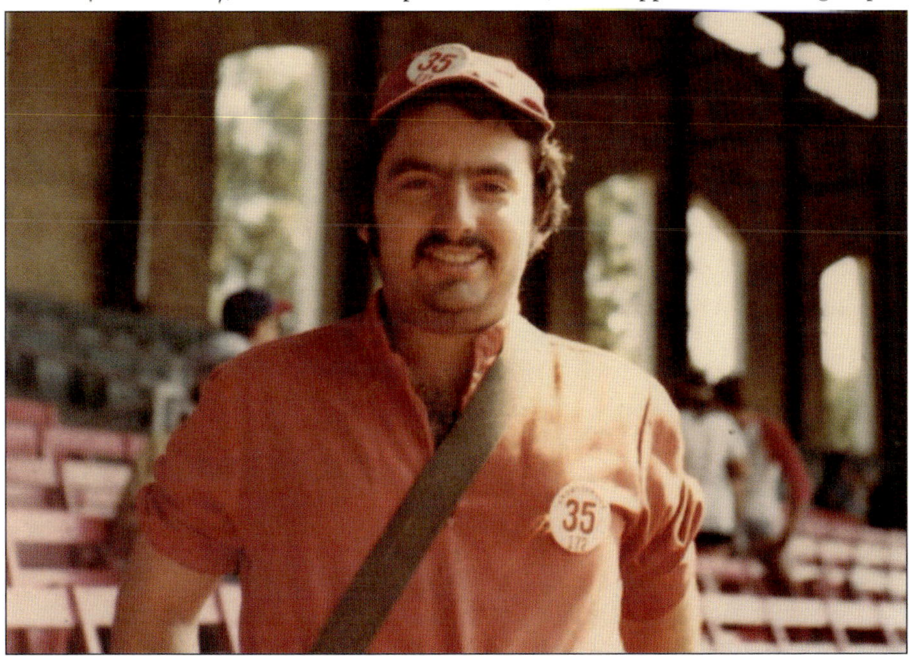

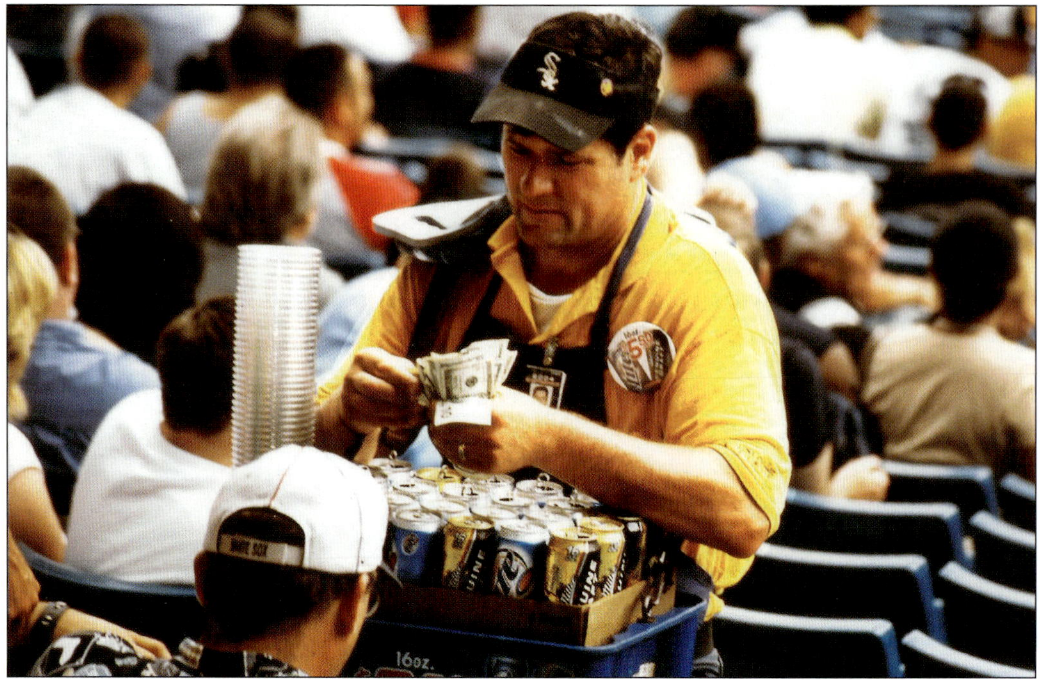

Beermen had to adjust to a new frontier in vending in the 2000s. Stands were being added on the concourse, giving fans many more avenues to buy a beer (and other treats too). The era of craft brews was approaching to broaden the horizons of thirsty fans seeking exotic refreshments, and these new factors gradually took a healthy gulp out of a beerman's earnings. One of the most significant changes at White Sox Park was that vendors were no longer required to pour beer into cups (as Frank Bellizzi, above, and William Dennis, below, were still doing in August 2004); they could simply give the can to customers after opening them. Surprisingly though, despite the obvious increase in speed per transaction, not all liked it. (Both, courtesy of Dave Levenson.)

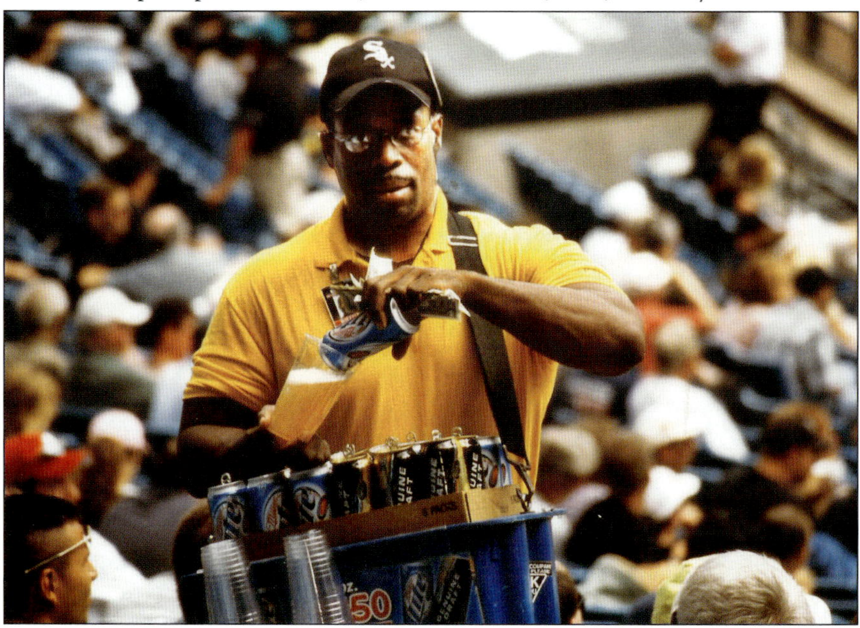

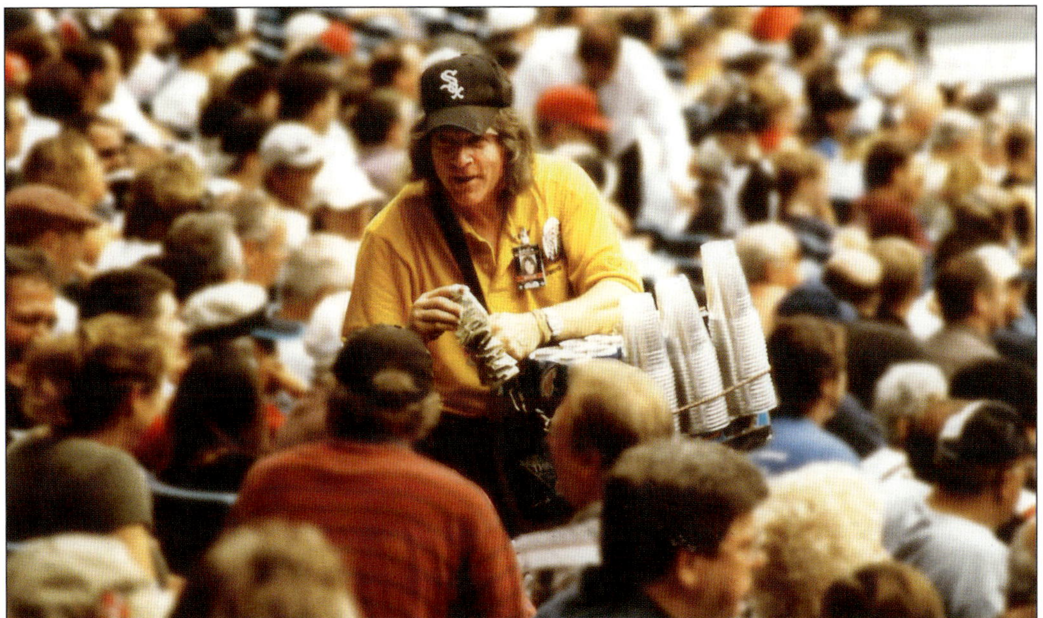

Seen here in August 2004, Roger Sosner (above) and Lloyd Rutzky (below) had to reinvent their vending methods in 2008 when beer was no longer dispensed into cups. It truly is a great idea to just hand out the cans when demand is very high, but what beermen soon learned was that for most games, when fans did not consume in mass quantities, an aisle that had just been serviced by a vendor might be virtually "dead" for 15 or more minutes. Thus, after the majority of aisles had had their refreshment needs quenched, it meant lots of time between purchases. That steadier flow of sales when pouring beer had a soothing rhythm for the vendors. Progress sometimes takes a while to get used to. (Both, courtesy of Dave Levenson.)

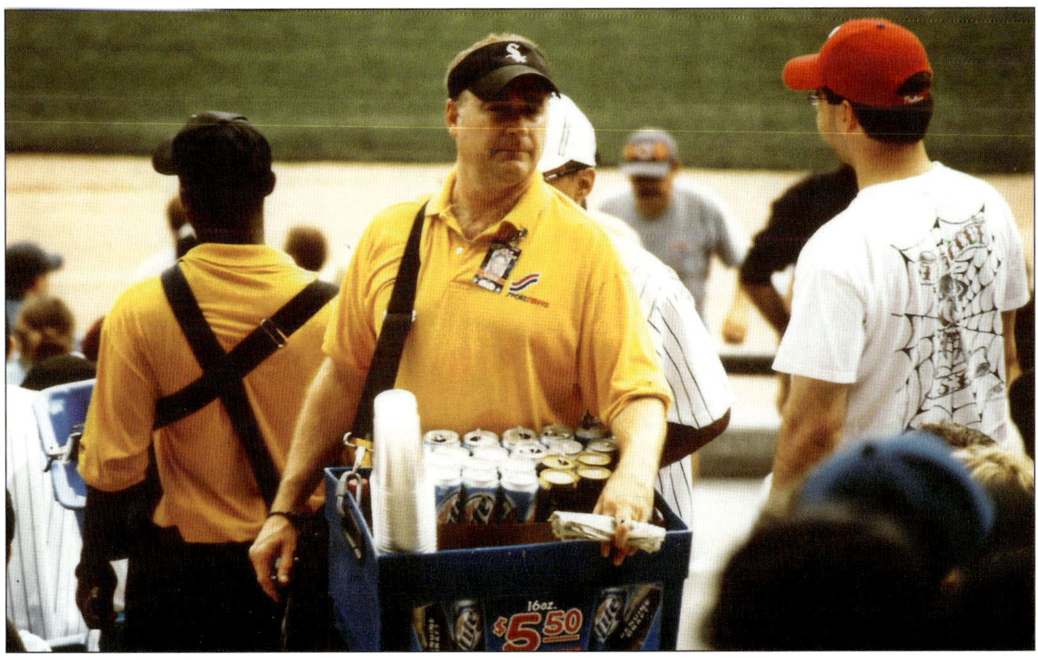

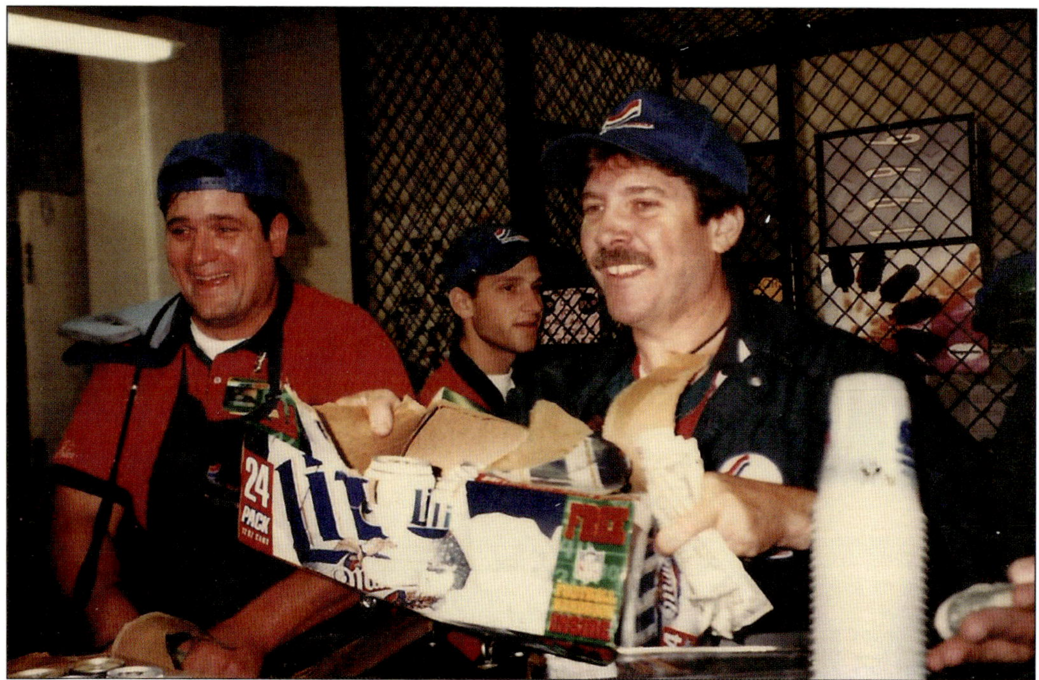

Working at the ballpark is not as simple as taking out an item and assuming everybody wants to buy it. If there was only one brand of beer to sell, vendors with enough seniority had to choose what location they wanted to work from—third or first base or the upper deck? Where would it be warmer or cooler? Where would there be less beermen, and who would be your competitors? Here on September 17, 1996, in the checkout line at the third-base commissary are, from left to right, (above) Frank Bellizzi, Nick Palumbo, and Arnold Lipski; (below) Bob Kraupner, Bo Daley, Anthony Donato, and Dennis Bresnahan. This night, third was the better choice, as first had cold winds and the deck had a sparse crowd. Bellizzi especially had reason to smile, as he had done over 12 cases to become high man.

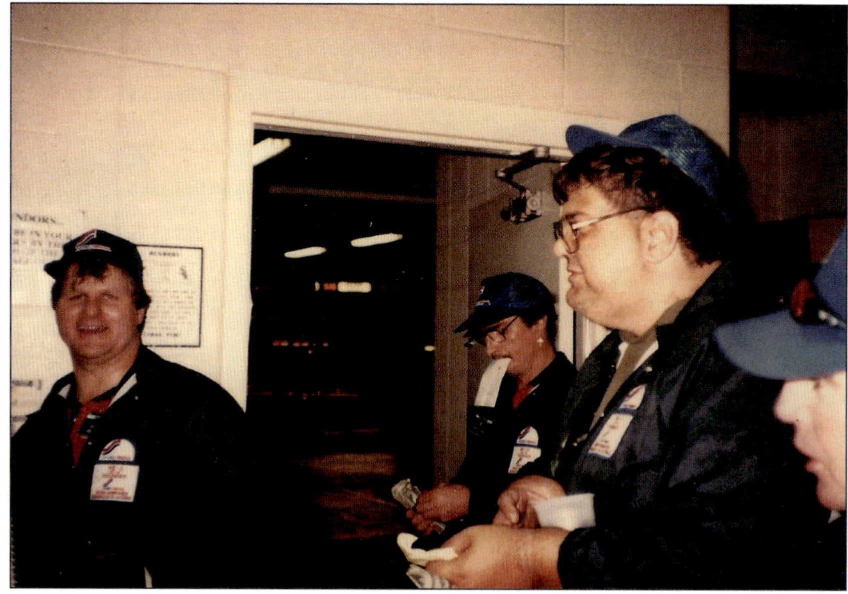

Two

Vendors Hit to All Fields

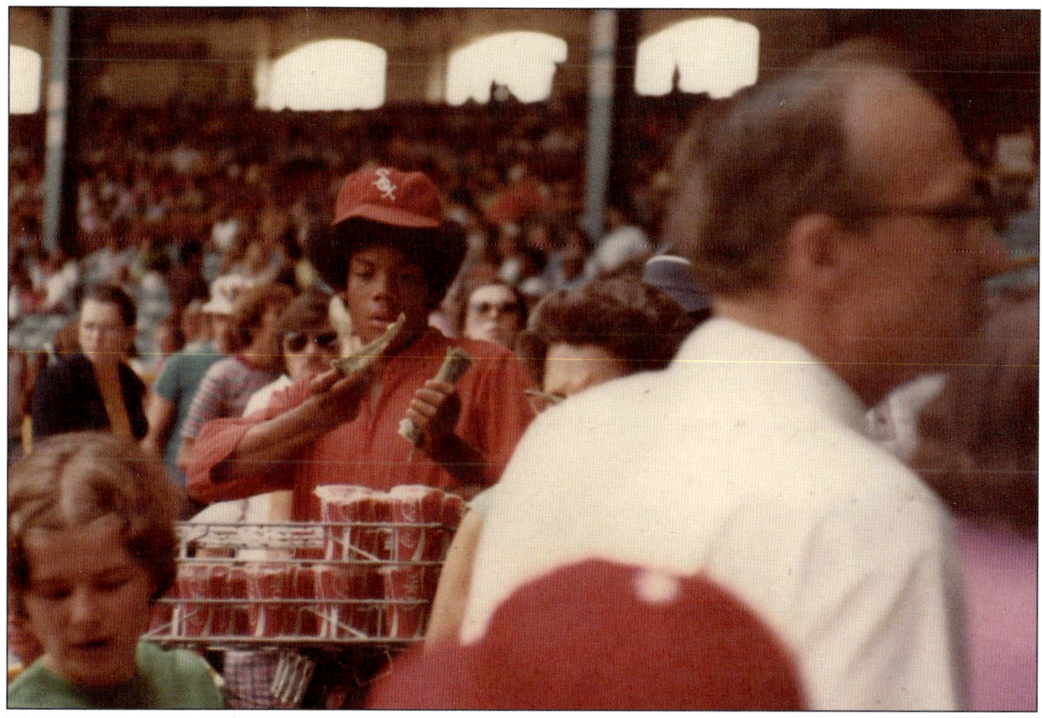

No surprise to see John W. Rogers Jr. carefully counting his money here in 1975 while hustling a double load of Coke. Eight years later, he founded the multi-billion dollar Ariel Investments. His father had been a member of the famed Tuskegee Airmen in World War II, and it was while attending White Sox games with his father that John Jr. met Lloyd Rutzky and became inspired to be a vendor. Later, he befriended fellow Chicagoan Barack Obama and became one of the president's economic advisers. (See page 93.)

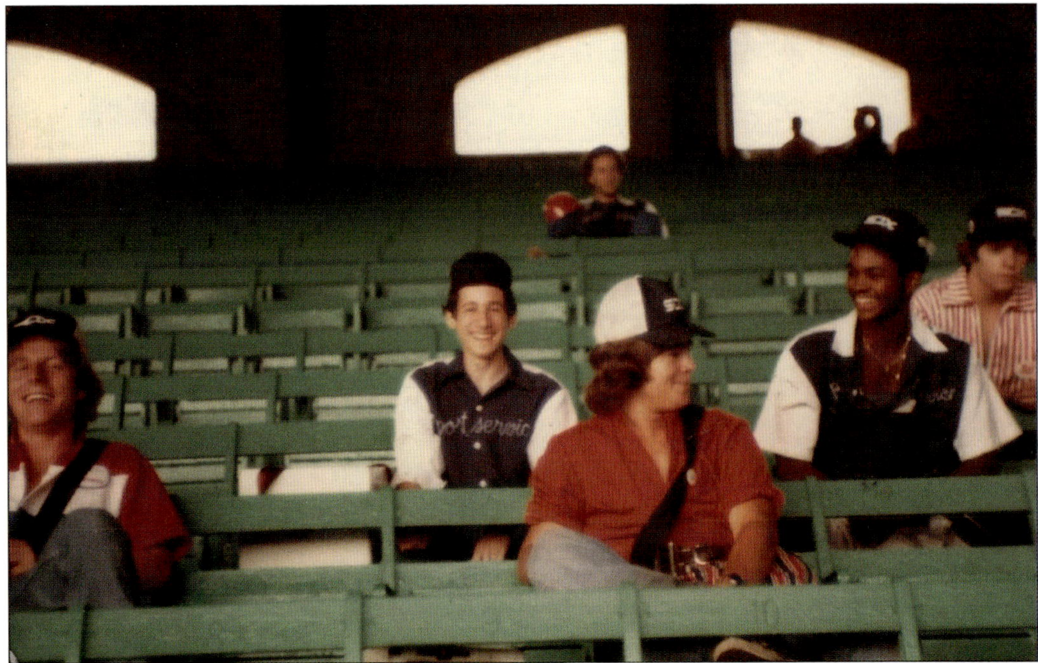

Notice the many different uniforms on display in these 1978 photographs. Above, on the left, is Charles Kellogg Bobrinskoy wearing red, white, and blue. He achieved great success as a vice chairman at Ariel Investments, working for his longtime friend CEO John W. Rogers Jr. (seen on the previous page). Leo Lindo (second from right in blue and white) became a doctor. However, Peter Guttmann (also in blue and white but with his hat on backward) and Phil Grazier (in red and white pinstripes at far right) would both tragically die young. Nobody, though, knows what became of Gary Pendel (in the orange tunic). Below, two months earlier in May and costumed in orange, Leo Lindo sells soda pop.

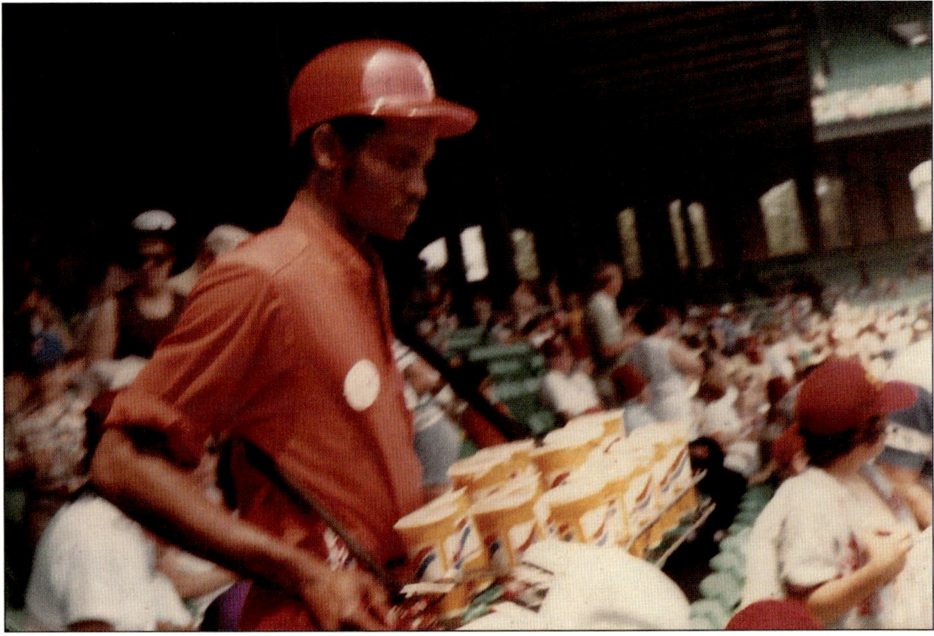

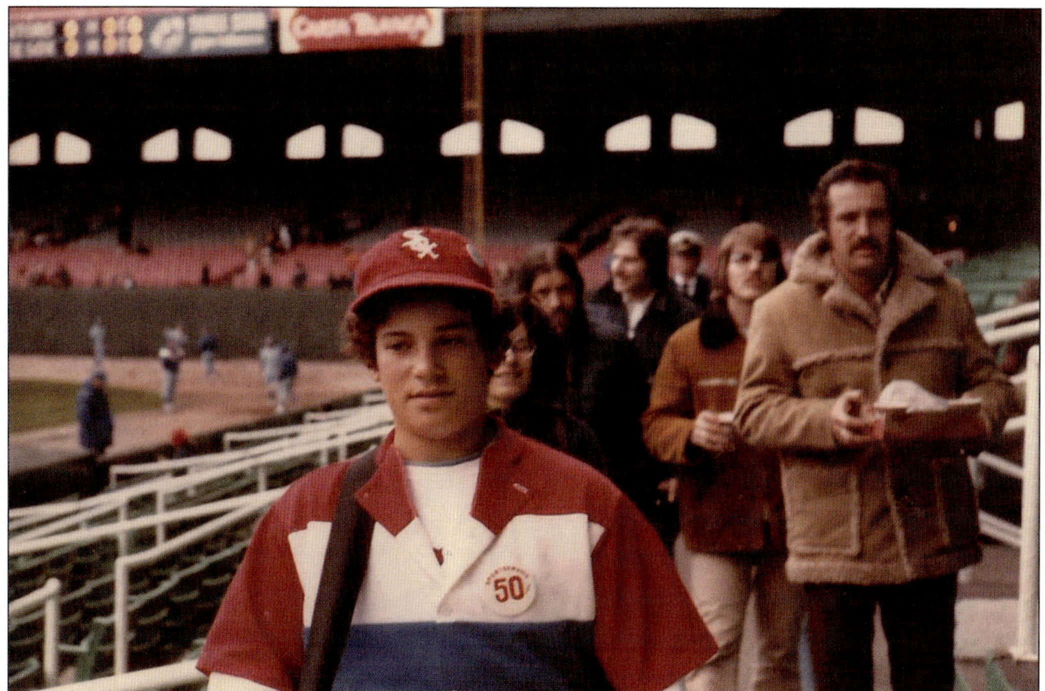

Many depended on carpools to the ballpark, especially Jordy Gelb, pictured above in 1977, who was only 14 years old. Luckily, he had an older brother, Randy, who could drive him along with other vendors, including two Levy and three Sherman brothers, and about seven others, including future sportswriter and radio personality Barry Rozner. Jordy Gelb eventually transported himself onto another team that at Bank of America Merrill Lynch, working with corporations on 401ks and individual investments. Seen below in 1978, John Chiropolos (left) and Tom Wangersham also traveled on to important careers. Chiropolos was employed by Frito-Lay, and Wangersham got involved at Chicago's Mercantile Exchange.

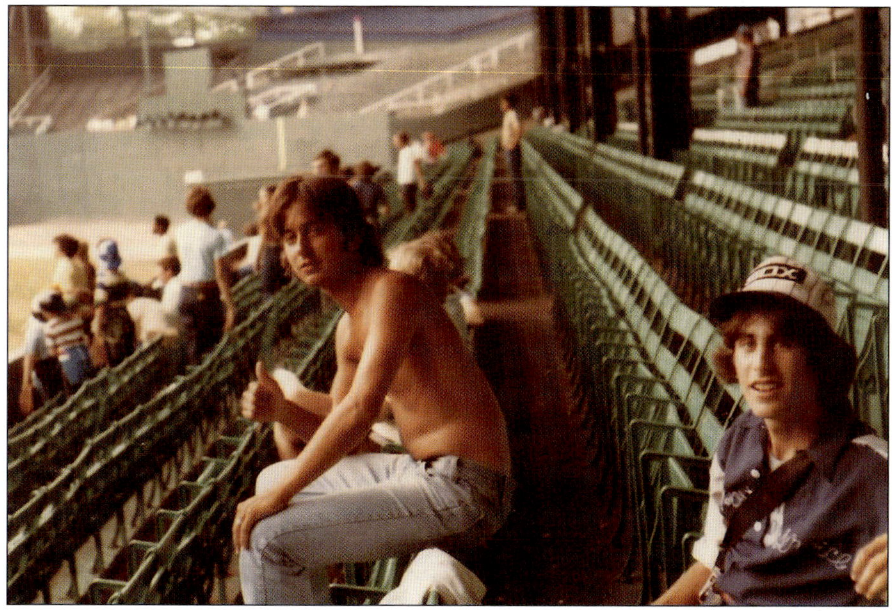

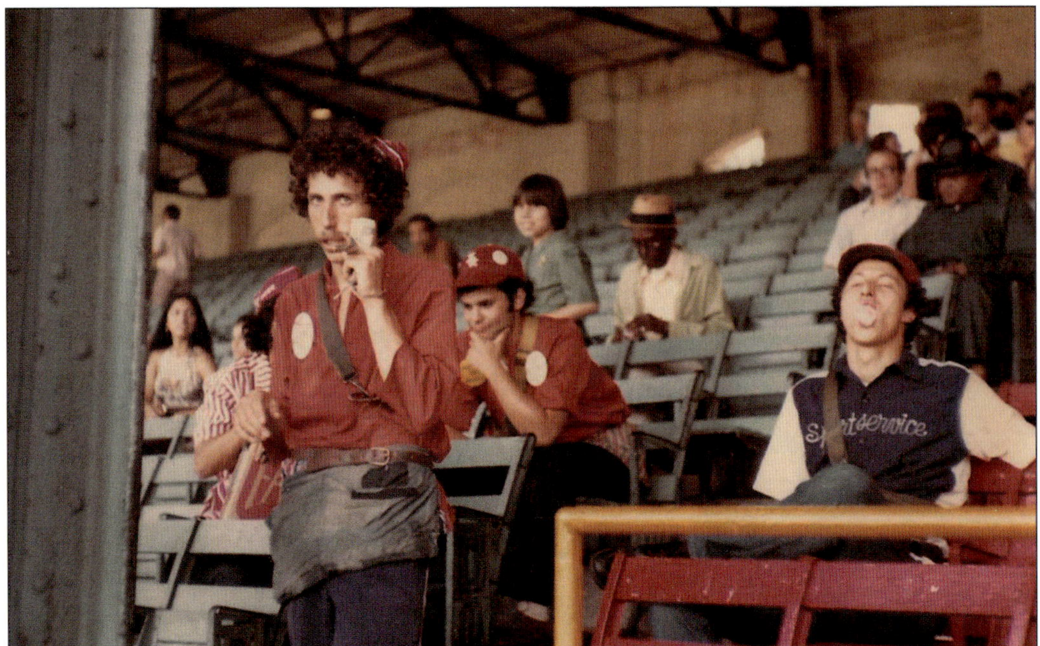

The "Law & Order" vendors seen on these two pages have been around much longer than the famed TV show. Above in 1975, "Exhibit A" has future attorney Lane Kaplan about to begin his opening argument of why the jury of fans should side with his client—beer. Meanwhile, Marc Perper, not yet a "mouthpiece," deliberates over how to approach the crowd. Brandon Medow (right), who became a Chicago patrolman in 1977, is on a stakeout awaiting evidence of beer drinkers. Below in 1978, before becoming a lawyer, Jack Beermann briefs a young man about his trial-worthy hot dogs. Beermann would go on to write legal textbooks for his students at Boston University and testified to them that as a beerman, he would win bets with customers who thought his last name was fake.

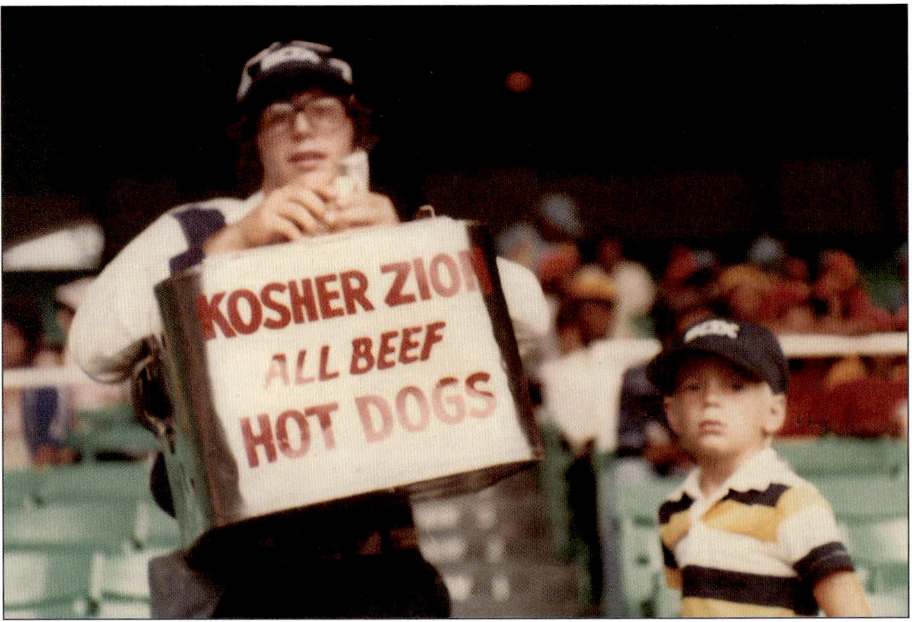

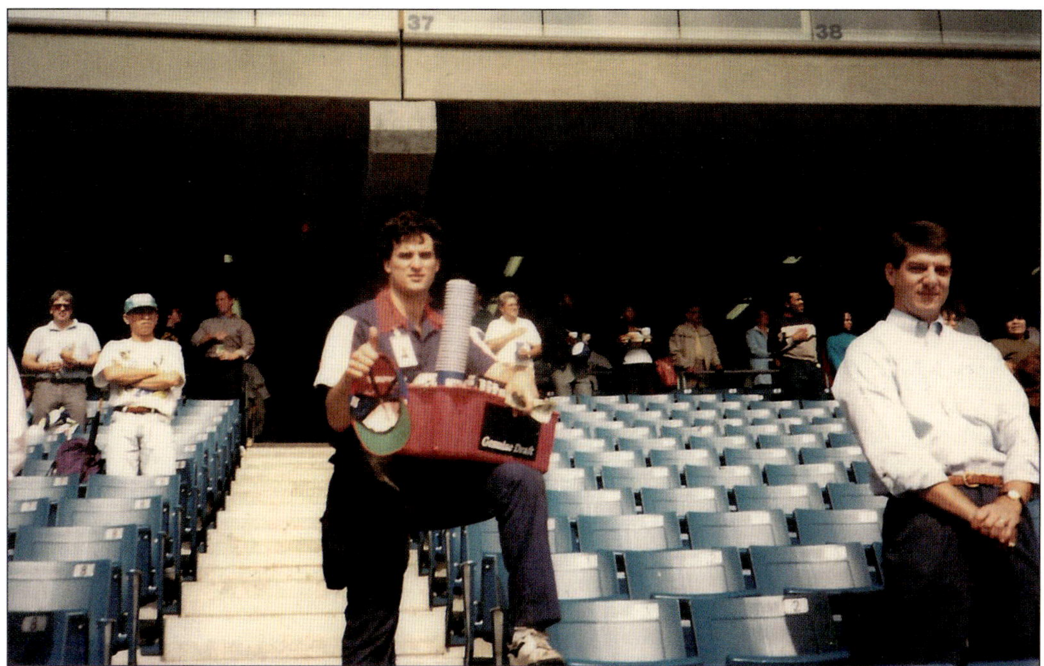

In the October 1991 photograph above, Daron Romanek "rests his case." Romanek would not become a counselor-at-law for a couple years, but when he did, his experience as a vendor served him well in his field of workmen's compensation. Before that, he was a public defender who once testified at the trial of the notorious Blackstone Rangers gang leader Jeff Fort. Below in 1978, Chicago policeman-in-waiting Henry Woodson (left) also rests his case—or rather, his beer tray—someday, perhaps he will have to deal with some of Fort's disciples. With him are innocent bystanders Ed Sherman (center) and Jerry Raphael.

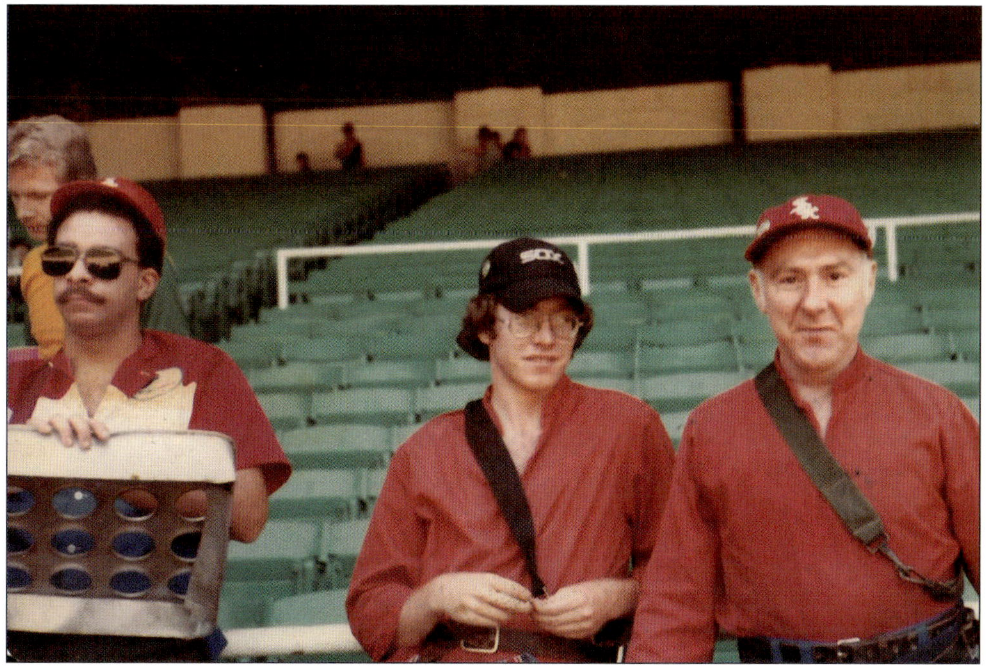

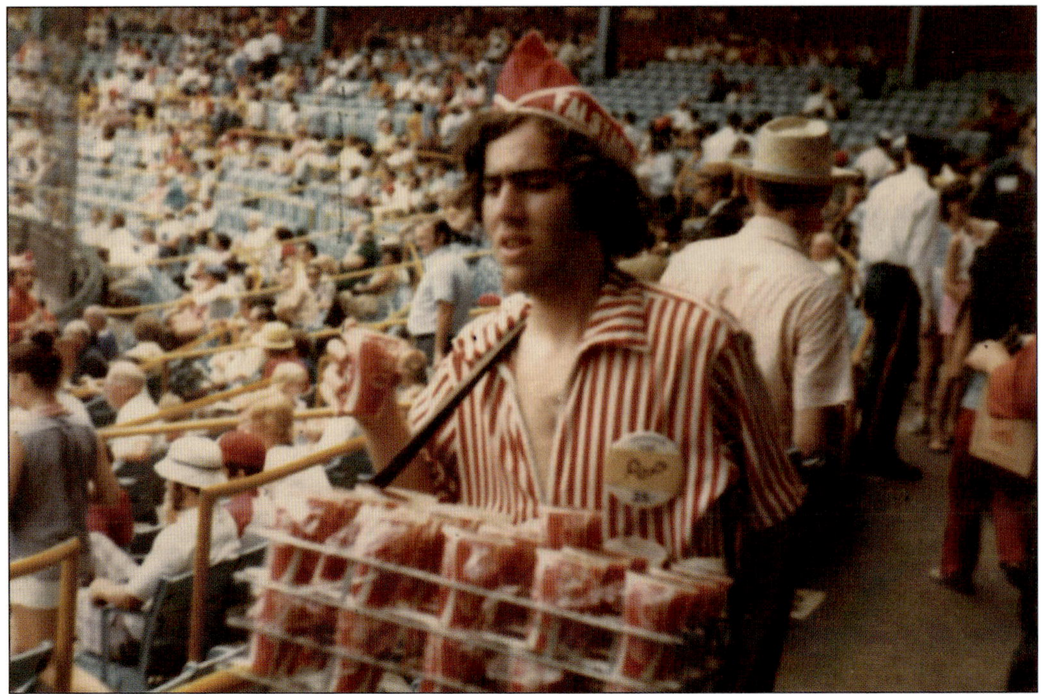

Art Newman had a distinguished career in vending and beyond. In the 1975 image above, he is a 20-year-old racing with a double load of Coke a year before he became one of the top men on beer. Below in 1978, he shakes hands while preparing for a future political campaign, as he would be elected the first ward alderman of north suburban Evanston from 1991 to 2005. He graduated from Chicago's Kent College of Law in the 1980s, and while there as its newspaper editor, he employed co-author Lloyd Rutzky as the movie critic. Rutzky then reciprocated by putting Newman's picture selling beer on the back cover of *Wrigley Field's Amazing Vendors*. And now, the Newman standard has been upheld, as his younger brother Gary holds a spot on the back cover of this book.

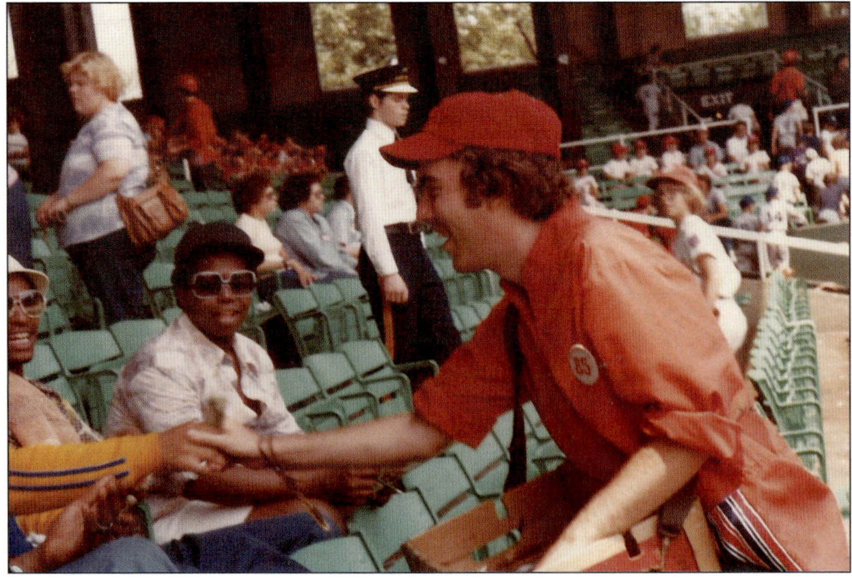

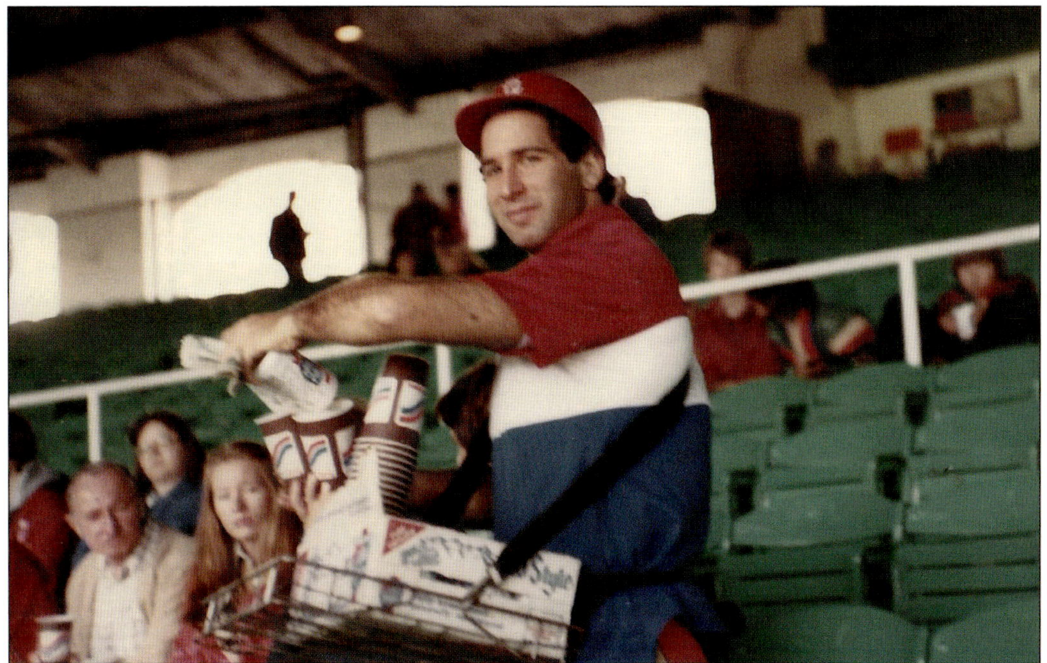

One might think that for vendors, a "pass out" meant a very exhausting day when sales were scarce—or for dentists, like the two future ones in these pictures, it might refer to the state they put their patients in when anesthetized for treatment. Yet in the world of ballpark salesmen, that expression referred to products being so highly in demand, that they would sell out immediately in every aisle. Eli Lawrence, seen above in October 1981 before becoming a DDS, enjoyed many such great days vending, as he was considered one of the best beermen. And there may never have been a greater pass out than on July 12, 1979, just three days after the photograph below of future dentist David Behm (left) and Evan Pomeroy was taken. That night, an over-capacity crowd arrived for the infamous "Disco Sucks" promotion.

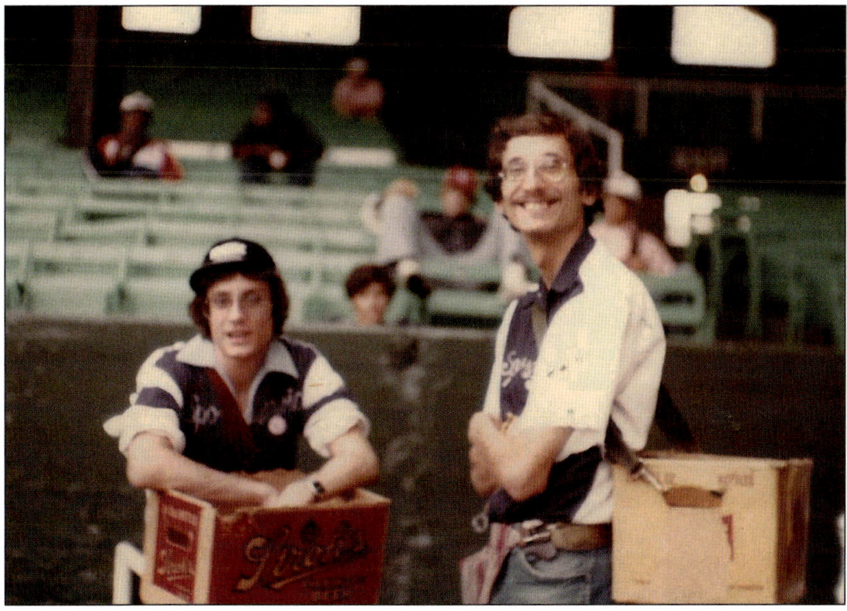

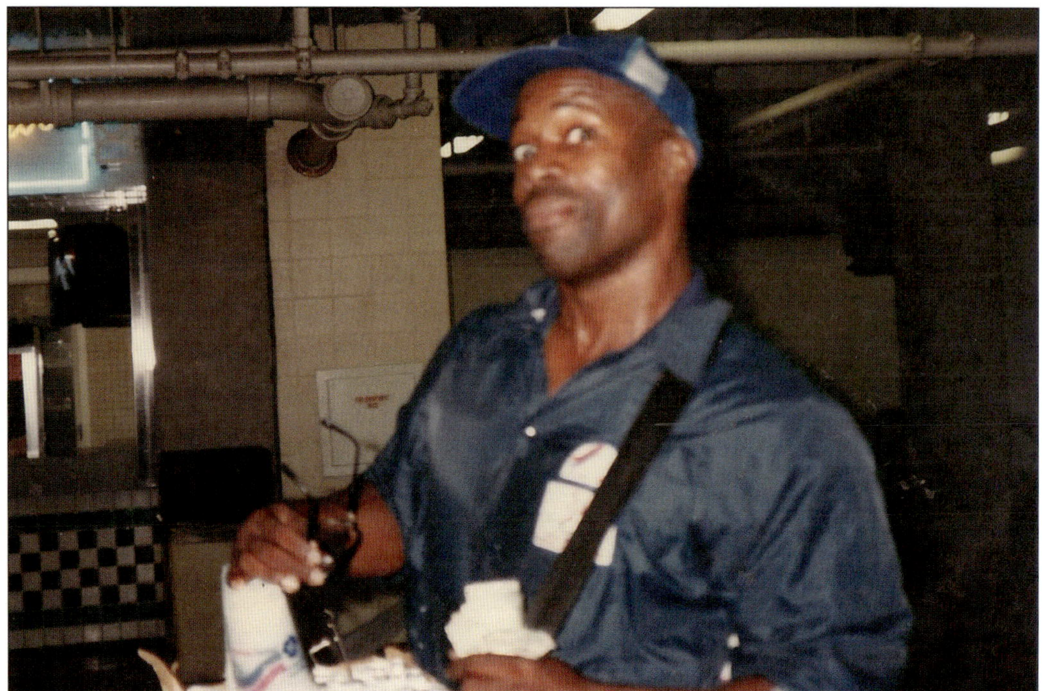

Above, William Dennis seems to be saying, "Look into my eyes," on September 26, 1997. Dennis was quite adept at explaining the statistical difference between a pass out and a "nightmare" in vending, as he became a college math teacher when his ballpark career began to wane. Specifically, a "nightmare" is how hawkers define an event that is the exact opposite of a "pass out." It means sales were extremely meager, and one would hope to wake up soon to find out it was not real. Bob Schwartz, seen below in 1975 with future delicatessen owner Steve Davis, also became a teacher when his vending career no longer was "adding up."

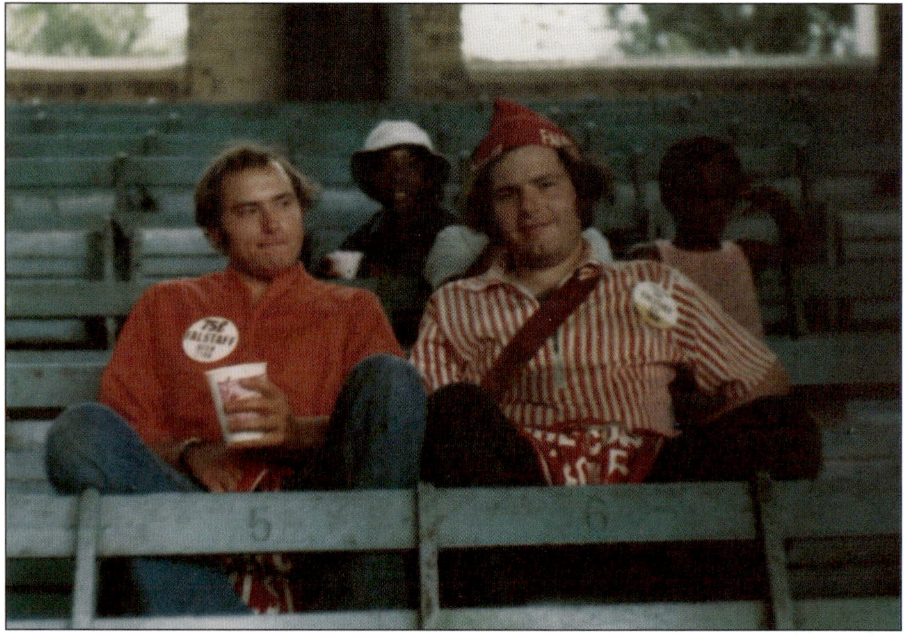

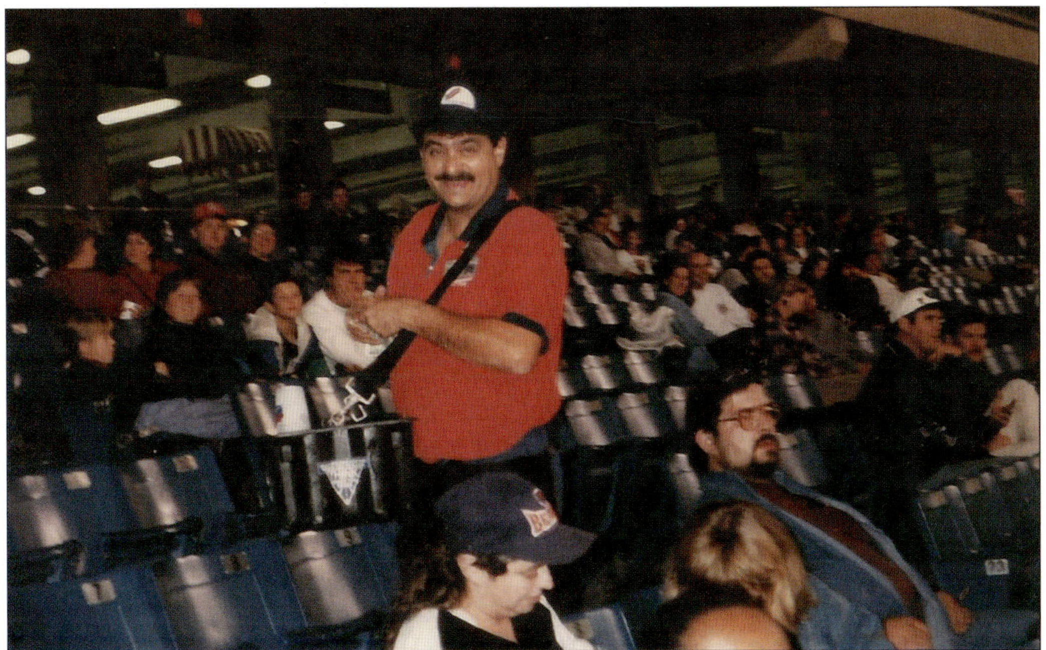

Describing a tough night at the ballpark as a nightmare, unfortunately, turned out to be inadequate when things were really, really slow. On September 26, 1997, Abe Rapuch (above) and Marv Mitofsky (below, with Glenn Smoler and his nephew Todd Smoler) try laughing about it or feigning a smile, but they were experiencing what would be termed a "death march." It was the last weekend of the season, and sadly, the White Sox, who had battled Cleveland most of the year for first place, had been "terminated." Many fans were no-shows for these games with last-place Kansas City, the weather turned colder, and beermen frequently cried, "I can't get rid of it," forcing even hard workers to "drop early" (meaning "check out")—also known as "going to the canvas."

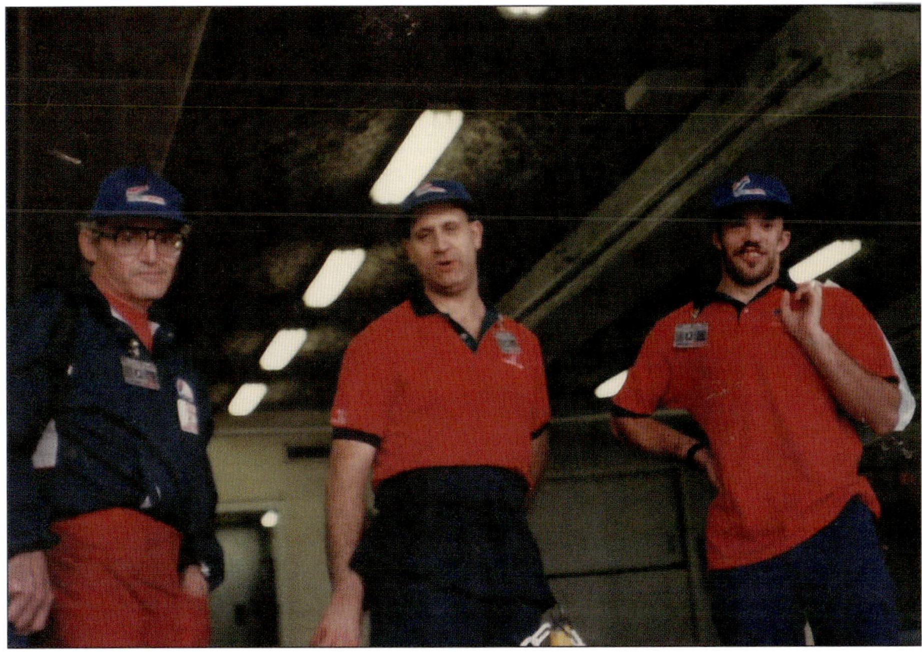

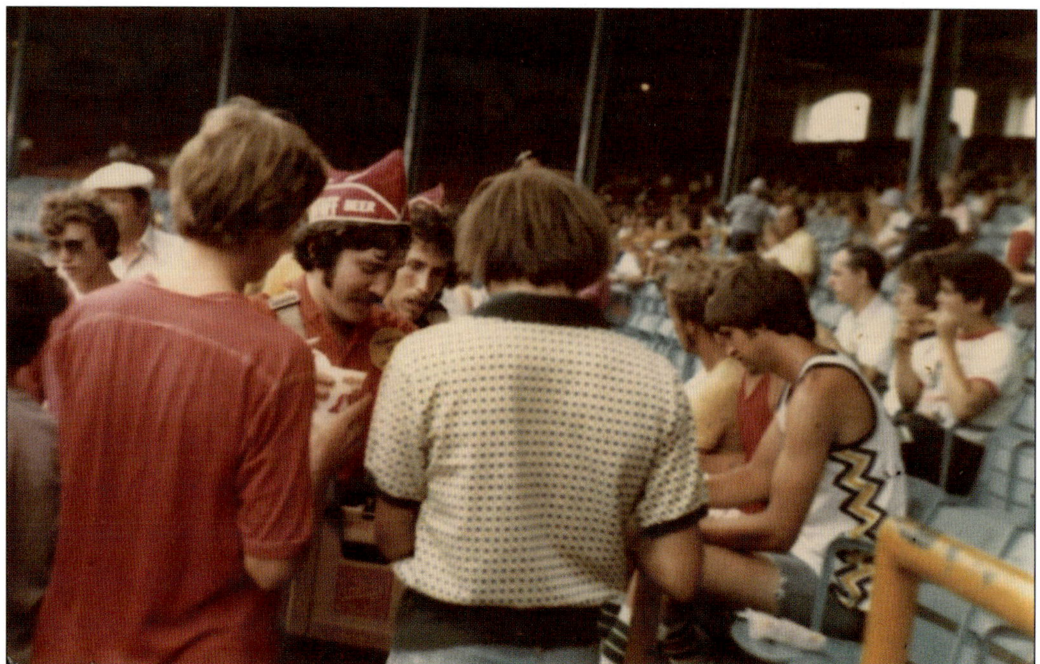

These three guys were beneficiaries of what has become known as Disco Demolition night. Pictured above are Arnold Lipski and Lane Kaplan in Falstaff hats during a fairly busy game in 1975; Seymour Pechter is below in 1978. However, on that 1979 evening, beermen were not merely crowded—they were mobbed more than 10 times greater than seen above. White Sox owner Bill Veeck's son Mike had dreamed up the anti-disco promotion with WLUP-FM 97.9 DJ Steve Dahl. Fans could come to the doubleheader for just 98¢ and a disco record that Dahl promised to blow up between games. A total of 50,000 fans were already in the park by the first game time, when less than 5,000 was the norm for an unscheduled first game. They threw records onto the field and rioted after the first game, and the White Sox were forced to forfeit game two.

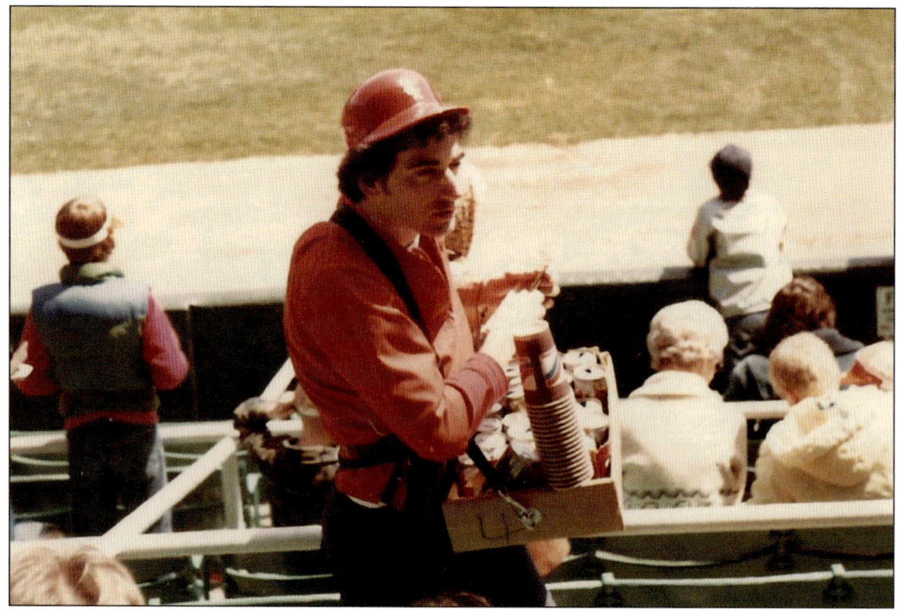

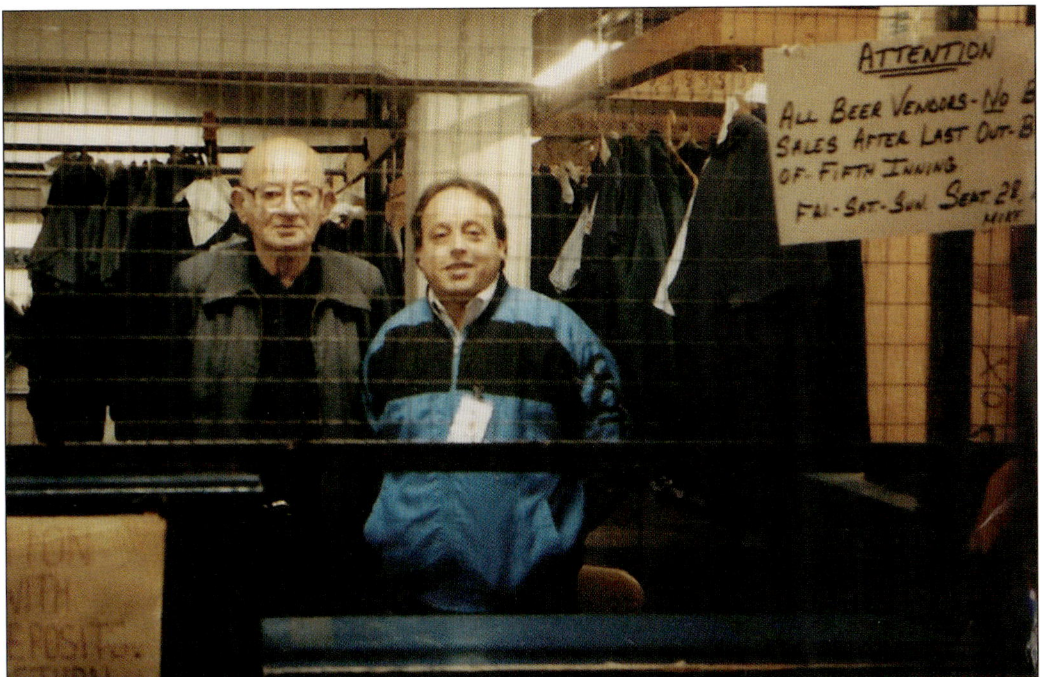

September 30, 1990, was the date of the last game at Comiskey Park in its 81st season. The White Sox defeated the Seattle Mariners 2-1 on a warm, sunny day with 42,849 in attendance. Vendors were delighted with the huge throng, but regretfully, management feared the fans would be too excited and shut off beer sales excessively early after five innings. Above, union stewards Phil Grossman (left) and Mike LaPapa stand near a sign that explains the policy. Seven years later, on the last Friday night of the 1997 season, LaPapa (below, center), who had been the chief union steward there since John Studnicka had passed away late in 1987, is flanked by his son Mike Jr. (left), who would take the steward's reins in 2012, and longtime family friend Tony DiFillippo.

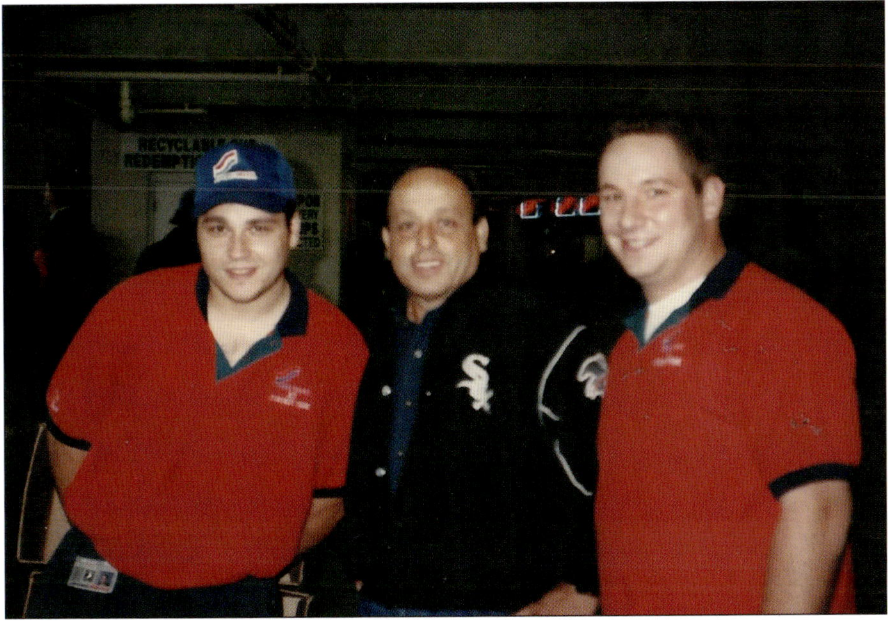

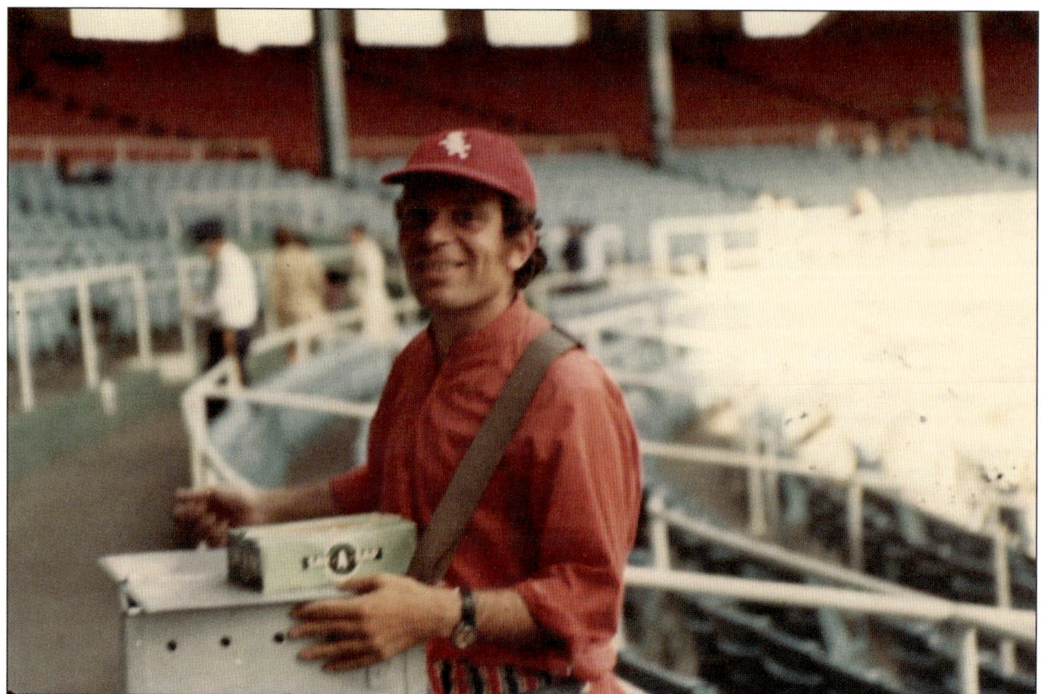

Captains Courageous was Rudyard Kipling's tale of rugged sailors in the North Atlantic a century ago. Fast forward to 1976, and imagine another salty yarn of vendors who charted their course for a somewhat less treacherous voyage fishing in White Sox Park for treasured commissions. Above is Jerry Shencup, a US Navy veteran from 1960 to 1966, and Leo Zimmer is below right; on top of being a vendor, he was also an optometrist, a banquet waiter, and worked at city hall, as well as a former US Coast Guardsman with the un-seamanlike nickname of "Sarge." Shencup rations out some tasty pretzels with Zimmer soon pouring many bottles of brew—ballpark booty to satisfy the cravings of all landlubbers.

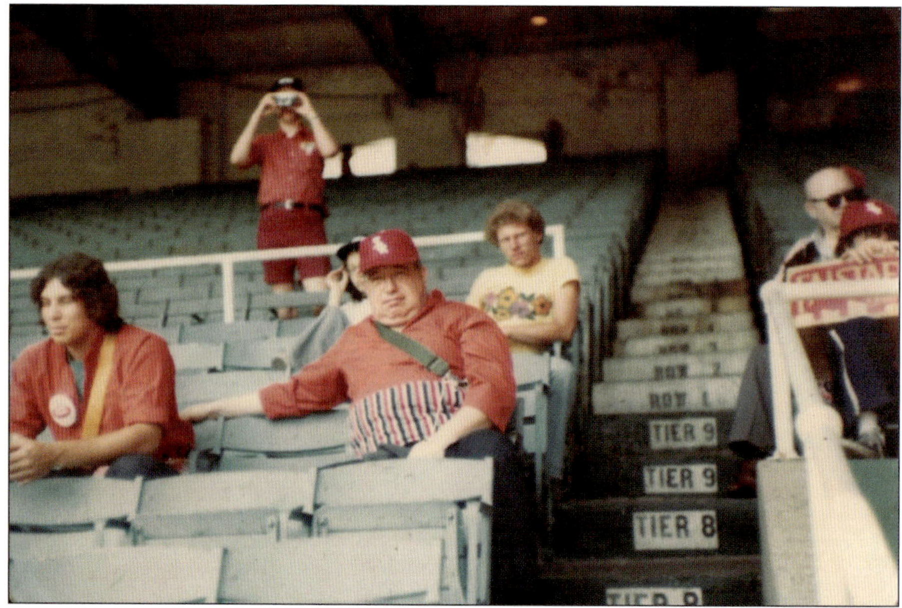

Three

Vendors Who Play Together Stay Together

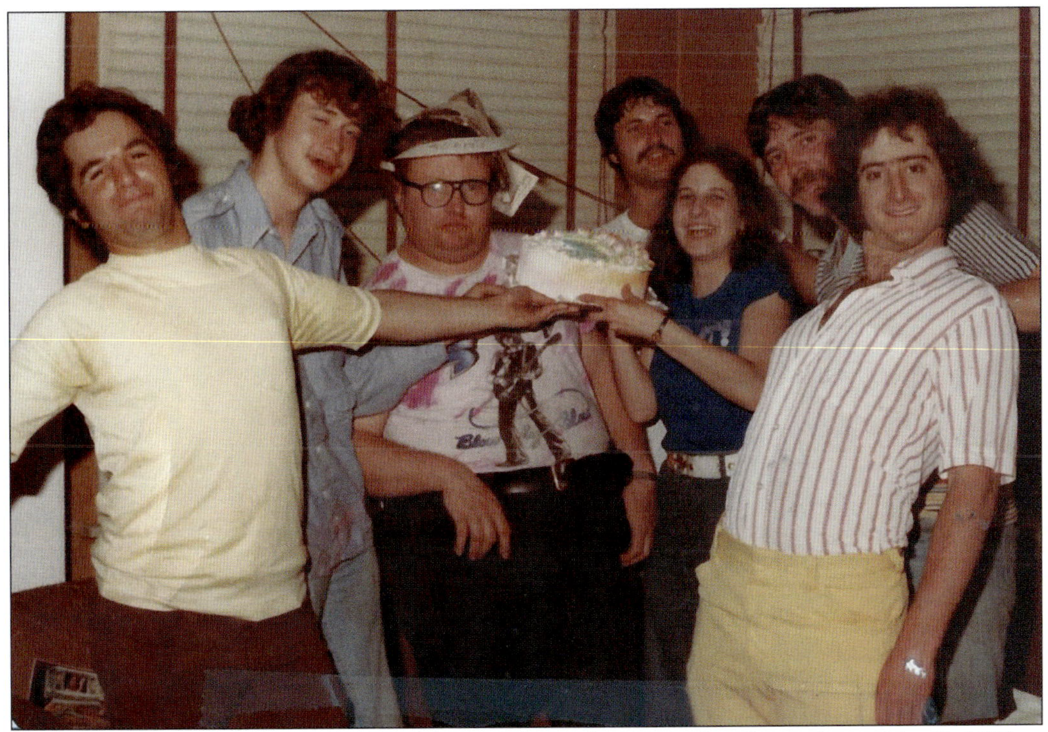

"Here's Johnnie!" Legendary Johnnie Skweres (center) is toasted with a cake on May 5, 1977, at his house. It was never determined if this was a celebration of his "thirty-something" birthday or a "mock bon voyage" party he concocted for another of his famed one-day airplane trips. Gathered around him to wish him well were, from left to right, Jay Lawrence, Wayne Fisher, Arlen Korer and his sister Melinda, Arnold Lipski, and Lloyd Rutzky. (Courtesy of Mike Gold.)

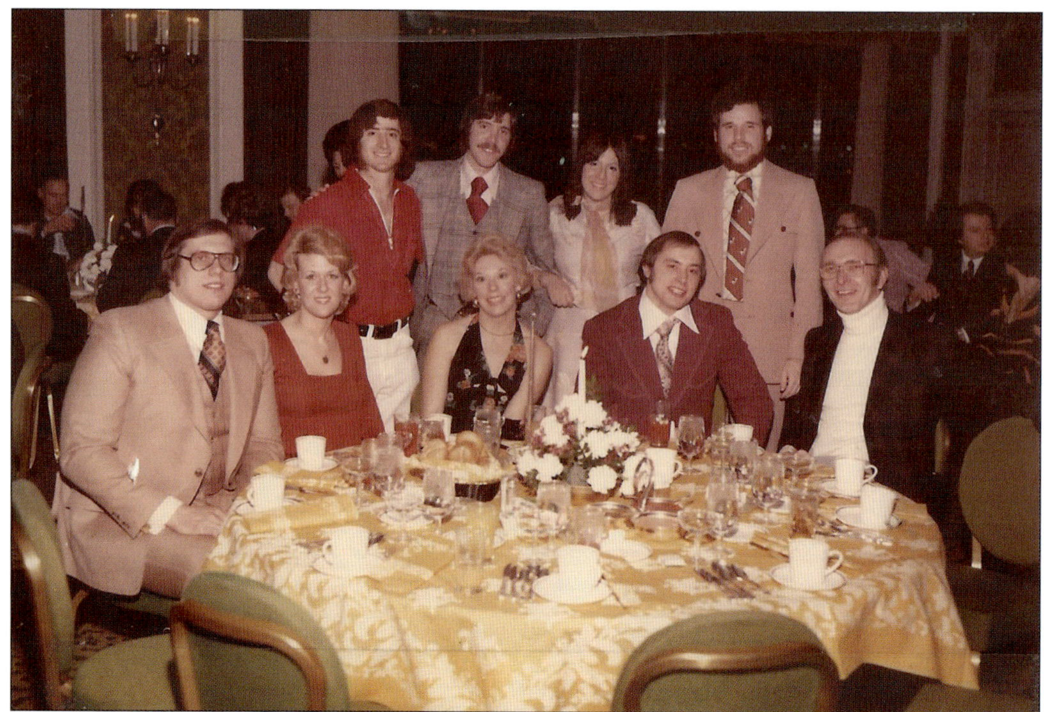

While this was not a meeting of Local 236, union president Nicholas J. LaPapa Jr. presides at this table, sitting on the far right on March 9, 1975. Union business was, however, being conducted, as this was a celebration of vendor Ira Levin's wedding. From left to right are (seated) Bill Bailen and his date, Bob Schwartz with his date, and LaPapa Jr.; (standing) Lloyd Rutzky, Arnold Lipski, and Mira and Darryl Temkin.

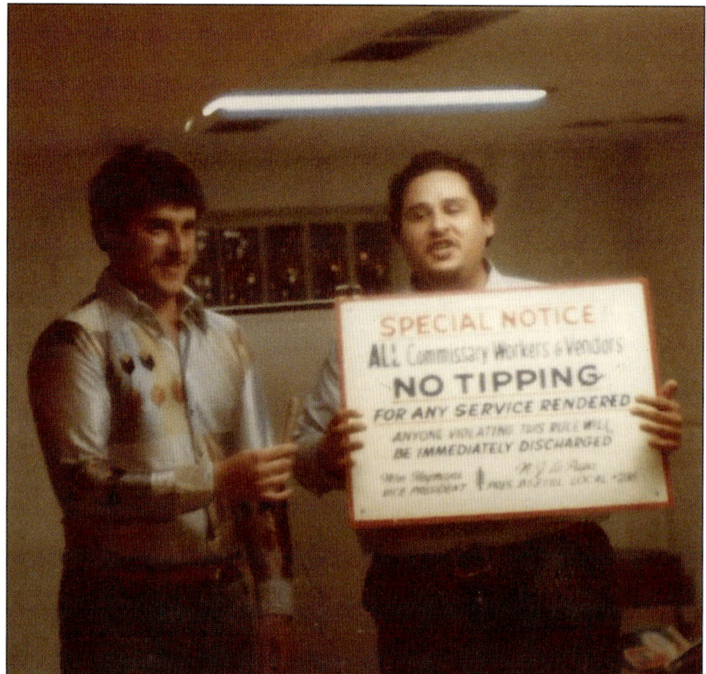

Vending business of another sort occurred during a famed All-Star week party at vending brothers Eli and Jay Lawrence's parents' home in 1978. Here, Mark Reiner and master of ceremonies Harlan Grabowsky exhibit a strange sign some unnamed person removed from the ballpark. Later, Reiner screened his newly filmed masterpiece about vending, *The Sound Of Money*.

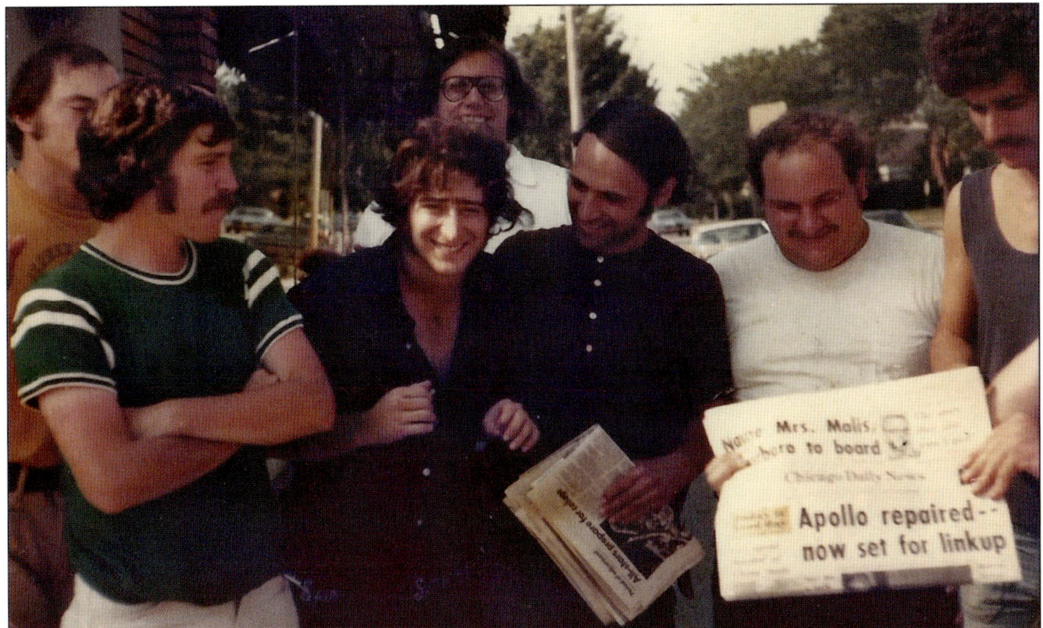

As the newspaper headline in the photograph above proclaims, there was a "linkup" going on in outer space. Meanwhile, back on planet Earth, the vendors were just "taking up space." Just call it fun (out of) the old ballpark. During the July 1975 All-Star break, the crew seen above orbits around Lloyd Rutzky (third from left); From left to right are Bob Schwartz, Arnold Lipski, Bill Bailen, Sherwin Tycher (seen on the front cover), Lewis Wilker, and Ira Levin. Below, in 1997, there appears to be some "exploration" of Rutzky (second from right) at the famed Jimbo's—a White Sox Park employees' hangout at Thirty-Third and Wells Streets—the successor to taverns Danny O'Brien's and McCuddy's that once were across Thirty-Fifth Street. From left to right are Dave Levenson, Frank Bellizzi, and Bob Kosiba.

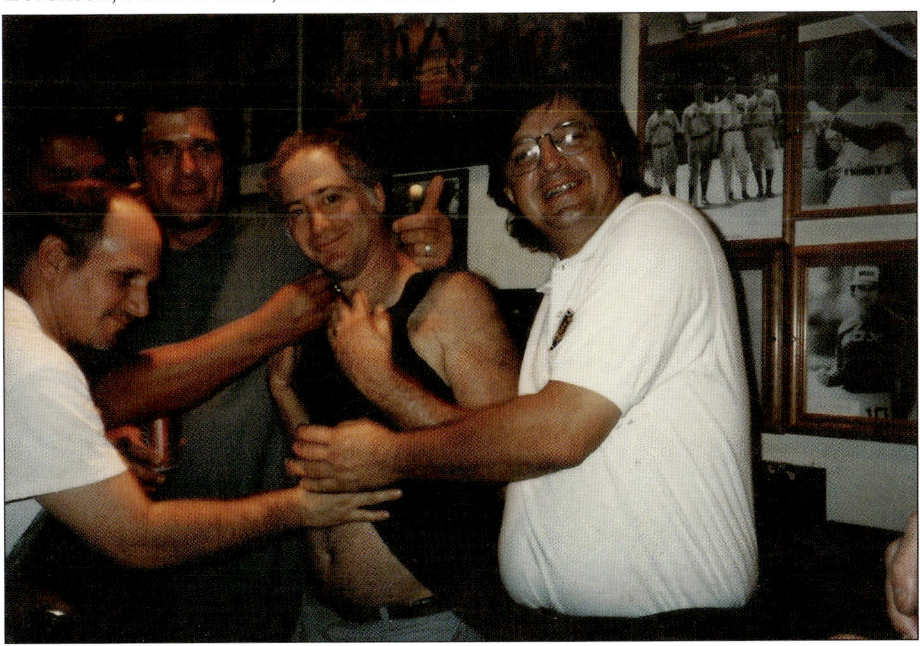

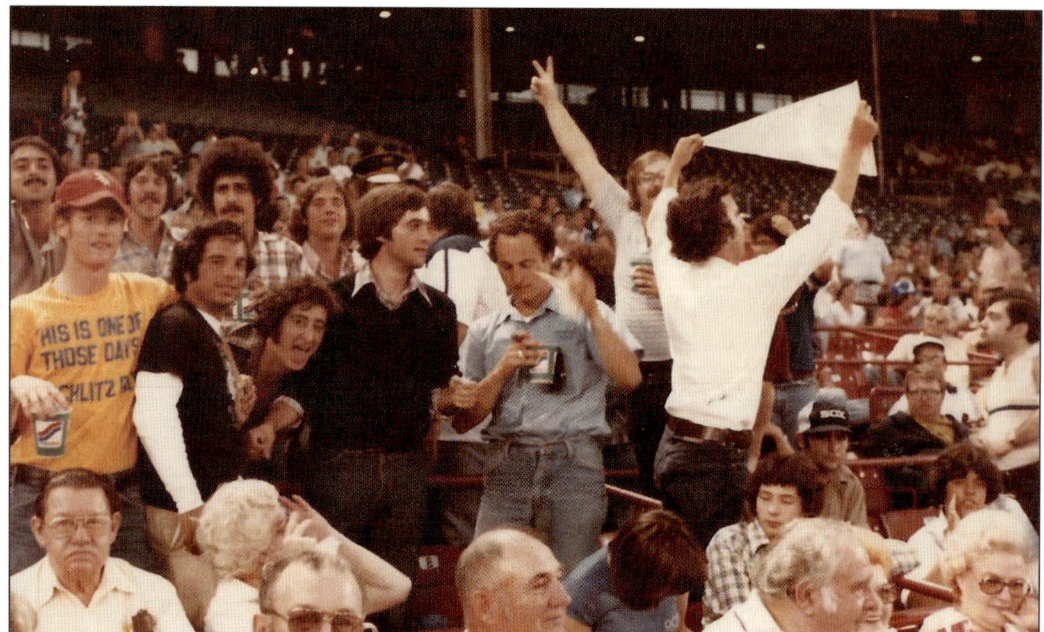

Vendors delighted in becoming fans every time there was a night off after a day game at Wrigley, providing a chance to see the White Sox play in Milwaukee—so would they be perfect guests in their rivals' house? Above, Corwin Glick, Gary Tuch, Arnold Lipski, Ira Levin, Jay Lawrence, co-author Lloyd Rutzky, Eric Eckstrum, Gary Newman, Brandon Medow, Dave Ashkanazy, Art Newman, Marc Perper, Johnnie Skweres, and Paul Pechter look a bit unsociable on July 17, 1978, as the Sox were getting beat 6-1 during a nine-game losing streak during a dismal season. (Courtesy of Mike Gold.)

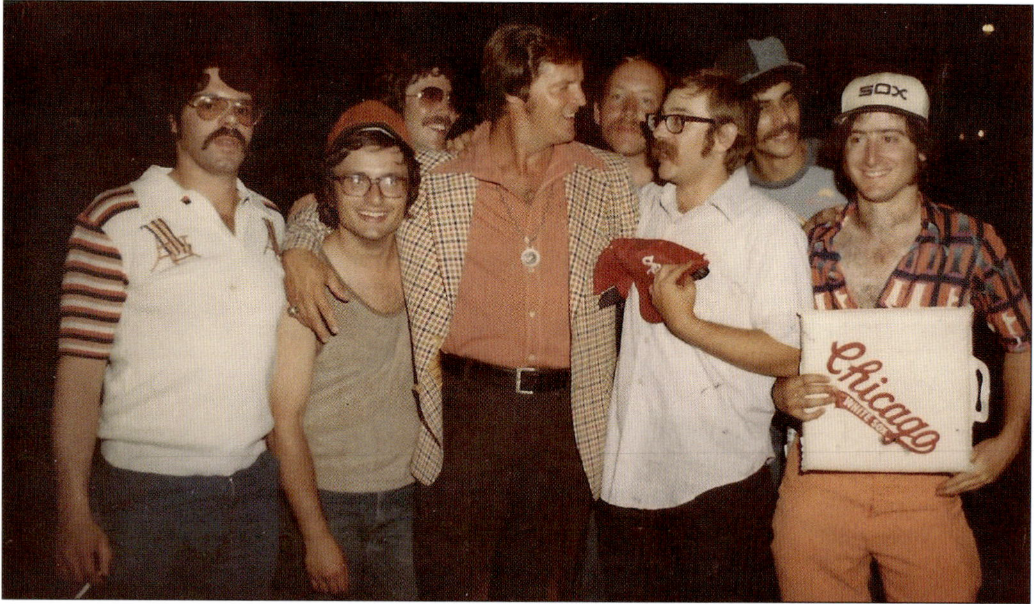

This was the result of a June 9, 1976, ballgame at County Stadium in Milwaukee. The Sox at least won this game 4-2. Congratulating the suit-wearing Sox pitcher Clay Carroll are Les Lasinsky, Brewers vendor Tony Capassio, Arnold Lipski, Dave Klemp, Dave Ashkanazy, Ira Levin, and Lloyd Rutzky (holding the seat cushion).

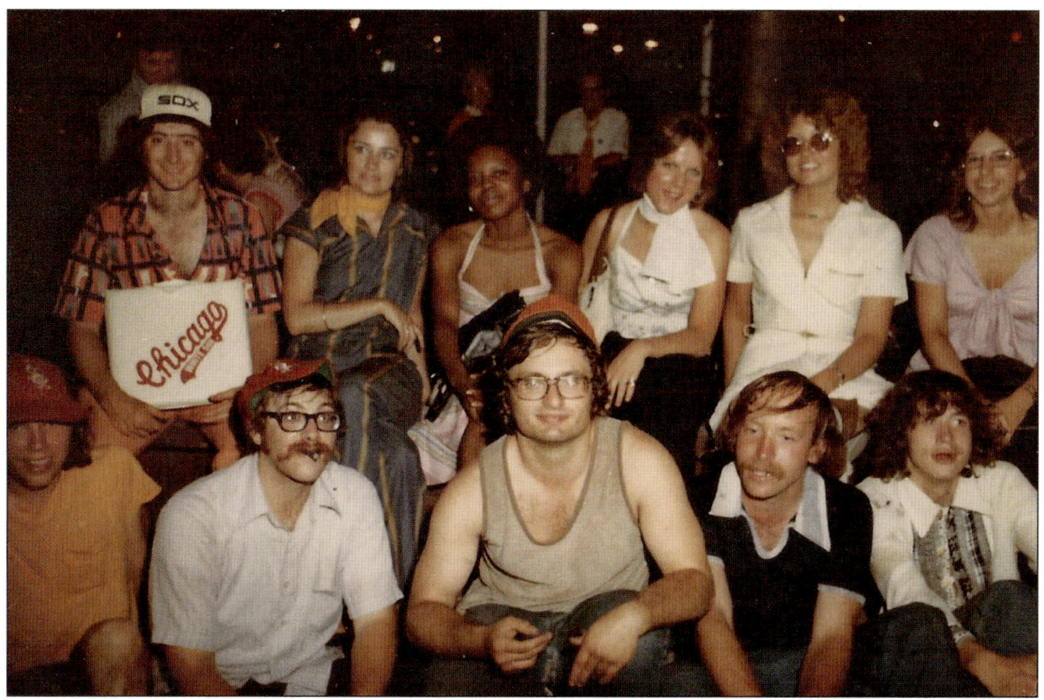

Also pictured on June 9, 1976, in Milwaukee, above, it appears that these scrappy chums had managed to befriend several lovely Brewer fans. However, below, the boys look like they had "struck out." (Both, courtesy of Mike Gold.)

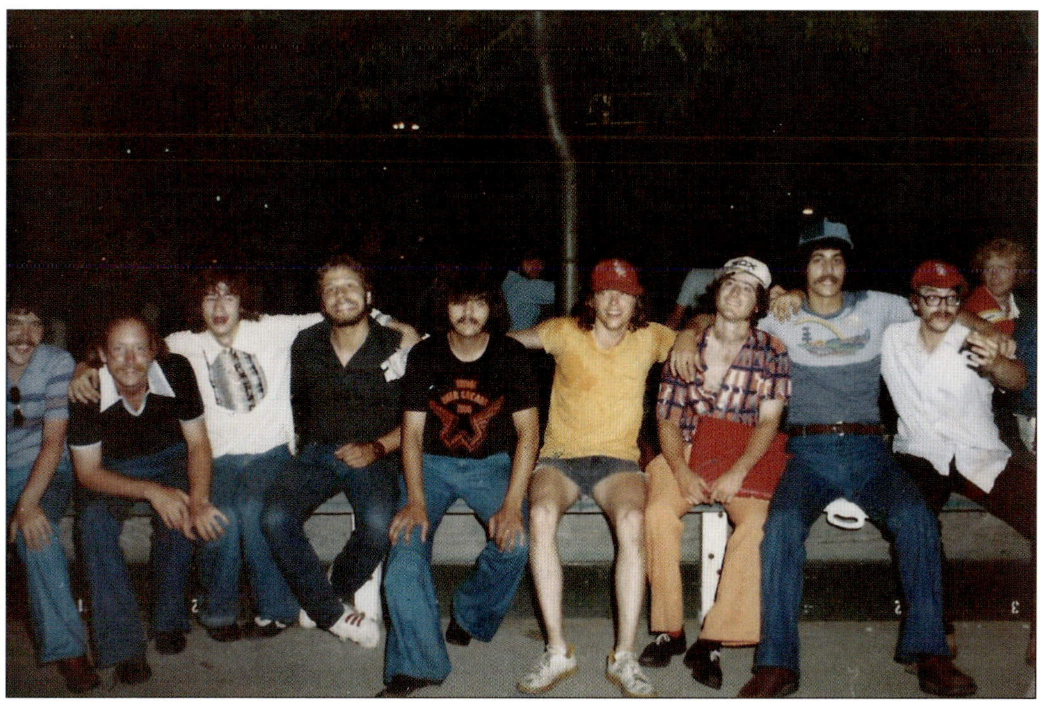

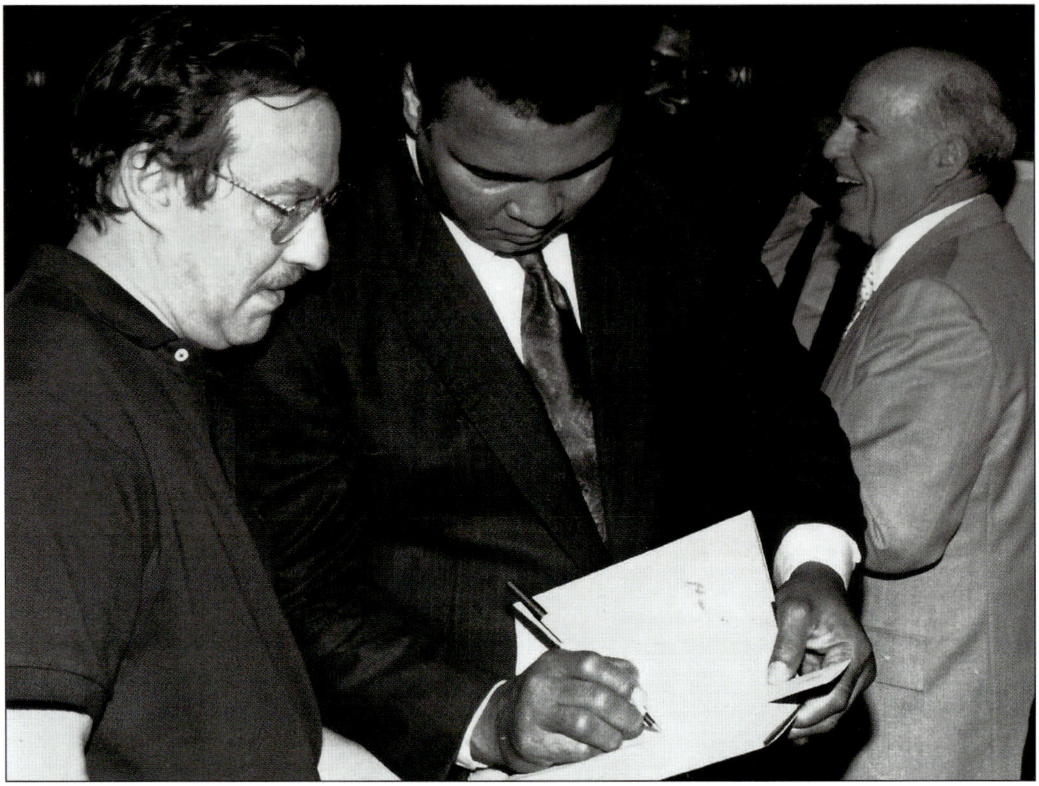

On September 25, 1962, Sonny Liston knocked out Floyd Patterson at Comiskey Park. Three other notables were also in attendance. Co-author Joel Levin and his brother Mitch were challenging their co-workers for most loads of Coke sold that night while future heavyweight champ Cassius Clay, later known as Muhammad Ali, came into the ring to harass and goad Liston into fighting him next. Thirty-three years later, Ali and Mitch (above) would "face off" in an autograph session hosted by Chicago Park District superintendent Ed Kelly (right). The Levin brothers were boxing experts who frequently gave lectures on that subject in the area. Mitch (below, reading paper) is not ready to come out of his corner to slug it out on beer, though, in 1976. His competition, Dan Ferrone (left) and Robert Lichtenstein, are also looking a bit "knocked out."

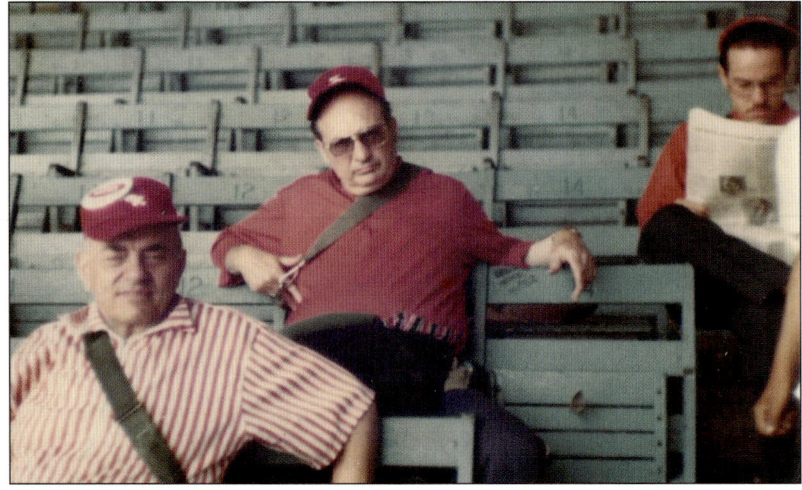

Four

The Legends

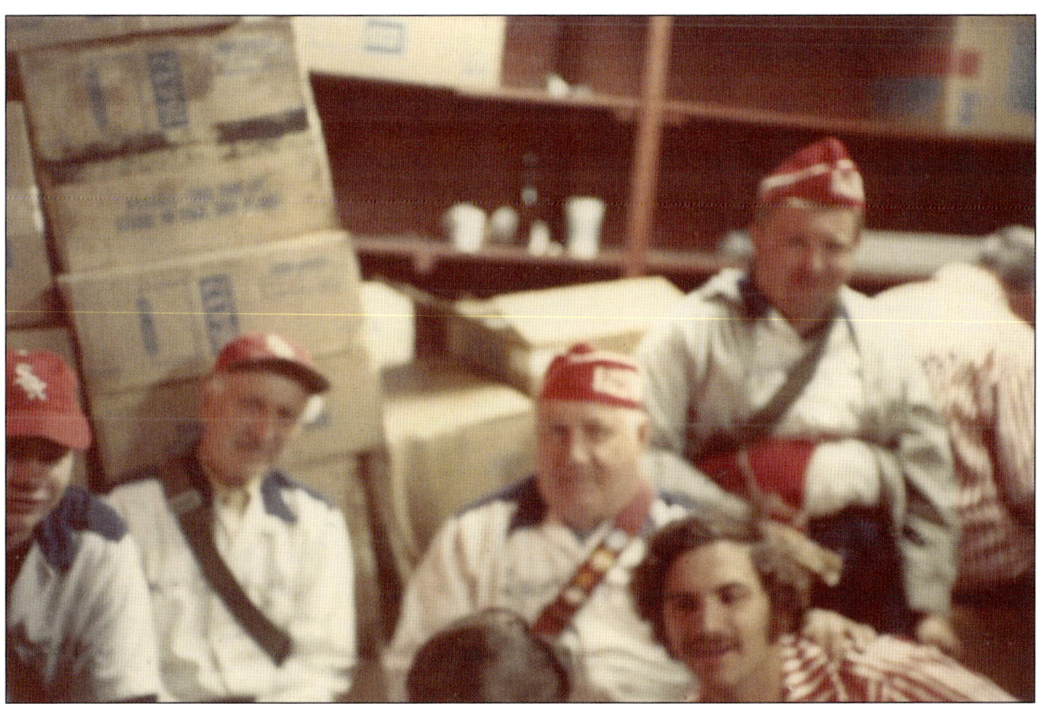

"Memories light the corners of my mind, misty water-colored memories of the way we were." Those are the immortal opening lines from the Oscar-winning title song from 1973's *The Way We Were*, written about the same time this 1972 "scattered picture" was being taken of "smiles we left behind." From left to right are Russ Virgo, Irving Newer, Lew Tidd, Johnnie Skweres, and Mike Ginsburg.

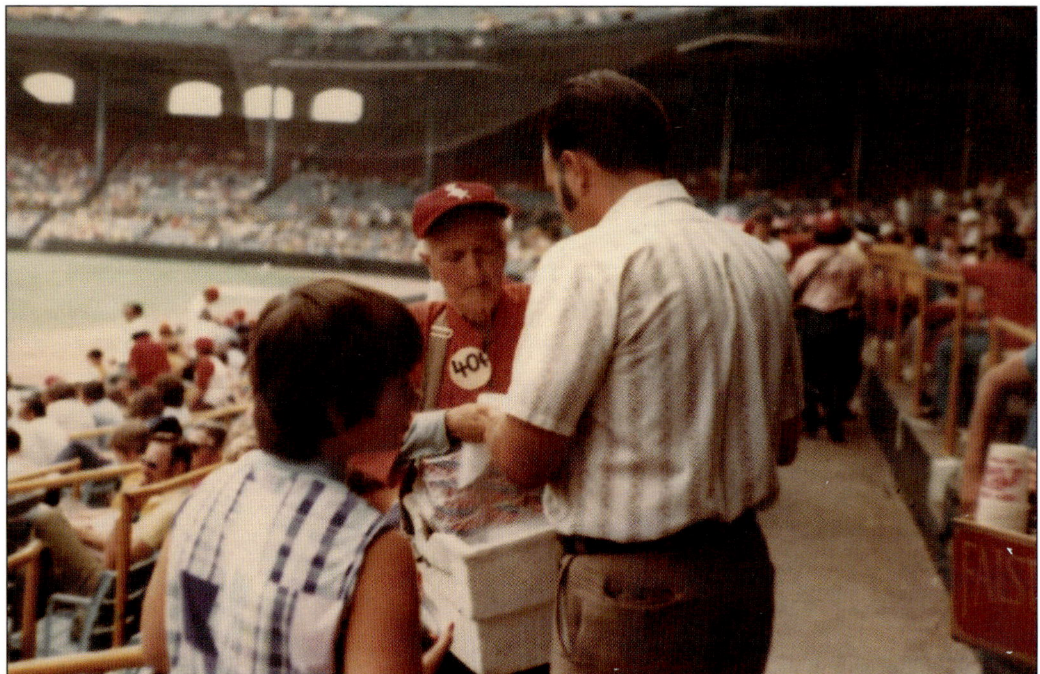

Wrigley Field's Amazing Vendors was dedicated to Irving Newer, also known as "Uncle Irv." Above, in 1975, he sells ice cream much the same way that made him so memorable on the North Side—in a styrofoam box with lots of dry ice to keep it chilled—and also doing his best to count the customer's money because of his failing eyesight. However, at Comiskey Park, the frozen treat was Dolly Madison sundaes for 40¢, whereas at Cubs games, it was Borden's frosty malts for a quarter. Below, just four years later and four years before passing away, he is seen selling peanuts, which were much lighter and easier to handle. Newer's vision had further deteriorated, as evidenced by his price badge being on sideways.

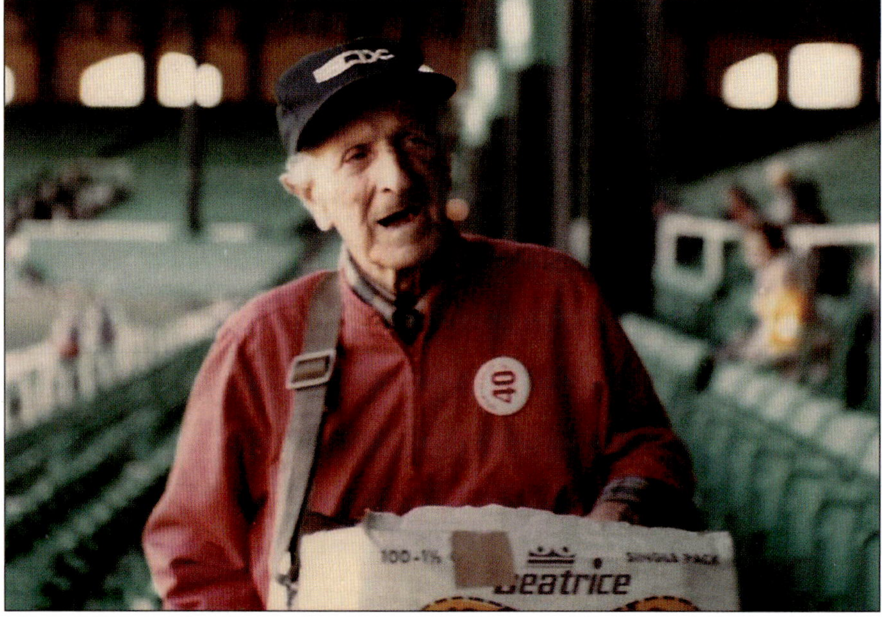

To the right, Arnold "the Chipmunk" Gorman does his best Napoleon imitation in 1972, with his hand across his chest. That is about as close, though, as anyone might get to mistaking him for "The Little Corporal." A much too kind-hearted soul, he never sold beer despite wearing a Falstaff hat and apron. Children's items were the agenda for this forever young-in-spirit legend. Marty "Mo" Moshinsky, seen below in 1979, is on "dogs" this game, though he sold everything (and knew everything, too). He was just as much of an icon as Gorman and had "nuttin' to worry about." They were both immortalized in *Wrigley Field's Amazing Vendors*.

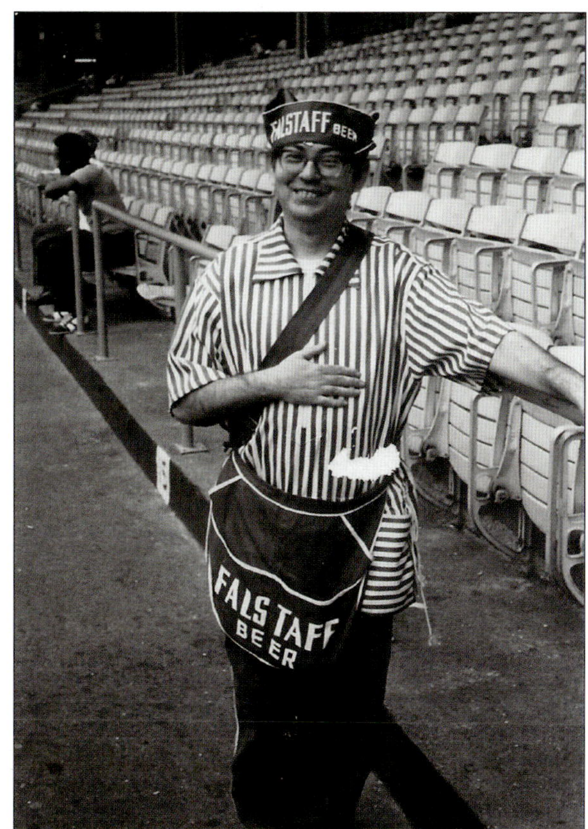

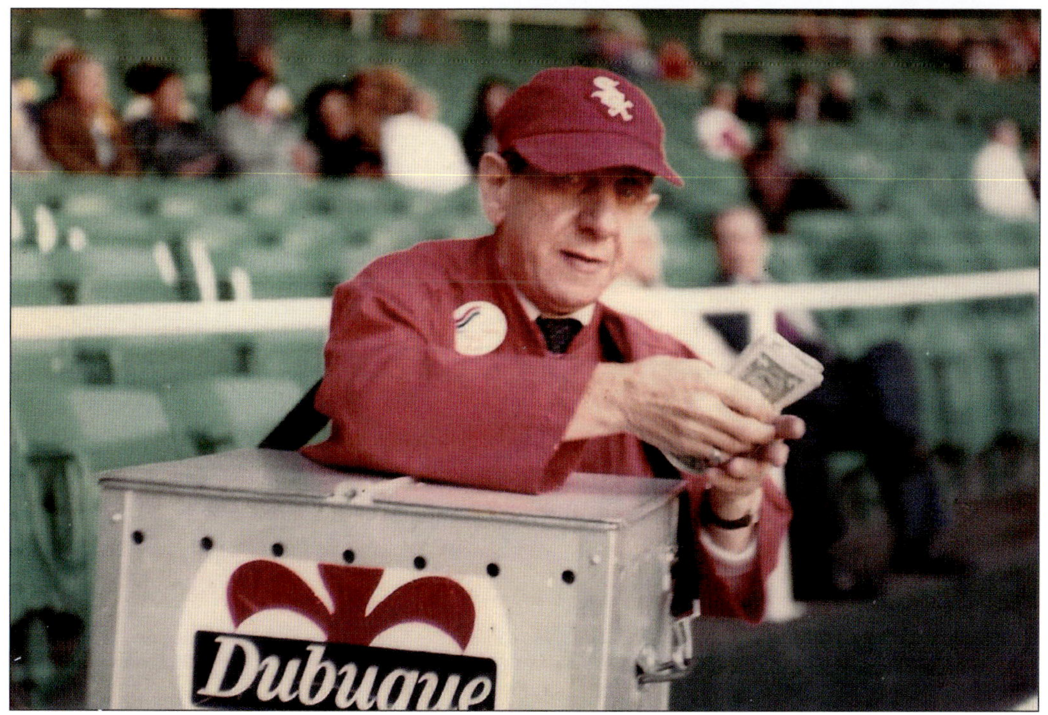

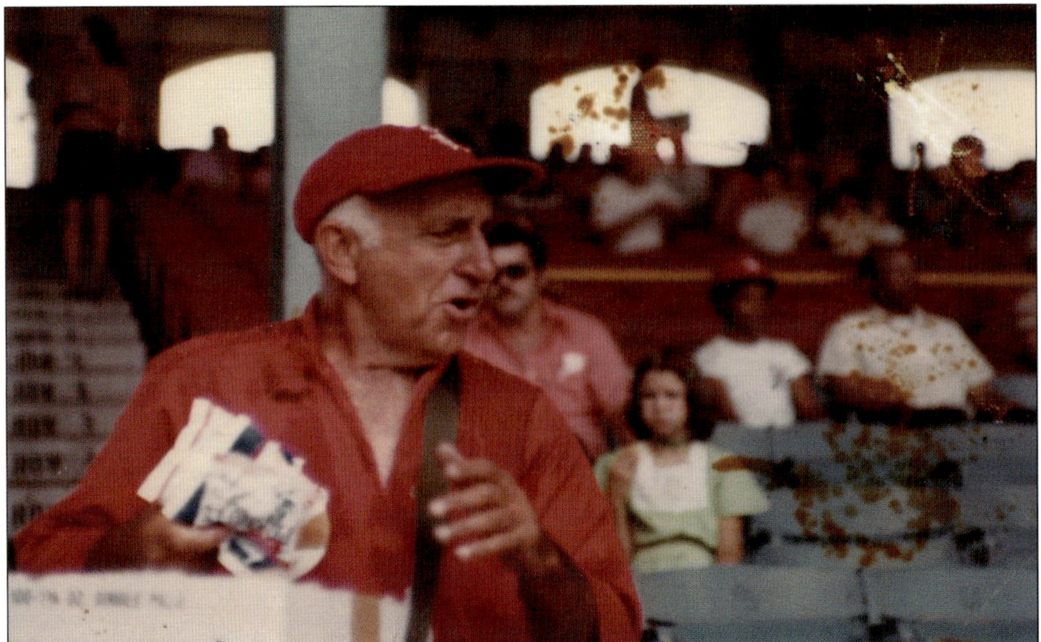

Bernie Lasinsky, seen above in 1975, and Johnnie Skweres, below in 1979, belong on the "Mt. Rushmore of Vendors" and richly deserve their enshrinement in this hallowed wing of *White Sox Park's Amazing Vendors*. Lasinsky was nicknamed "the Roadrunner" because he was a perpetual-motion vending machine, even when selling peanuts on a 90-degree day, versus hawkers half his age. Despite mumbling Don Rickles–like insults and having no time for anybody's behavior, he was much beloved by all, even if most of the time he was running them over. Skweres (as seen on page 77 and also featured in *Wrigley Field's Amazing Vendors*) was a renowned traveling "soldier of fortune" and he and his one-of-a-kind quirky remarks will live forever in the annals of vending history.

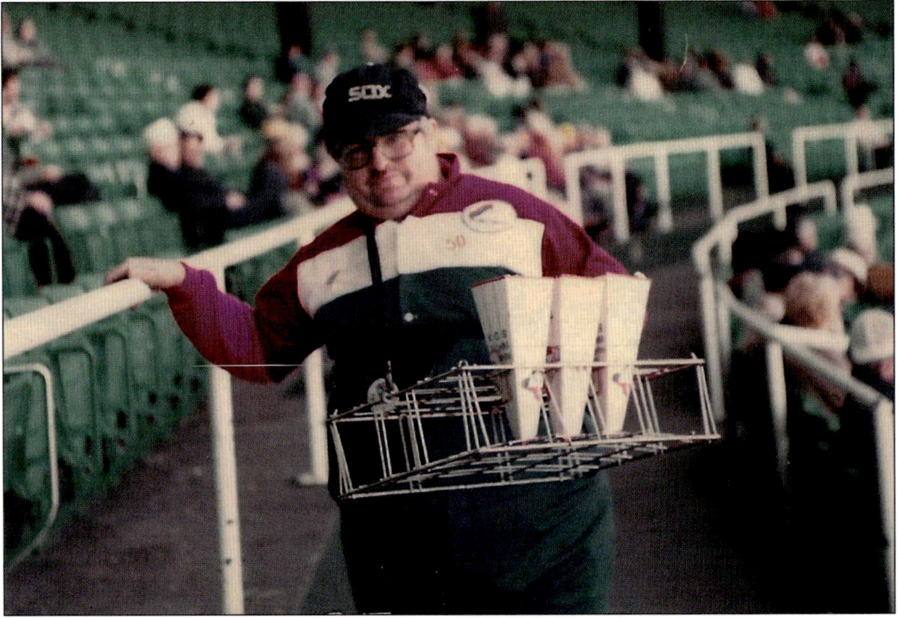

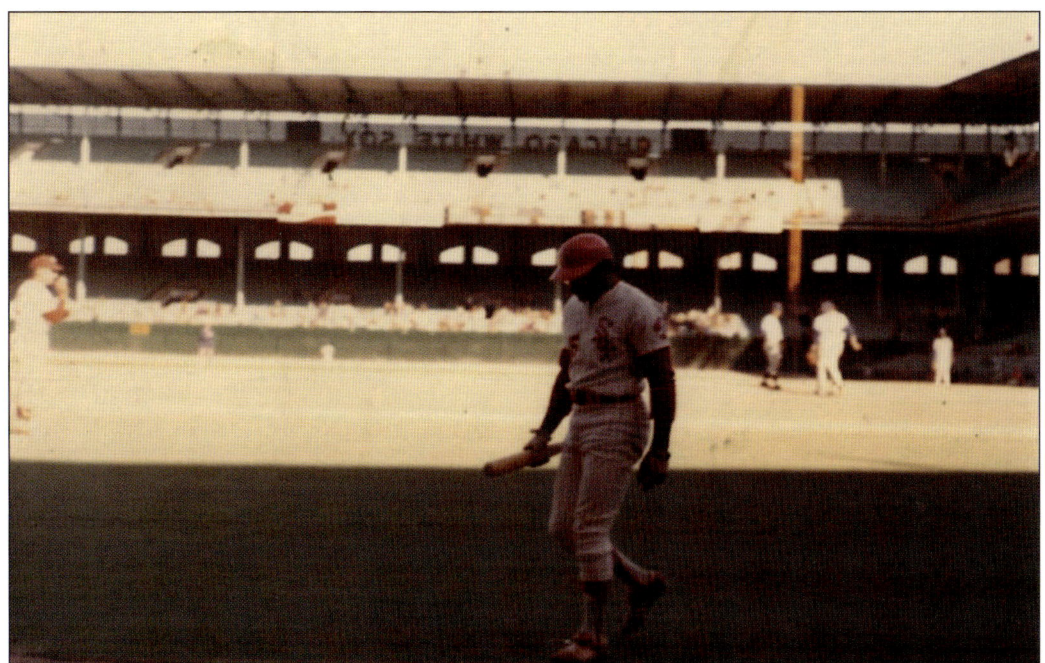

Vendors are constantly asked, "Do you watch the game?" Many focus on making money and pay little heed to the diamond doings, but co-author Lloyd Rutzky would never have stayed in this job for long if he could not see the events on the field—and there may never have been a player he paid more attention to than White Sox slugger Dick Allen, who won the American League MVP in 1972. Allen would hit the ball with such authority that the fans were spellbound every time he swung, including when he struck out (above). Another crowd pleaser was Sox shortstop and future manager Ozzie Guillen (right), who celebrated the Sox winning their division with Rutzky on September 27, 1993, at an employee party held by White Sox general manager Ron Schueler.

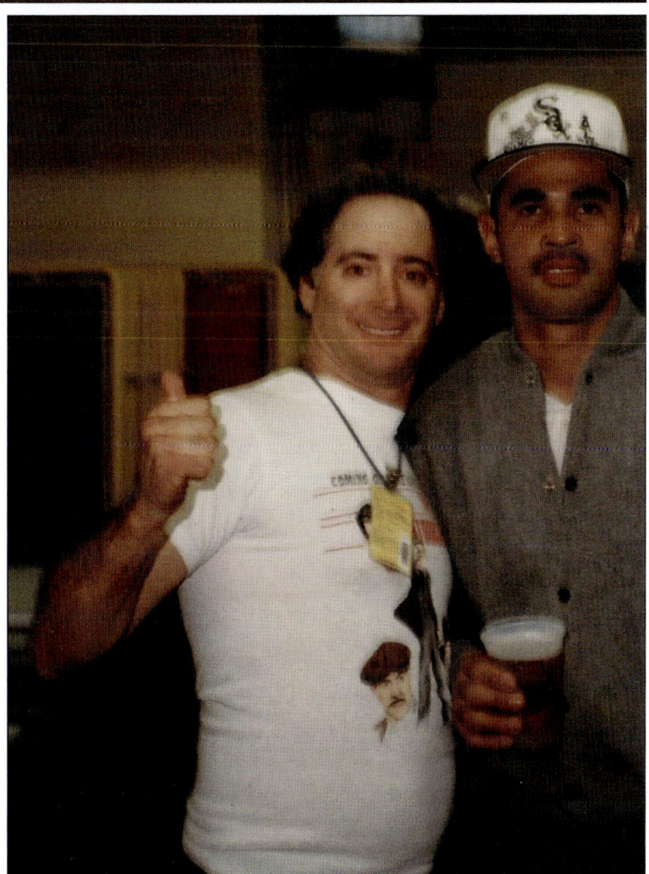

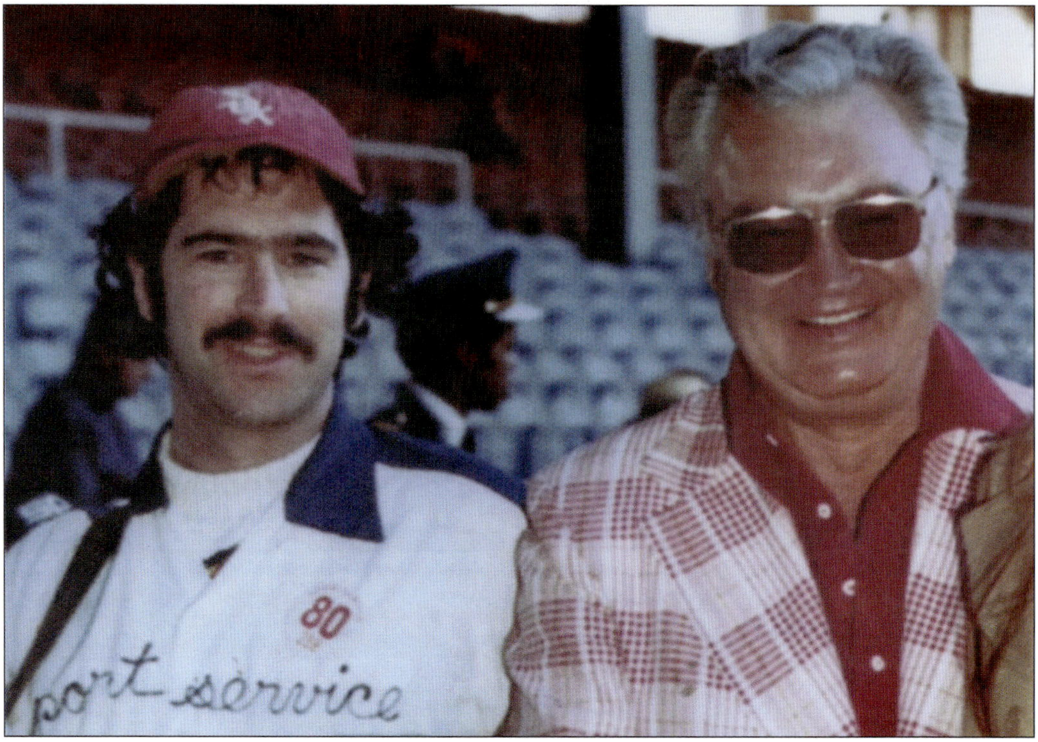

Harry Caray, above right in 1977, loved to "take himself out with the crowd." He mingles here with beerman Paul Smulson, who would eventually hang up his vending strap and put on a dental surgeon's smock. He was as controversial at the ballpark as Caray was—Caray often being critical of his team for being outplayed, while Smulson faced criticism from competing beermen for his methods in outselling them. Smulson, below right in 1976, is pictured in the left-field seats with Alan Rose. The center-field bleachers are in the background. On August 23, 1972, the White Sox's Dick Allen crushed a 485-foot homer out there, which Caray nearly caught with his famous butterfly net while doing a special broadcast. That blast helped give the Sox a 5-2 win to lift them into first place. (Above, courtesy of Paul Smulson.)

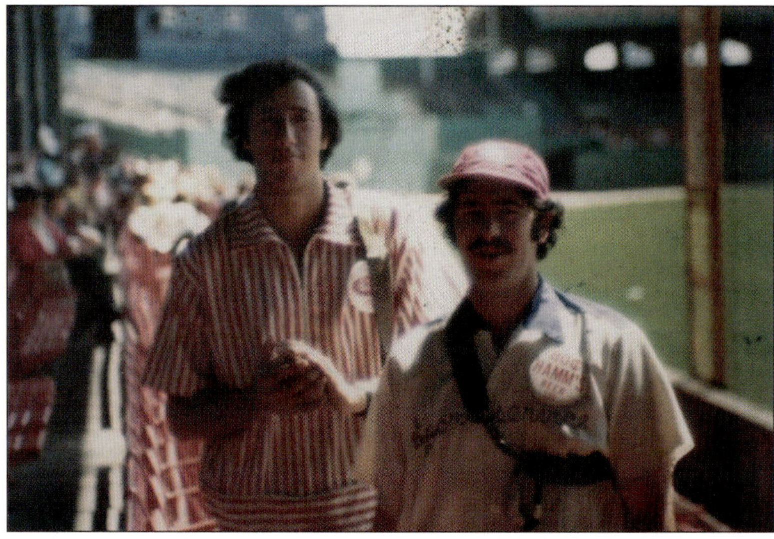

Perhaps the greatest maverick owner in sports history was Bill Veeck (right). He is sitting in Comiskey Park's outfield stands with the fans in the first year of his second stretch as owner of the White Sox in 1976. Veeck sold the team after 1980; he had also owned the team from 1959 to 1961 and previously owned the Cleveland Indians and the St. Louis Browns. In the 1930s, he was a popcorn vendor at Wrigley Field and, later, a treasurer for the Cubs. Beloved player Minnie Minoso (below left), an icon of the "Go-Go-Sox" in the early 1950s before a trade to Cleveland after 1957, was reacquired by Veeck in 1960, and again in 1976 and 1980, and was hired by new owner Jerry Reinsdorf as a goodwill ambassador for the team here in 1991. (Right, courtesy of Mike Gold.)

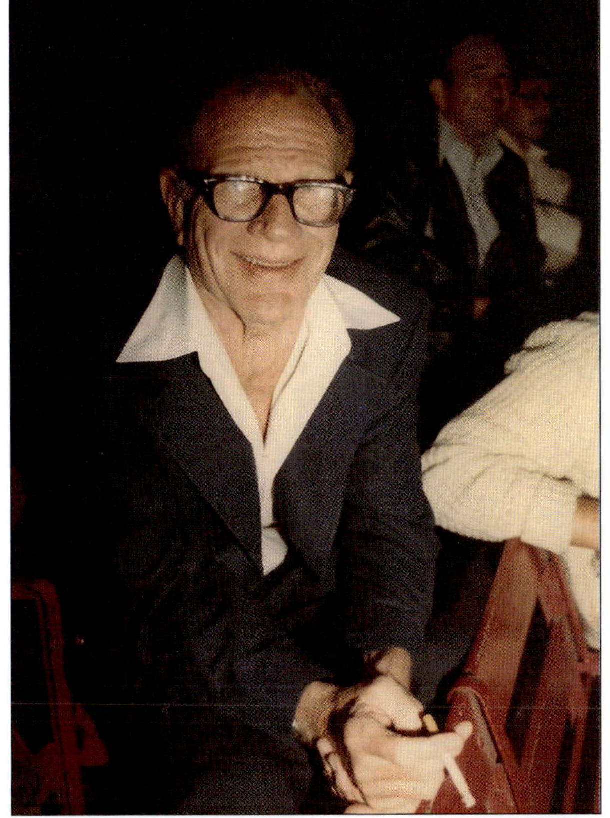

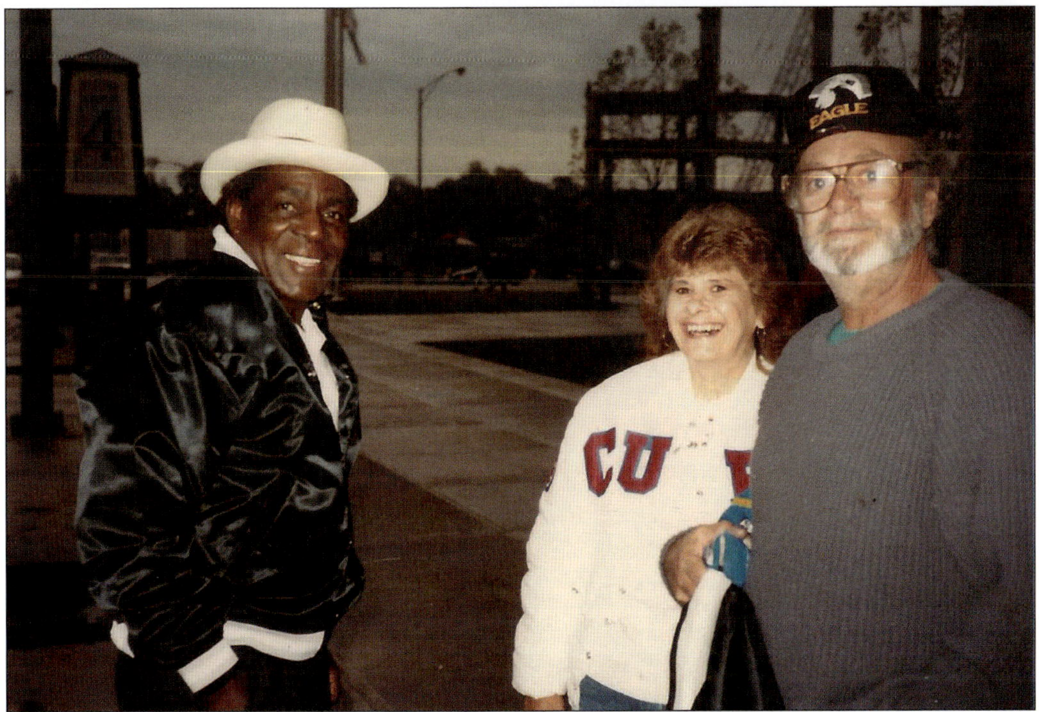

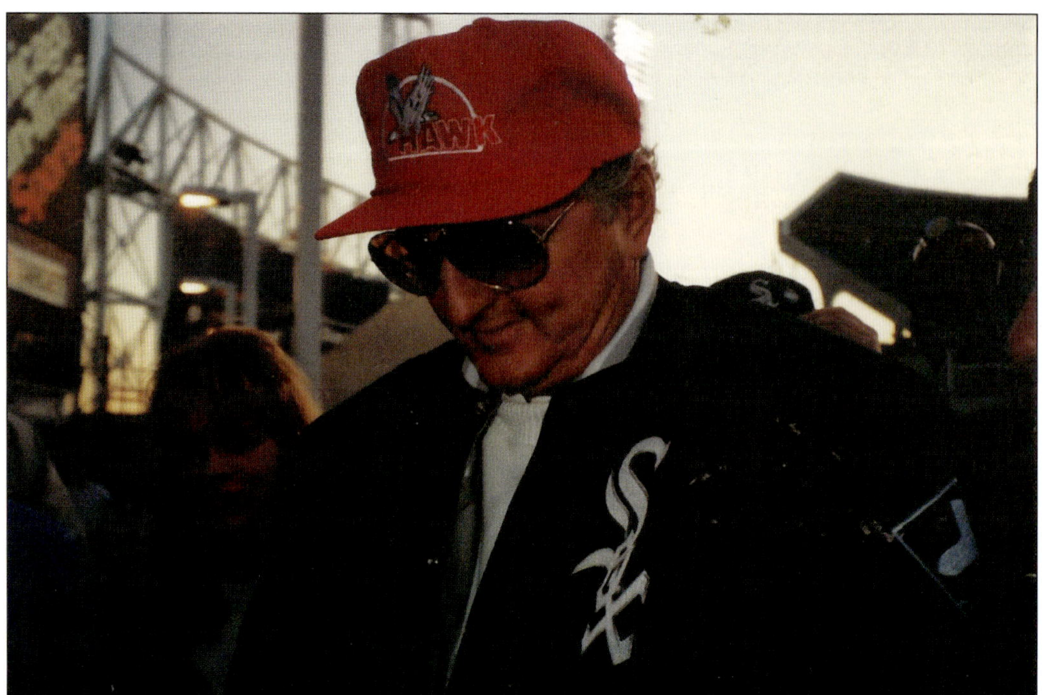

Ken Harrelson, wearing his personalized "Hawk" baseball cap, tensely confers with fans on October 5, 1993, before the White Sox battled the Toronto Blue Jays in the first game of the American League playoffs. Among a long line of memorable team broadcasters, Hawk was among the most beloved, retiring after the 2018 season. A noted major leaguer, being a 1968 All-Star, and leading the American League in runs batted in that year for those "other" Sox from Boston, he started announcing games for the ChiSox in 1982, was their GM in 1986, and resumed White Sox broadcasting in 1990 when he was partnered with Tom Paciorek (below left), seen celebrating with Lloyd Rutzky on the night the White Sox clinched their division on September 27, 1993.

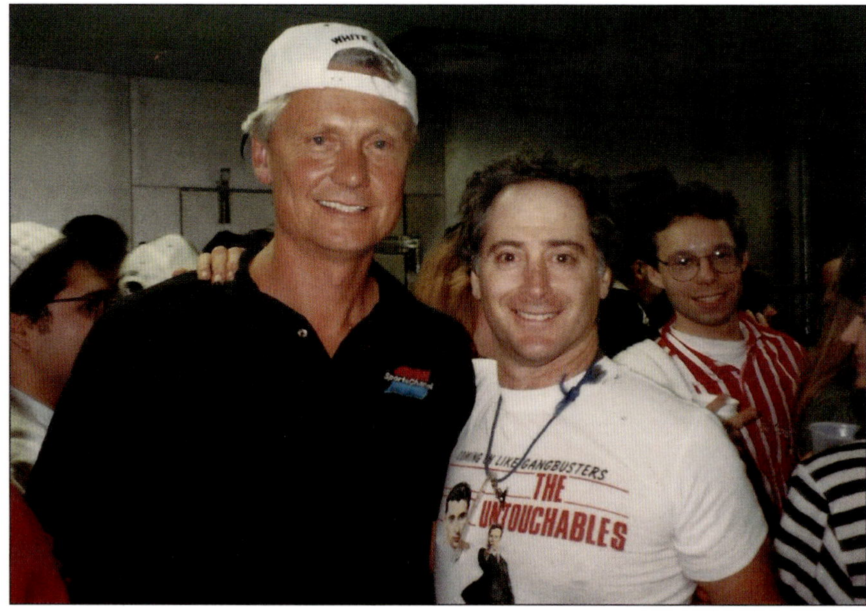

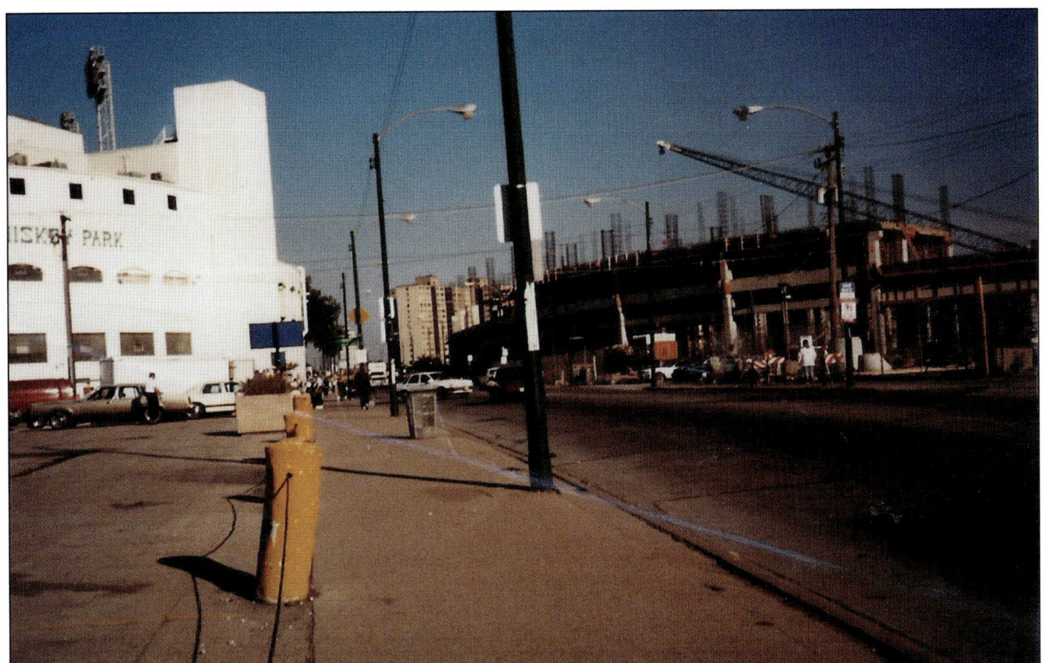

On July 1, 1910, the White Sox played their first game at the newly built Comiskey Park at the corner of Thirty-Fifth Street and Shields Avenue. They lost that game 2-0 to the St. Louis Browns. Three straight World Series were played here, from 1917 to 1919, with the Sox winning in 1917, losing in 1919, and the Cubs losing there in 1918 because Comiskey Park was larger than the Cub's home field. It also hosted the first All-Star game in 1935 and the 1959 World Series. Comiskey (above, left) is shown on September 30, 1989, exactly one year to the day before the last game was played there; across the street to the right is what would be its replacement being constructed. What was still left of Comiskey Park is seen below at left with the brand-new ballpark at right in its first season of 1991 on June 20.

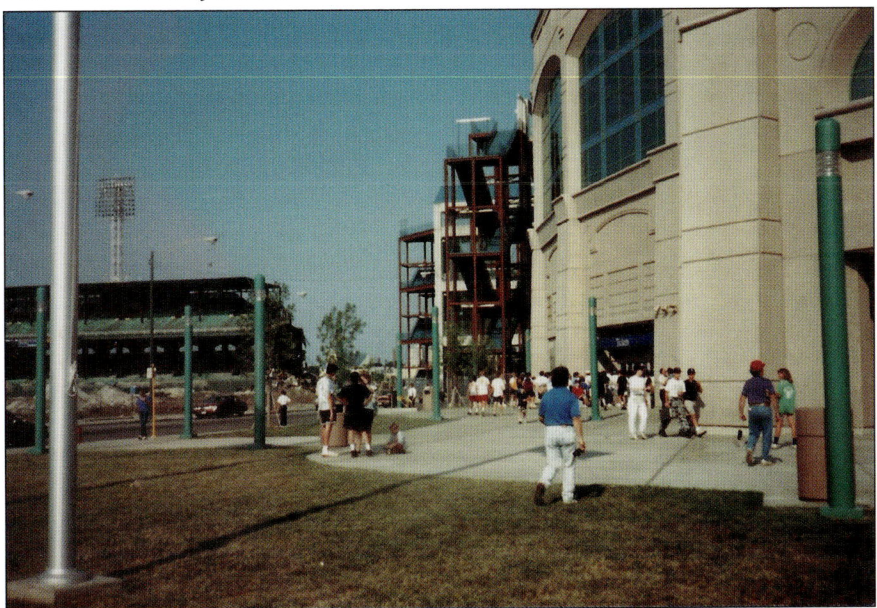

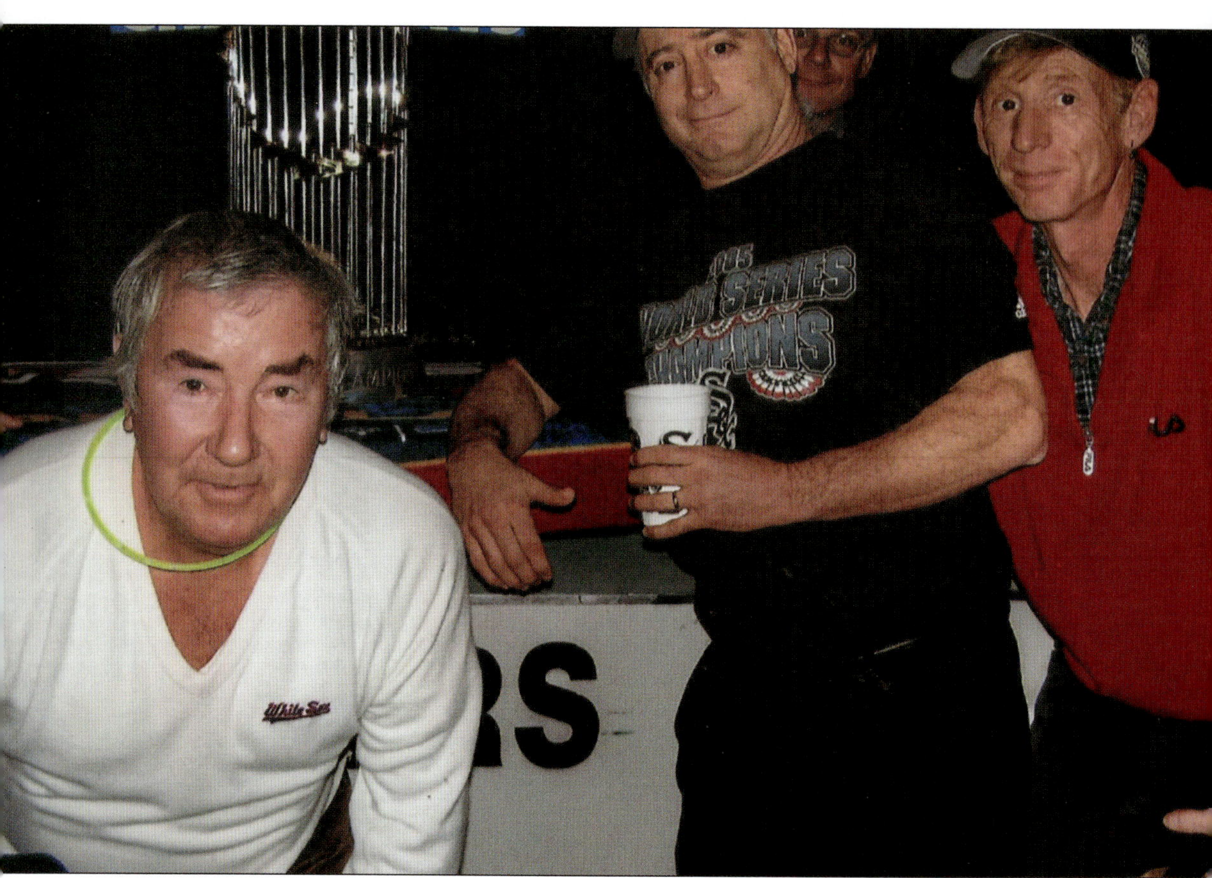

Ozzie Guillen reaped eternal glory managing the White Sox in their miracle season of 2005. The World Series trophy was back on the South Side for the first time in 88 years. The White Sox's last trip to the Fall Classic had been in 1959, losing four games to two to the Los Angeles Dodgers. The Sox's last World Series victory was in 1917, beating the New York Giants; their first world championship had been in 1906 over the crosstown Cubs when the White Sox played at West Side Park, just four blocks south of their current home. Here, basking in the glow of this long-awaited triumph that November are, from left to right, Jimmy Rochford, Lloyd Rutzky, and Gary Tuch at an employees' celebration at what was then called U.S. Cellular Field. (Courtesy of Michael Ginsburg.)

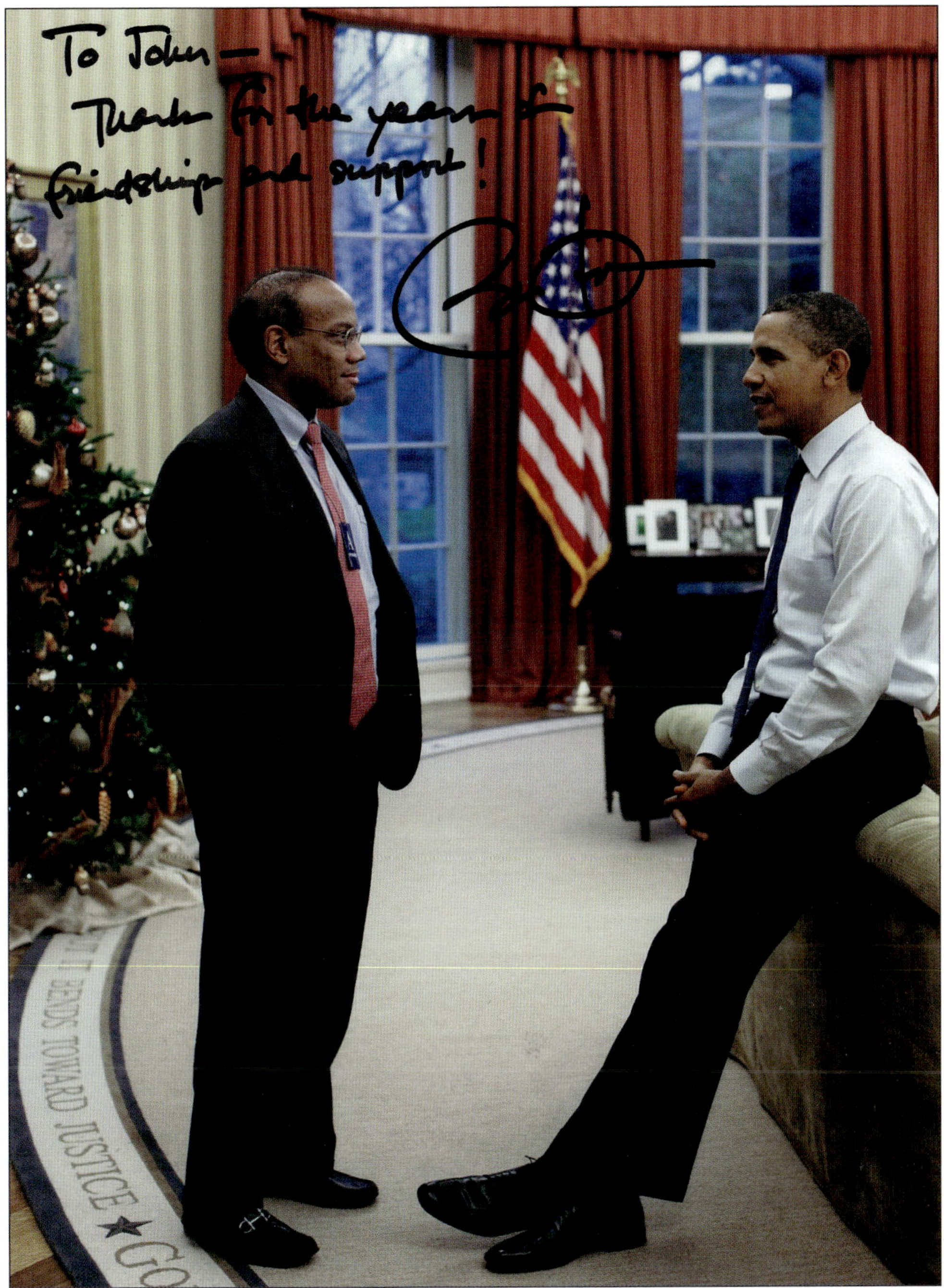

John W. Rogers Jr., approximately 35 years beyond his Coke-selling days (see page 65), confers here in 2010 as an economic adviser with No. 1 White Sox fan Pres. Barack Obama in the Oval Office. When Obama was president-elect, his headquarters were at Rogers's Chicago branch of his firm, Ariel Investments, directly across from Grant Park, where Obama gave his famed "Yes We Can" acceptance speech, in which he said, "If there is anyone out there who still doubts that America is a place where all things are possible, who still wonders if the dream of our founders is alive in our time, who still questions the power of our democracy, tonight is your answer."

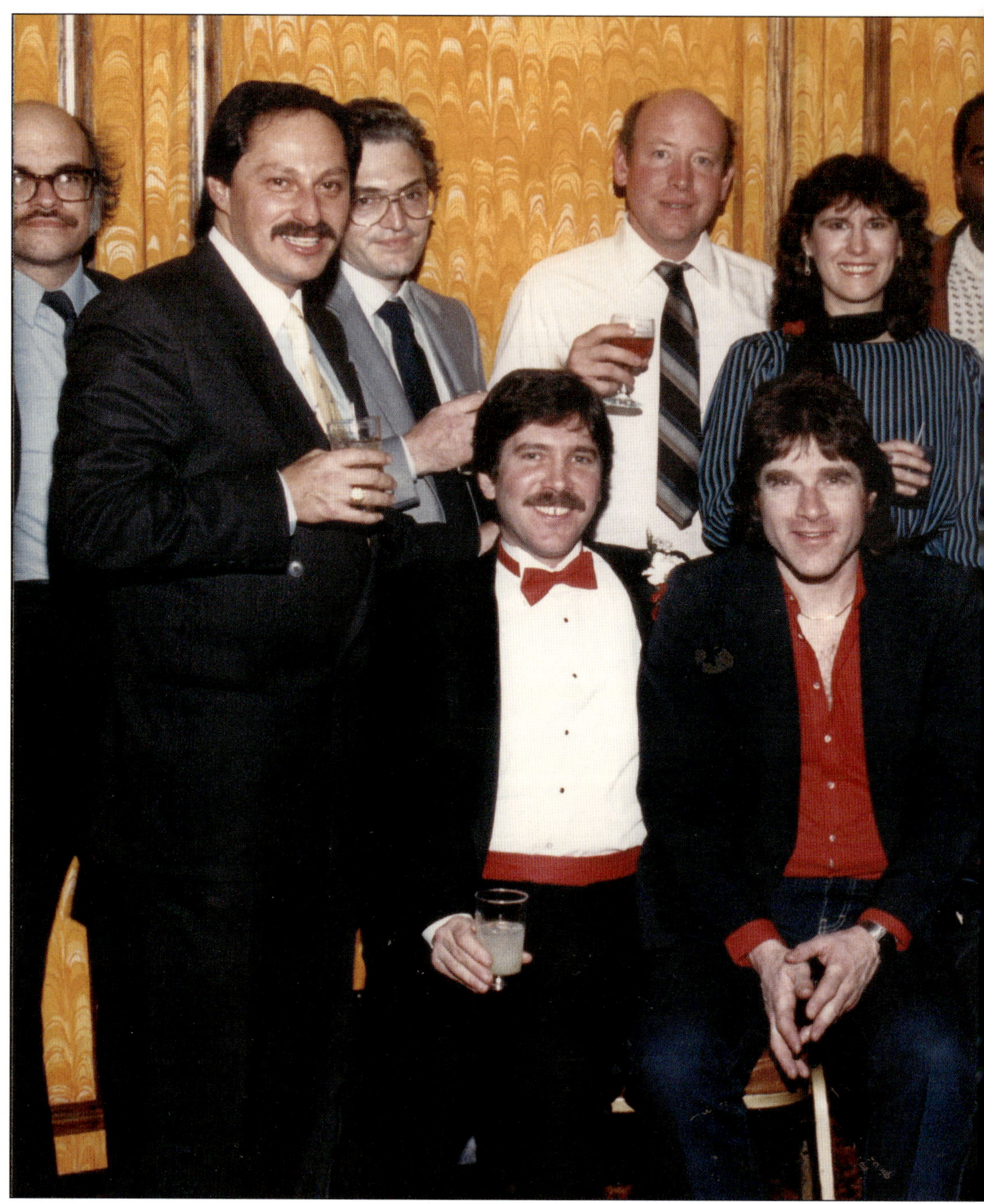

Suitably suited up to say goodbye, White Sox Park's amazing vendors gather for a group portrait on November 15, 1986. The occasion was Lloyd Rutzky's wedding to Helita Young, whom Rutzky had actually met at Comiskey Park, where she was a season ticket holder. Here is the guest roster and the pages where most of them can be found in this "album." From left to right are (first row, seated) Arnold Lipski (pages 25, 64, 74, 77–81); Roger Sosner (48, 63); Abe Rapuch (73, 81); Wayne Fisher (77, 80–81); and front-cover man Sherwin Tycher (79); (second row, standing) Bobby "K" Kletnick (58); Morrie Rosenblatt; Marv Mitofsky (10–11, 73); Dave Klemp (40, 80–81); Klemp's

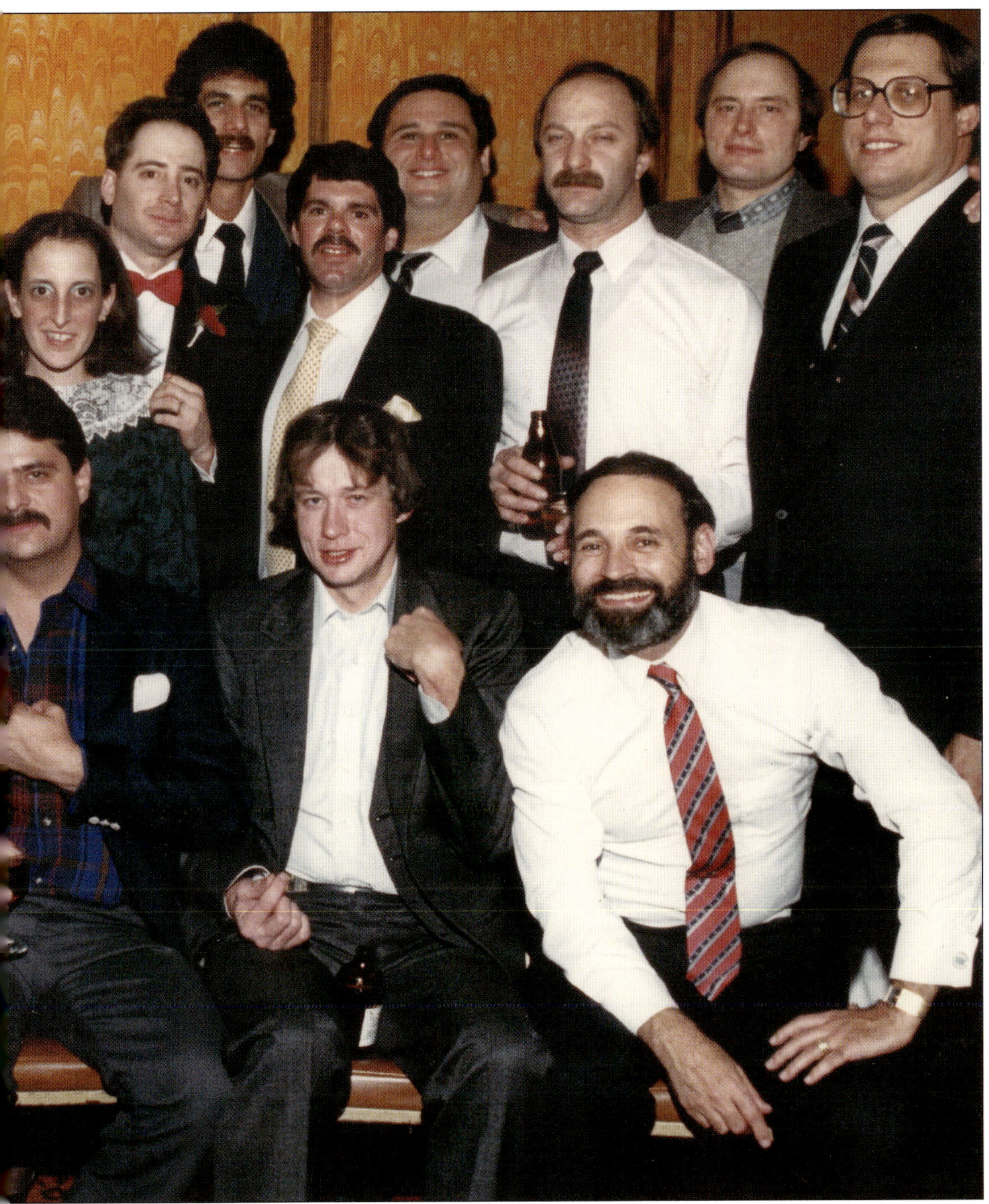

wife, Sandy, who was a vendor but is not pictured elsewhere in this book; Mel Mormon (27, 40); Lloyd's sister Alise (12–13); Lloyd (11, 43, 45, 56, 63, 77–81, 87, 90, 92); Ira Levin (10–11, 53, 79–81); Les Lasinsky (80), who was not a vendor, but whose uncle was legend Bernie Lasinsky (40, 86); Harlan Grabowsky (78); Alan Federman, who was not a vendor and also is not pictured elsewhere in the book, but who employed Ira Levin in his clothing store; Bob Schwartz (72, 78–79); and Bill Bailen (78–79).

Consistent with our mission to preserve history on a local level, this book was printed in South Carolina on American-made paper and manufactured entirely in the United States. Products carrying the accredited Forest Stewardship Council (FSC) label are printed on 100 percent FSC-certified paper.

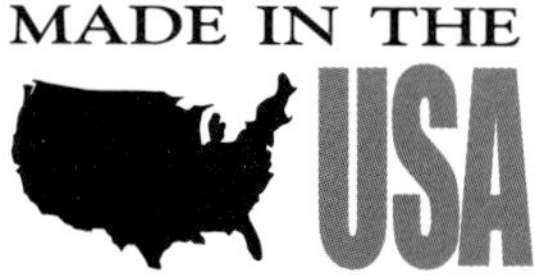